UNITED
QUEERDOM

About the Author

Dan Glass is an award-winning activist, mentor, performer and writer. He uses music, performance and protest to catalyse love, soul, revolution and justice in communities confronting injustice. Dan is an educator from Training for Transformation (TfT).

Dan has been named one of *Attitude Magazine*'s campaigning role models for LGBT youth, GaydarRadio Heroes Awards for Gay Rights activism and a *Guardian* 'UK youth climate leader' for famously superglueing the Prime Minister. Dan was recently awarded 'activist of the year' at the Sexual Freedom Awards 2017 for contributions to sex-positive, queer, healthcare and human rights movements for social justice.

theglassishalffull.co.uk

UNITED

QUEERDOM

From the Legends of the
Gay Liberation Front to
the Queers of Tomorrow

DAN GLASS

ZED

United Queerdom: From the Legends of the Gay Liberation Front to the Queers of Tomorrow was first published in 2020 by Zed Books Ltd, The Foundry, 17 Oval Way, London SE11 5RR, UK.

www.zedbooks.net

Typeset in Galliard by Swales & Willis Ltd, Exeter, Devon
Index by Rohan Bolton
Cover design by Alice Marwick

Printed and bound by CPI Group (UK) Ltd, Croydon, CR0 4YY

A catalogue record for this book is available from the British Library

ISBN 978-1-78699-876-7 pb
ISBN 978-1-91344-162-3 hb
ISBN 978-1-78699-879-8 pdf
ISBN 978-1-78699-877-4 epub
ISBN 978-1-78699-878-1 mobi

Contents

Contents

Part 3: Space

Foreword

Yet another day mincing your way through life trying your hardest to get through it?

Me too. Every g*d damn day over the last two weeks here in London a friend has been homophobically attacked or 'batty bashed' and screamed 'faggot' at whilst getting their heads get kicked in.

No, it's not the 1920s, when we had to hide in underground bars. It's not the 1950s, waiting for the 'The Wolfenden Report' to be released in the House of Lords to tell the world that, shock horror, we homosexuals 'cannot legitimately be regarded as a disease'. It's 2020 for crying out loud! In the last five years alone LGBTQIA+ hate crime has doubled and all minorities are living in fear as BREXIT ushers in a fear-mongering culture of 'the other'. Something has to be done.

So come here and put your feet up. Every day, the world we all face forces us all, whatever our identities, to perform to the status quo in order to survive. Now you can relax, release the tension in your shoulders and just be yourself. Change can happen. Nothing is absolute.

But how can I be so sure?

Because for 50 years the Gay Liberation Front (GLF) have taught humankind this lesson in the most dazzling and spectacular fashion. Emerging from the Stonewall uprisings in New York 1969 it wasn't long before they catalysed a movement here in Britain that led to 'Pride' today, but not as we know it.

At the pumping heart of the GLF mission is the aim of 'Absolute freedom for all'. A principled opposition against all oppression; standing in solidarity with everyone everywhere facing horrific discrimination and abuse. Fast forward to 2004 and Pride in London was officially changed from a protest to a parade, instantly de-politicising its purpose, as if there is nothing left to fight for.[1]

This is intentional. It is not helpful for people to question power. It is not helpful for ordinary people to be conscious.

It is helpful, however, to question everything, if you think that an injustice to one is an injustice to all. That building a movement based on solidarity and difference allows everyone to celebrate weirdness and defy what is 'normal'.

If you, queer or not, want to explore how to navigate and interrogate a matrix of injustices and pierce through the worldwide web of inequality that faces us every time we walk out the door, then read on. I hope you revel in the testimony, stories, ideas and toolkits for action. Stoke the fire in your heart and take back what's been stolen from us to live in dignity and pride. As the late great popular educator, Paulo Freire argued, we must 'read our own reality and write our own history to transform the world around us'.[2]

If we want to have a hope in completing the GLF journey for absolute freedom for all, then put the kettle on and enjoy.

But don't get too comfortable. I'll see you on the streets. Here's why.

Language and Abbreviations

History is written by the winners, that is why 'United Queerdom' proudly uses 'Queerstory' instead.

'United Queerdom' proudly capitalises all cultures, ethnicities and groups of people instead of just the ones that dominate society.

ACT UP	AIDS Coalition to Unleash Power
CAB	Community Advisory Board
CIC	Community Interest Companies
FOTJA	Friends of the Joiners Arms
GLF	Gay Liberation Front
LGBTQIA+	Lesbian, Gay, Bisexual, Transgender, Queer, Intersex +
LGSM	Lesbians and Gays Support the Miners
LGSP	Lesbians and Gays Support the Printworkers
NAACP	National Association for the Advancement of Coloured People
NGO	Non-Governmental Organisations
NHS	National Health Service
PFI	Private Finance Initiative
PiL	Pride in London
STAR	Street Transvestite Action Revolutionaries

TfT   Training for Transformation
UKI   United Kingdom Independence Party

Acknowledgements

United Queerdom is dedicated to Melania Geymonat and Christine Hannigan who were harassed and pelted with coins by homophobes on the no. 31 bus to Camden, North London on 30 May 2019, the two men holding hands who were violently attacked on London's South Bank on New Year's Day 2020 and everyone affected by rising LGBTQIA+ street attacks.

Big love to everyone who was part of the actions documented herein and all my loved ones who have been my 'home away from home' whilst writing this.

And happy 50th birthday to all the GLF, you disgraceful bunch of perverts and nancies – I've only got one thing to say to you:

'HOW DARE YOU PRESUME I'M HETEROSEXUAL?'

PART 1
SEX

1

Chicken Soup

Every great dream begins with a dreamer. Always remember, you have within you the strength, the patience, and the passion to reach for the stars to change the world. (Harriet Tubman)[1]

If you don't have roots then how can your leaves turn to the sun? Roots connect us to our past, help nourish our present story and lead us to our future. When they are broken it can take a lifetime to recover. When we find them, a whole world of possibility can unfurl.

Until the age of ten I spoke so little my family thought I might be deaf. The remains of my orthodox Jewish biological family came to London after the Second World War under a cloud of death. The fog seeped through the next generations. The mental pathologies of war and migration can confuse children already sensitive to sadness and the war seems to never end. Everyone was still in hiding. No-one, especially me, could come out.

Born of a long line of Jews, spanning Holland, Poland, Romania and Germany, my grandparents were hunted during the Nazi Holocaust. My parents and my generation didn't find out about their stories until my grandparents were very old and their minds stopped looking forward and instead reverse crashed into the past, regurgitating the horror within. As a child every Chanukah, Rosh Hashanah and other key festivals, when our family would meet, at some point in the evening, the Holocaust would come into conversation. I could literally time it. Every new TV show, theatre show or documentary about the Holocaust was a must-see. Sitting around the dinner table surrounded by shelves of enormous books, with page after page of auto-biographies connected by train tracks to Auschwitz, gas chambers, concentration camp inmates with 'Juden' signs, identity codes for the persecuted including yellow stars for Jews and pink triangles for homosexuals – my heart ached.

'Never. Again. Ever.' I heard on repeat every Holocaust Memorial Day and I became curious as to why some people seek to transform their traumatic experience, and others to perpetuate it.

Often war survivors open up to their grandchildren first so as to protect their children as only when they are old do they feel they can release. This is the bitter sweet my grand-mother left me. We all carry our maternal grandmother's pregnancy stress, bewitchingly called the 'Mitochondrial

Eve', the matrilineal most recent common ancestor of all living humans. When our life began in our mother's eggs during our grandmother's pregnancy, the stress through epigenetic markers started their journey through the generations. At the time, the gravity of this was unknown to me.

Post war, Michalina my Polish grandmother, wore glamorous make-up and a sweet smile that disguised a raging defensiveness at the world. Occasionally, like a tiger ready to pounce, the sheen dissolved. Once in a restaurant we sat together and the waitress was slow to take our order. Maybe she was tired, hungover or stoned – not rare for teenagers like me. Watching her intensely, Michalina suddenly retreated into her seat. 'She knows we are Jewish', she whispered in my ear, whilst grabbing my arm ready to flee. And we were off. No time to waste.

Soon after I remember sitting with her after school one day slurping chicken soup, spellbound whilst she began to pour her heart out. She sat there teary-eyed talking on repeat about the day she said goodbye to her family not knowing if they would ever see each other again. She told me her Holocaust survival stories and what happened to the Jews of Cracow, Poland. Knowing that I was both Jewish and gay entering adulthood, I couldn't help but wonder, where was the other half of me? It took me months to finally pluck up the courage to ask her, 'What happened to the homosexuals? Did they fight back?'

Startled, 'Sssh Daniel! Just eat your chicken soup. It's getting cold', she simmered at me.

So that was that.

I knew she survived thanks to the Polish underground resistance movement providing her with false papers. She recalled this to me until the day she died. During the 1943 Warsaw ghetto uprising, the largest of all the Jewish open-air prisons in German-occupied Europe during the Second World War, she lived as a nanny and an undercover Jew in the anti-semitic 'Jagielski' household. She was 17.

It came as no surprise then, that Michalina had a deeply ingrained awareness of the depth and range of human emotions. She had an incredible instinct on how depraved humankind could become having witnessed it at its extremes. Her experience included nightmarish effects of calculated destruction and human wickedness, of the depths of people's courage to struggle, of how much one's spirit can withstand and ultimately how we can continue to confront injustice to liberate each other.

Soon after she died a letter was found on her bedside table.

His (Mr Jagielski) anti-semitic tendencies became clear to us when during the ghetto uprising, when the sky was red with fires and soot laid out on the streets, the fall-out of the flames, I made an inadvertent remark about how cruel the Germans were to the Jews. 'Michalina' he said, as that was my name, 'this is the only way to get rid of these vermin.'

As a child my eyes were forced open to issues of injustice and the banality of evil. Once opened they could not be shut. As philosopher and political theorist Hannah Arendt reflects in her seminal work *The Human Condition*, which analyses the Holocaust, 'The sad truth is that most evil is done by people who never make up their minds to be good or evil'.[2] The nasty residue this left for me was a critical awareness of the dangers of blind faith in structures that damage society, the dangers of indifference.

Against the backdrop of silence and death, the engine of my soul began to hiccup and purr – could homophobic trauma ever be a force for change?

2

An Inalienable Right

The love that dare not speak its name. (Lord Alfred Douglas, poet, journalist and the lover of Oscar Wilde)[1]

Depression, abandonment issues, drug addiction, fear, instability and self-destruction are all consequences of being submerged in a society that ignores you, erases you and tries to throw your entire identity under the bus. There's no easy road map to queer empowerment, we have to travel it for ourselves.

Fast-forward 20 years and I wake to a new dawn. Last night, I dreamt of my boyfriend Dan's neck and the way he makes small yelps in his sleep like a dog looking for love and attention.

This morning, I thought of his eyes. Those times when we are locked together and regardless of the drama and the tumultuous roller coaster, our love for each other is as deep as the sea. I know, pass the sick bucket. And to think that this is a man with the same name. LOL. Ridiculous!

We met five years ago in 2015 in Berlin. I was working on a project with grandchildren of Nazis, Jews, Roma and other descendants, like myself, to make sense of our inheritance 70 years later. He was grieving the recent loss of his father. Both of us on a quest to find belonging in a lonely world.

I remember so vividly the hot times in the early days we fell onto the pillows and stared into each other's eyes. That look of simultaneous bliss and terror, so bittersweet. To know that the pain of loneliness, so raw, could actually end. Now we are two cuddle queens. The 'hankie code' has been a prominent colour-coded form of clandestine identification for queers over the centuries to share their sexual preferences; my favourite code is not a hankie but the 'teddy bear'. I'd rather a good hug and some soul classics than a leather orgy, any day.

It seems that none of these adventures in queer freedom-seeking and queer family-building would be possible without Dan – or perhaps that's just the unhealthy codependency singing sweetly. The love-force we have cultivated together to take on the world of inequity is both fragile and extraordinary. It's a sculpture, something we, or indeed anyone whose relationship falls outside of societal norms, have had to carve out delicately and ferociously at the same time. Every day we face the challenge of stigma, belittling, disregard – not to mention the relentless systematic marginalisation in society.

Our love is a threat to the system and my fuck, can it feel good.

We wake up every day to centuries of compounded internalised shame, walk past homeless queer youth on the streets as we get our milk from the shops and end the day speaking with more queer friends who are struggling to stay afloat. Yet without hope we are nothing and without celebrating our heritage we stay small.

The history of the queer liberation struggle is one of individuals who built movements and took on the often lethal task of raising the profile of oppression of queers to such heights that the public could no longer claim ignorance. They knew their work was sacrificial; internment and death was the fate of many of them.

I have my own heroines: Willem Arondeus bridged the connection of my heritage. A queer anti-fascist in 1943, he blew up the records office that the Nazis were about to pilfer from saving thousands of lives. Just before he was executed his last words on this planet were 'Let it be known that homosexuals are not cowards'.[2] The Queen of the Stonewall uprisings is Marsha P. Johnson, a queer trans person of colour, who catalysed the protests against the homophobic police invasion at the Stonewall Inn in 1969.[3] Today we have many legends such as model and trans activist Munroe Bergdorf, refusing to be co-opted by L'Oréal by speaking out against racial injustice and systematic oppression, truly in the spirit of 'All injustices are connected'.[4]

Queer culture has never been a walk in the park (well actually it has been a mince in the bushes, but more of that later) and so every day we have to shake off our fatalism and understand that progress is made in a myriad of ways. Without meaning to sound like an extra in the film *The Exorcist*, I feel ghosts all around.[5] I am sure many queers do. The concept of 'Hauntology' resonates deeply – that being the feeling of 'the priority of being and presence with the figure of the ghost as that which is neither present, nor absent, neither dead nor alive'.[6] Not just the ghosts of my family murdered in the war who I've learned about in my past, but the ghosts of my living present that I'm only beginning to find out about. Where are our queer icons and elders, and what framework should I use to make sense of myself and understand the world?

Denied, killed, lobotomised, silenced.

When there is no affirmation of your existence, you can't understand yourself. When there is no sense of being or purpose in the world you turn in on yourself. Especially when you're a child.

As a teenager at my local secondary school, survival was the only lesson I learnt. During my whole formative education I didn't hear the word 'gay' used once in a positive light, only in an attack when someone's head was being flushed down the toilet (bog washed) or kicked like a football on the school bus. That was our homosexual identity and our destiny. I presumed this was just the way things were. I pretended to shrug the shame off, but its tentacles were already making a home inside me.

A five-year-long study commissioned by LGBTQIA+ mental health charity Pace, resulting in *The RaRE Research Report*, found that 34 per cent of young LGBTQIA+ people under 26 surveyed had made at least one suicide attempt in their life. Forty-eight per cent of young trans people had attempted suicide. This is compared to 18 per cent of heterosexual and 26 per cent of cisgender young people – cisgender people being those whose gender identity matches the sex that they were assigned at birth. The two main causes of such high rates of self-sabotage might be chilling, but should come as little surprise: homophobic or transphobic bullying and 'struggles about being LGB or trans within the family and at school'.[7]

If you are not incubated when young, whether by family or by society, you are unlikely to emerge from childhood fully nourished. I only realised much later in life how profoundly corrosive this culture of silence was. A misty landscape so all-consuming that I hadn't even been aware of what might exist beyond it. These unequal social relations are what Freire animates as a 'culture of silence', stating

> Every person, however ignorant or submerged in the 'culture of silence', can look critically at his or her world through a process of dialogue with others, and can gradually come to perceive his personal

and social reality, think about it, and take action in regard to it.[8]

When I was 12 years old and the house was empty, I went to the kitchen and took knives upstairs to kill myself. As a child trying to make sense of the world in an orthodox religion, where being gay was an abomination, I was so depressed I felt like I was trapped in a cave with no way out. Alone in the house, I stared at the sharp blades, not knowing where to start.

Suddenly a voice sounded, 'Is anybody home?' It was Jenny, my mum's friend. The sweet shrill in her tone was such a contrast to the horror show upstairs. The moment had passed. This is a memory I will carry with me for the rest of my life.

I hadn't thought about that night until recently when I started to witness the rise in homophobic hate crime and saw myself, queer friends and those stigmatised by sexually repressive notions of society turn in on themselves. I'm very lucky to have made it through that night with the knives but, like many queers, there are other skeletons in the closet, buried deep, that are too painful to access.

Sometimes you have to have a good look at the shadows, as it's often the shadows that haven't had enough attention. There is great beauty in interpretation. I always thought of looking into the abyss as a metaphor for chaos and meaninglessness. The harder you focus on this the more life feels chaotic, meaningless and traumatic. Perhaps dwelling on trauma makes us become bewildered, stunned, victimised, makes us suffer from it and start looking into the abyss. But if we zoom out and dig at the roots of what catalysed the traumatic episode, whether in our lifetimes or before, we can begin to frame ourselves within it, construct narratives around it and eventually see how it has damaged or strengthened us. Then we begin to stare at trauma but not necessarily into the abyss. It is a paradigm shift that enhances rather than depletes our story. If we can explore the root causes of trauma and unpick its many interweaving drivers, we are better placed to mobilise for political action through humanising and loving intent rather than reactive hostility.

If we leave the abyss as it is, lingering social stigmas will never be smoked out. Whatever our sexual preference, if we stare stigma in the eye and integrate it into our present reality, then the ingredients that make up Pride – self-respect, dignity, pleasure in our personal and cultural existence – begin to bubble to the surface.

In 1988 the highly controversial Section 28 legislation outlawed the promotion of homosexuality as 'a pretend family relationship'.[9] 'Children are being taught they have an inalienable right to be gay. All of those children are being cheated of a sound start in life', said former British Prime Minister Margaret Thatcher on 9 October 1987 at the Conservative Party Conference, Blackpool.[10]

Simultaneously vague and all-encompassing, it forbade 'the promotion of homosexuality' in public institutions at the height of the HIV/AIDS epidemic, exactly the time society desperately needed mass consciousness raising. A coincidence? I think not. For all I knew, my teachers were being silent for fear of losing their jobs and were busy organising behind the staff room door in the Section 28 resistance movements.

The silencing around necessary medical treatment effectively sentenced people living with HIV and AIDS to death. In December 1986, Sir James Anderton, Chief Constable of Greater Manchester Police, said that HIV and AIDS patients were 'swirling around in a human cess-pool of their own making'. Anderton could have easily lost his job given the public outcry against his hideous homophobia that resulted in phenomenal outrage on the streets, but Thatcher was there to save him.[11] Only when his daughter publicly came out as a lesbian did his venom-ous bigotry slow down. Treated like second-class citizens, teachers across the country were terrified to mention the word 'gay', or even tackle homophobic bullying, lest they lose their jobs. Deadly homophobia raged on up and down the country. After a health committee meeting at South Staffordshire Council at the height of the epidemic, Bill Brownhill, Tory Leader at the time, said:

> I should shoot them all . . . those bunch of queers that legalise filth in homosexuality have a lot to answer for and I hope they are proud of what they have done. It is disgusting and diabolical. As a

15

cure I would put 90% of queers in the ruddy gas chambers.[12]

So much for 'Never. Again. Ever', as Michalina said. She was 17 when she saw the Warsaw ghetto burn. I was exactly the same age when I entered my own prison by declaring my homosexuality in school. A modern-day suffocating ghetto that deliberately banished homosexuals and so many others in a sexual warfare that has contributed to the wide-ranging AIDS epidemic across the world. Since the beginning of the epidemic, 75 million people have been infected with the HIV virus and about 32 million people have died of HIV.

Headlines such as 'Poofs in pop' pounced across the newspapers hounding stars including musician Freddie Mercury and TV star Kenny Everett as 'diseased vermin'. Intimidated LGBT+ members fled the Church after being called 'Pulpit poofs'. *News of the World* went so far as to disclose the home address of gay *EastEnders* – my favourite TV drama – star Michael Cashman.[13]

Although Section 28 was repealed in 2003 by the Labour government, it seeped into the atmosphere of the time, compounding and encouraging societal homophobia until it became government sanctioned. Its fumes still roam about the pipes of our archaic education system, thick enough to suffocate most sense of belonging out of our LGBTQIA+ youth.

In 1988, when it was introduced, I was 5 years old and definitely a camp queen waiting in the wings of life.

I was completely oblivious that across the city in central London ordinary people just like me were creating an alternative on the battlefield. A giant pink-paint-splattered bus with 'Repeal Section 28' on its side occupied Piccadilly Circus whilst activists abseiled into the House of Lords and the streets were full of people in defiance chanting 'Homosexuals! Homosexuals! Lesbians! Lesbians! Pinko Commie Queers! Pinko Commie Queers! We're all Poofs! We're all Poofs!'

If only civil disobedience and freedom fighters were given such a stake in our young imaginations.

As a teenager, instead of turning up to school to learn about how to fit neatly into the straight and religious world that I was being offered by my school and synagogue, I found a lucky escape route – the London rave scene.

Launching myself head first into late 1990s free party counterculture I revelled in the fast beats, huge crowds and the thrill of taking over corporate space for public good. I read adverts on smoke-filled toilet walls inviting the public to 'Kiss-ins', 'Protests against homophobic murder music', 'Stop Clause 28', 'Outrage!' protests, 'Reclaim the Streets' and 'Never Going Underground'. What was the meaning behind these bold posters screaming 'ACT UP! FIGHT BACK!', 'SILENCE = DEATH' or 'ACTION = LIFE' with pink triangles turned upside down from the ones I knew so well from my family's Holocaust-laden bookshelves? Seduced and tantalised it felt like I was entering the gates of queer Narnia to another world – but what did it all mean?

By the age of 14, I already knew four boys in my local Jewish scene who had committed suicide. In conservative Judaism not only does homosexuality bring shame but so too does suicide as it is not your body to take, but g*d's. So the tragedies face a double silence. Unsurprisingly, my surviving mates and I fled to the bright lights of London's West End, or what we called 'running from the synagogue to Soho'. I'd learnt this strategy before – if something endangers your life, flee; make peace with yourself and find a way to find light at the end of the tunnel while you're at it. Thank you Nan.

My favourite queer nightclub in London was called Ghetto, behind Oxford Street in the heart of glittery Soho in central London. Religiously every week I was caught in the toilets shagging or doing other things I wasn't allowed to do, usually got kicked out, and within an hour I was let back in. It was a place which deeply understood the queer soul. In a society that imprisons our psyche we need to let loose more than most. 'Fuck the Pain Away' was the night-clubs anthem and that was no coincidence. If I ever get the chance to see the bouncer again who stood outside those famous pink ghetto walls, I'd give her my equivalent of an OBE, because she allowed me to be my own queen.

It wasn't all fun though. Anxious to never return to my home, school and synagogue, to avoid the silence of queer invalidation that struck like lightning in my soul, I did everything I could to avoid it. Shady memories and hazy flashbacks: of being found by the police on Blackpool beach covered in bruises; being so drunk lying marooned in the middle of a noisy Hackney traffic island; or sleeping in a Soho alleyway and going home with men twice, maybe thrice, my age. However, one clear memory cutting through the fog was my first protest. Our Hebrew Sunday school in Golders Green allowed us to go to Carmelli's, the kosher bagel shop, at lunch, whereas McDonald's, being deeply unkosher, was banned. So with a few friends we organised a 'We Love McDonald's' sit-in at the school grounds, complete with all accessories, including McDonald's hats, flags and my favourite – unsurprisingly – 'My Little Ponies' from the 'Happy Meals'.

The Rabbi went ballistic. I was out.

'What have you done?' my Dad raged at the gates. And so the rebellion began.

My new magical nocturnal Soho-life swept me into an underworld of mystery. As a result I spent most of my spare time being late for school, wholeheartedly distracted and hence in school detention.

Here I wrote my first poem 'Up the Dirt Track' – on shame, pride and my total pleasure in exploring anal sex.

Sorry I was late for football again sir
I've injured myself
Can't sit down as my backsides taken a stir
But you know, here we go
In truth, I've been living the dream
And only now, I begin to see what it all means

19

I've always wondered what's the fuss
With all this straight wanderlust
We're living a lie
In a big fat straight pie
I wanna love you John
But inside I cry
An abomination, the Jews say
Make them change, the Christians pray
A sin (to rim) shout the Muslims as they go grey.
G*d don't seem to like it our way

But it's your loss you schmod
As you ignore your G spot
Without being a gay
For come what may
This raucous world of Vauxhall, Miami and Berlin
Of GHB, Diazepam and Ketamine,
Would be replaced by missionary, marriage and mort-
gage buy-ins
We may not be perfect, I know
As the drink, drugs and superficial culture
Makes our spirits lay low

But let's remember before we all go,
Shakespeare, Aristotle and Oscar Wilde
All liked a good blow
And thanks for your kind discussions of marriage
equality (with conditions)

But I'd rather have fun with all this gaiety
So one day my mind may shrivel and go black but who cares?
Cos right now it's time for payback
And, deep down, we all know
It's magic up the dirt track!

After school was done and I was out of detention I began to speak more openly when witnessing the despair and suicides of many young LGBTQIA+ friends. To bring truth and justice to 'Never Again Ever' for everyone means standing with other oppressed groups even if they aren't the same as you. Not conforming or limiting ourselves to one identity stops us from being pigeonholed or 'othered' by 'dominator culture' – the fear-inducing rigid maintenance of a society premised on hierarchical superiority.

Living in defiance against conventions can sharpen our gifts as intelligent human beings and provides us with a loving toolkit to enable a sense of justice for all.

I didn't realise how soon I would need this toolkit when just a few years later I would be diagnosed with HIV.

3

Shafted?

I was born in 1983, it was a time of the leather-clad punk lesbian Rebel Dykes,[1] a grassroots spirit of 'Do It Yourself' (DIY), collective organising, sex positivity, AIDS health-care fundraisers, creativity, squats, community activism, street life, resistance, and co-organising amongst struggles where Women's, Black, Queer and Anarchist struggles rose up against rising inequality to resist Thatcher's Britain.

It was also the year that 'HIV' was recognised as 'HIV' rather than 'GRID' – 'gay-related-immune-deficiency' – or the 'gay plague', 'gay disease' or 'gay cancer'. Picture this: all of a sudden masses of healthy people were dying very rapidly from an unknown condition. Fear and anxiety through institutionally generated ignorance gripped the social imagination. Governments and health professionals were not responding to the crisis. Something had to be done.

However, until I found out I was HIV+ I was quite happily promiscuous and care-free. There was so much loving during those years and then the whole reality of HIV just hit me. It was like someone suddenly slammed my face against the window and changed all the rules.

I remember vividly the night I met him. A devilishly handsome guy I met in one of my favourite clubs in Brighton when I was at university there. Short brown hair. Sharp blue shirt. Nice jacket. Gold earrings. A really beautiful guy. It was, all things considered, an amazing night. He was so gorgeous, from top to toe. I do remember scrabbling around for condoms at some point. Using a condom, then not using a condom.

Then a week later, the 'seroconversion' rash attacked. At the time I thought it was just a really bad bout of flu. Eventually I dragged myself to the doctor's to get blood tests and was swiftly called back for the results. Because of Section 28, known by that point as 'Clause 28', I'd never heard about HIV in school, or the need to look after or protect myself as a queer person, or anything so silly and dignified. My only frame of reference was from watching the 'falling AIDS tombstone' adverts stating 'Don't Die of Ignorance' or my beloved *EastEnders* where Mark Fowler sped off on his motorbike after seeing 'AIDS Scum' graffitied on his wall. The images that defined a generation.

Doctor Seaton, a smiley man with wise eyes was there to break the news to me. He sat cautiously staring at me in his surgery room and told me the news.

Stunned and confused for a minute or two I then heard 'HIV positive? You mean like Mark Fowler?' topple out of my mouth.

'Who's Mark Fowler?' he quizzed.

I was shocked – 'how could he not know?'

'CD4', 'Viral load' – a test that measures how strong your immune system is – and other medical terms that made no sense to me started tumbling out of his mouth. It felt like a waterfall smashing me on the head.

All I wanted to know is what does this mean in terms of my sex life. What positions can I still do? What about blow jobs?!

'There's a lot more to it than blow jobs, Dan', he said.

'Oh … ….' My brain was finding this hard to compute.

After another ten minutes of scientific explanation I began to feel really sick. All I had going round and round in my head was 'did he – the handsome one – know?'

A week later we bumped into each other by the ice cream van on the seafront and slid ourselves backwards underneath Brighton Pier.

'I think you should go get some check-ups … you may have HIV', I nervously said, watching the waves curl up around our feet.

'Er … OK, sure', he twitched, and I never saw him again.

A few years later I was struggling desperately to find an outlet for the pain. Stored in a box in my mind, wrapped tightly, I kept my 'HIV', but I knew the damage was being done. One stormy night the box was blown apart. Recently my heart had jumped out of its cage for a delicious guy I met called Thierry. I thought he was completely out of my league so when he showed interest I went to his flat with a well-prepared speech.

'Erm Thierry I just wanted to tell you something, erm, I can leave straight away no problem, I know the taxi number already', I said shaking.

'What's wrong Dan? Spit it out.'

'Er, er I don't really know how to say this, there's no really nice way, so er I'm HIV Positive', I whimpered.

'Don't be so fucking patronising, do you really think you're the first person with HIV I know?' he threw back.

Shocked, this was not the usual response I had had before.

'I don't need you to tell me about how I should respond to HIV, as a gay man, as someone who witnessed Section 28 and importantly as a human being on this planet – I should work it out for myself.'

'Oh, oh sorry.'

Then he warmed, turned to me and grinned.

'Now get your clothes off and get in my bed.'

Waking up a new human after a night of outrageously hot sex I didn't expect any more nice surprises until he fed me breakfast and reached on top of the shelves for five hours worth of films about HIV+ activism.

'Here we go, fasten up', he winked.

What an education it turned out to be, as the cold caves in my mind cracked open to the heat of the sun.

This wide-spread, diverse and sassy movement totally changed the world. ACT UP took to the streets, occupied politicians offices and drugs companies headquarters and sprayed fake blood over government buildings to demand tangible action to put the HIV/AIDS crisis right up the political agenda. They set out to bring about legislation, medical research and treatment to ultimately bring an end to the horrific loss of lives. ACT UP are living proof that when people get together to bring about a much-needed change, things can and do change for the better. Thanks to their efforts, HIV medications and treatments were made available and have been crucial in saving thousands and thousands of lives.

ACT UP were also part of the reason I was smiling like the Cheshire Cat that morning.

'Learn your queerstory – remember "Aids Coalition To Unleash Power – ACT UP! FIGHT BACK! FIGHT AIDS! Until there is healthcare for all"', Thierry beamed, and then sent me on my merry way.

Play with fire, watch your fingers burn – I know. But in all situations, as life is so short, hold tight the strength of those around you, fight ignorance everywhere and trust that fate is never absolute. Thirty years ago, the hopeless-ness of the pharmaceutical industries brought my HIV activist heroines out in force to demand medication. Now the medical results from this struggle provide hope for many (but not nearly enough – the struggle continues) with HIV across the world.

Life can be strange, but sometimes, it's fucking glorious.

Newly emboldened after such a long time feeling so glum, I confided in my mate Tilly. I knew her incredible levels of empathy and instinctive aversion to bigotry was just the medicine I needed. It was exhausting disclosing my status to beloveds. Some were distraught, others baffled and a few unfortunately still thought it was the 1980s. 'If we drink out of this bottle of buckfast [an infamous energetic tonic wine, drunk a lot in Scotland, that is my favourite drink] can I get HIV+?' 'Can we share this sandwich Dan?' and 'am I at risk if we share a toilet seat?' were some of the responses. One friend even bought me a drink as if that might be our last, which yes, I took full advantage of.

But when the drinks were drunk, the conversations over and the moon was shining through my curtains, I lay awake, exhausted.

'How can I deal with this Tilly?' I asked.

She smiled that mischievous grin I know so well. 'Why don't you do a coming out show to all your nearest and dearest at once. We'll get a venue and do a big raucous show about being HIV+ and the realities of it, but in a celebratory way, rather than a "We're all gonna die" kind of way.'

So that's how I came to publicly expose my HIV+ status in a coming out show launched to celebrate the 25th anniversary of ACT UP and all they have done to help so many people have courage. It was almost like the TV show *Stars in Their Eyes*, where people take to the stage to fulfil their dreams and blast through predictable stereotypes – best described as 'HIV Cabaret'. Scripted and created by people living with HIV, it is a coming-out project using a combination of methods to discuss the theme of HIV including live spoken word, physical theatre, bicycle stunts, live dance, music and true-life story-telling. The show began with a funeral procession. It then evolved to embody the rollercoaster of emotions from diagnosis, to dealing with prejudices and crass media representations, denial, trauma, disclosure, sex, substance abuse, the families you have to shed and the networks of support you have to create in order to survive and thrive. Alongside HIV stigma-busting quizzes and performances I began to tell my story from infection to what it now means to me in terms of friends and lovers.

Back on the 'Shafted' stage, cast as my nurse who gave me my initial HIV test results was one of the most incredible humans I have ever been lucky enough to meet – Cathy McCormack. Cathy was critical in the make-up of the show through mentoring the cast on how to bring life to stigmatised situations.

'You can either choose to internalise prejudice and stigma, or you can confront it and accept that it is society's problem, not yours. It's being outspoken and saying "it's your fear, not mine, let's talk about it"', she mesmerised us all in her thick Glaswegian accent.

A few years earlier I'd had the fortune to meet Cathy McCormack as part of a healthcare-activist panel in

Glasgow. I was sitting in the audience spellbound by how such a huge heart and phenomenal mind could squeeze into such a tiny body. A popular educator and expert in critical community psychology, Cathy had the audience captivated, articulately weaving an extraordinary web of how the powerful remain powerful and the weak obedient. At the heart of this was her extraordinary commitment to 'actions speak louder than words' and the legacy of her community's transformation when it refused to obey the barbaric politics of inequality of the government and instead fought back. From her flat in Easterhouse, one of Europe's largest post-war housing schemes and one of the most deprived communities in Britain, she launched the first community solar-power housing project in response to the fungus dripping down her walls into her and her children's lungs. As Cathy says, 'a social, economic, and propaganda war where the rich and powerful do everything in their power to promote their own welfare regardless of how many people they make poor, hurt or kill in the process' – the dynamics of systematic injustice in relation to my journey began to dawn on me.

Excited about curating the finale, Tilly had a plan. As an artist she is an expert in creating the 'you did what?' factor. This is the moment when the instant the performance or action is over, people have to take a rain-check that the bizarre events they just experienced actually took place. At the end of the show I was blasted across the audience in a cloud of glitter out of a giant cock-shaped human cannonball.

Shafted?! asked the question. 'Are you shafted?!' Yes, people living with HIV+ are likely to be oppressed unless we fight back. When you're diagnosed with HIV+ you grieve for the loss of your health, your pride, your dignity, family and libido. It's about resistance not as a cerebral choice, but coming from your own lived reality. It was outrageous and ridiculous to pull off – with very high stakes. Real stigma-busting is a delicate road to walk. It's taking a heavy issue and making it digestible.

The show then became not just its own island but a centrepiece in a wider body of activism in response to austerity cuts and welfare reforms that were devastating essential healthcare support services needed to contain the epidemic. After one of the shows many of the cast and the audience took the giant cock to Atos corporate headquarters – Atos at the time being one of the two profit-making companies given half a billion pounds by the government to 'assess' people on disability benefits, before their contract was terminated following widespread public and political anger over the tests.[2] With loads of people with HIV and some friends we went to their office and, using the cock as a battering ram, blasted the doors open. We did get some shifty looks on the High Street but as Einstein said 'No problem can be solved from the same level of consciousness that created it'.[3]

Soon after the show I took the concept of 'pretend families' to heart and became more cut-throat as I started to cut out the 'fake elders' in my life. I'd recommend it. There are those who have forgotten that being connected by blood lines and having been cultured in a society that insists upon unconditional love from their children doesn't mean respect is something you don't have to earn.

Life throws situations our way that force us to totally rethink our support networks, or, as I like to comprehend, 'who is aboard our love-ship'. This empathy then helps us interrogate and transcend the 'blame culture' that navigates presumptions that people are born malicious and accept that everyone is a product of their own conditioning and is on their own journey. A difficult pill to swallow, as I was soon to find out.

At a Jewish festival meal a few years ago we were all sharing what we were doing with our days. I had just returned from the unveiling of the plaque of the legendary Mark Ashton over Gay's the Word bookshop.[4] Mark was a key activist in Lesbians and Gays Support the Miners (LGSM) and many other intersectional groundbreaking movements that are documented in the amazing film *Pride*. Mark died of AIDS aged 26.[5]

'Have you seen the film *Pride*?' I asked.

'Yeah, I thought it was shit', my uncle said.

'Oh, okay why is that? Was it the content or the production of the film?' I managed to spit out whilst biting my tongue.

'All of it. What's the point of it?' he continued unabashedly.

To be an inspirational 'elder' – to love, heal, educate and empower – in a society which doesn't have any cultural framework for it and to break through the dominator culture that idolises rampant materialistic hyper individualism is something to be praised. Elders don't have to be old, in fact they can be children – they can be anyone who guides us to be free.

So I cleared out my belongings and left the meal. That evening I took myself to my local gay bar, Dalston Superstore, to have a drink in tribute to the many 'elders' in my life who I think about everyday but don't express wholehearted gratitude to nearly enough. You only have so much brain-space, and once you get rid of the bad presences which suck your life force, you have space to cherish the good ones.

For so long and for many reasons many queers have never had any figures in our lives who teach us how to love or to be human. For me, Thatcher's barbaric Section 28 legislation reinforced the religious fundamentalism at home. Nowhere to learn, nowhere to turn. Some of them were comfortable in their domination and some of them were too wounded by what came before them, namely the Nazi Holocaust, or both.

It wasn't until I met LGBTQI+ activists, old and young, that I found connection and solace in the activist struggle for freedom. It wasn't a coincidence. It was an active search in the wilderness for validation, survival, community, purpose, power and love.

If I was run over by a stampede of unicorns tonight I would want my dying, spluttering words to them to be this

You were the first ones who said 'gay' not as a derogatory slur or as a whisper in case somebody heard, but as a form of beauty. You were the ones who came with me to the hospital to get my HIV medication. In contrast, since my diagnosis, none of these fake elders have even said 'Gay' or 'HIV', as language is either a roadmap to accountability, or avoidance. It was you, my queer activist community who taught me how to overturn stigma and be sexually free. You were the ones who taught me how to be a feminist, self-reflective man, while what I witnessed as a child was scrambling mentor-less men, complete disconnection, patriarchal violence or male suicide. You were the ones who taught me to break the cycle of victim and perpetrator. To challenge domination in all its forms – in the heart, home, streets, forests and apartheids in this world and laugh, create, agitate, dance and seek joy and utopia amidst this broken, wild but beautiful world. I love you.

With my birth family I could never openly explore the effect of criminalisation on my psyche. When I read Jeanette Winterson's spellbinding novel *Why Be Happy When You Can Be Normal?*, where she said 'I did not know that love could have continuity. I did not know that human love could be depended upon', I wanted to pay tribute to the rocky road of embracing yourself.[6] And one month later I had 'when one door closes another one shuts' tattooed in rainbow leopard print across my thigh.

Throughout this time I was incessantly digging, hungry from the pit of my stomach for a life denied. When I found Gay's the Word bookshop through watching *Pride* and found books about Section 28, I became angrier by the second.

'Here, read *Blowing the Lid: Gay Liberation, Sexual Revolution and Radical Queens*, it is a first-hand account of the birth of the modern Pride movement by Stuart Feather', said Uli, the hottest queer bookstore assistant in London Town, with a twinkle in his eye, 'I think you will like it'.[7]

Oh hello. Five minutes later by a tree in the sun in Russell Square it was time to get stuck in and I dive straight into the iconic GLF demands first written in 1971.

1 That all discrimination against gay people, male and female, by the law, by employers, and by society at large, should end.

2 That all people who feel attracted to a member of their own sex be taught that such feelings are perfectly valid.

3 That sex education in schools stop being exclusively heterosexual.

4 That psychiatrists stop treating homosexuality as though it were a sickness, thereby giving gay people senseless guilt complexes.

5 That gay people be as legally free to contact other gay people, through newspaper ads, on the streets and by

any other means they may want as are heterosexuals, and that police harassment should cease right now.

6   That employers should no longer be allowed to discriminate against anyone on account of their sexual preferences.

7   That the age of consent for gay males be reduced to the same as for straight.

8   That gay people be free to hold hands and kiss in public, as are heterosexuals.

It seems that so many of the issues, 50 years later, are as oppressive as they were before. Rushing home I couldn't wait to explore more, and what struck me most was this.

FREE OUR HEADS

The starting point of our liberation must be to rid ourselves of the oppression which lies in the head of every one of us. This means freeing our heads from self-oppression and male chauvinism, and no longer organising our lives according to the patterns with which we are indoctrinated by straight society. It means that we must root out the idea that homosexuality is bad, sick or immoral, and develop a gay pride. The aim is to step outside the experience permitted by straight society, and to learn to love and trust one another. This is the precondition for acting and struggling together. (GLF Manifesto)[8]

The next day I took Stuart's book to my local, The Joiners Arms pub on Hackney Road. By night it was a delicious, wild, anarchic queer rave, and by day a pioneering, filthy and gorgeous haven for London's misfits and deviants that set the standard by initiating London's first living wage in pubs. We got wind that it was soon to be shut down by luxury property developers.[9]

'Is it true?' a few of us firm Joiners fans asked its legendary mischievous landlord David Pollard.

Newly inspired by my new book and chewing on words in 'Free Our Heads' I was adamant. I knew something deeper had to be done, that something could be done. A University College London (UCL) report by Urban Labs was soon released, documenting the closure of marginalised spaces and the resurgence in London's queer communities in response.[10] Between 2006 and 2017, the number of LGBTQIA+ clubs, bars and performance spaces in London plunged from 121 to 51 and many more of the smaller queer venues were closing too. London's queer community now faced total erasure. Once the Joiners closed we realised just how serious an issue this had become: if it could happen somewhere so in-demand, it could happen anywhere.

Even the most commercially viable bars, some open since the 1960s, have succumbed to the ominous knell of gentrification.

Legendary ACT UP activist and author Sarah Schulman defines the processes of gentrification in her book, *The Gentrification of the Mind*, so clearly:

To me, the literal experience of gentrification is a concrete replacement process. Physically it is an urban phenomena: the removal of communities of diverse classes, ethnicities, races, sexualities, languages, and points of view from the central neighbourhood of cities and their replacement by more homogenized groups. With this comes the destruction of culture and relationship and this has profound consequences for the future lives of cities.[11]

As it stands, anything independent and alternative in the heart of the capital is just keeping the space warm for yet another chain-bar or the next batch of designer flats. Space is essential to understanding queer freedom – not just at Pride once a year in central London but 365 days a year in all our neighbourhoods. Understanding ourselves is essential to our growth.

We needed to politicise our world on our own terms. From one conversation in the smokers' area it emerged that we wanted to do something more than just firefighting. We wanted to celebrate giants like the GLF and so 'Queer Tours of London – A Mince Through Time' was born, a tour project that, against the backdrop of the mass closure of LGBTQIA+ spaces, supports London's current queer activism, culture and performance in all its glory.

All very well, but I didn't know any elders to ask. On the off-chance, I emailed *Blowing the Lid*'s author, Stuart

Feather, because 'G*d loves a trier'. We met a week later and the rollercoaster ride began. With razor sharp wit and an uncompromising, defiant attitude dripping from every word we hit it off immediately and to put our intentions into action we responded to an artists call-out. That winter the National Archives planned to take over Soho's recreated Caravan Club. The original Caravan Club was invaded and torn apart by police disgusted by 'rotten sissies' in 1934. The owners received years of hard labour. The event we prepared was to celebrate the 50th anniversary in 2017 of the Sexual Offences Act which had led to the partial decriminalisation of homosexuality. Stuart and the GLF were part of the movement that made it happen. We decided to call the open-mic cabaret night 'Auntie Sharon', a symbolic name that pays tribute to all the queer people in our family tree who went missing with their stories left untold, to name, recognise and acknowledge all our queer ancestors electrocuted, beaten and killed before this legislative change 50 years before.

Just as the 'Shafted' show released the grip of HIV stigma on me and my beloveds and softened the blow of internalised stigma, 'Auntie Sharon' served to cement the GLF decision to create a new generation of queer community.

Questions buzzed around my mind like giant dazzling butterflies. How can we challenge co-option and exhaustion and decolonise our minds from heteronormative conditioning and fight until queer liberation is complete? What does that look like? And what are the stepping stones to get there?

A few months later, on a windy December evening, 100 people gathered on the cobbled streets of Covent Garden in central London in a wild array of colour. Everyone was clutching a personal item – a photo, a piece of clothing, a flower. 'Auntie Sharon' the open-mic cabaret was about to begin. We asked people to bring with them an image of someone, personal or unknown, to contribute to a collective statue of those who have made us who we are today in an act of collective consciousness and a ritual of grief and celebration never seen before.

Cramped in the Caravan Club interior it is easy to imagine the fug of smoke and queer bodies which filled the tiny private members' club. The bar's exterior was covered in blown-up 1930s police reports and scandalised letters of complaint from undercover police seeing 'sexual perverts, lesbians and sodomites, dancing very close together and wriggling their posteriors'. At gay clubs then and now, sex, drugs and swing have always mingled with grief. We started the night playing 'Fuck the Pain Away' as my mind tingled back to stomping the dancefloors in clubs around the corner. As the song faded, one after another guests, young and old recalled predecessors thrown in jail, beaten to death and consumed by AIDS. Waves of goosebumps passed through the room as one by one the audience stood at the queer grief altar at the front to share their loss.

'I don't know what's worse – being explicitly targeted as a gay man or invisibilised out of existence as lesbian or trans?' shared an older glamorous lady followed quickly by a wild-eyed nervous but striking young man who trembled as he recalled coming out to his father the previous week.

Lyndsay then came bounding next to the stage. An activist from Lesbians and Gays Support the Migrants (LGSM), a movement inspired by Mark Ashton and Lesbians and Gays Support the Miners in the 1980s.

'Right now multiple queer women are trapped in Yarl's Wood detention centre, facing deportation back to face violence and persecution in Commonwealth countries.' She breaks off.

'At the last anti-deportation centre demonstration I was trying to see their eyes but I couldn't reach them, I couldn't talk to them, I couldn't hold them, all I could connect with were the tissues they were waving behind the prison windows', said Lyndsay as she held her heart and found her chair.

Kat Kai Kol-Kes, sparkling in a shimmering black outfit, then came out from behind the curtain and got ready to perform a song from her musical.[12] It was a tribute to American Matthew Shephard who in 1998 was battered to death aged 22, sparking a global movement against LGBTQIA+ hate crime.[13] After the song she said, 'I spent years wondering if I should step in front of a bus', slowly pronouncing each word, giving it its own stage, 'or if it's better than being tied to a post and beaten to death', giving the audience a knowing hug with her eyes, and stepped down.

Next up came Nell, with fiery red hair and a floor-length sequined dress, who opened their lungs and embraced the room, 'Our entire queer culture is perceived by the outside world often as being about getting screwed, high, exploited, or being promiscuous – in one sense or another, but there's more than that to being queer … it is about being together, being free'.

One speaker to go and I winked at Andrew that it was his time to stand up. In 1970, Andrew was a journalist at *The Times* in Fleet Street. The first demo for the GLF was held in Highbury Fields on 27 November that year. Andrew read about it and thought 'I've got to get down there' and joined the GLF the following Wednesday. He suggested that the country needed an LGBT newspaper, and urged it be called 'Gay News' – 'gay' then being the defiant new term covering all genders and all queers. It became the first legal LGBT+ paper since the partial decriminalisation of homosexuality in 1967.

He knew acutely about the homophobic persecution 'Auntie Sharon' brought to life that night, as he recalled 1960s gay clubs where you were not allowed to touch while dancing. He and the GLF were hounded by police for their 'radical drag' stunts as they dressed up as nuns in the Albert Hall, shutting down queerphobic religious festivals and bookstores selling material that medicalised homosexuality as a sin. Creating radical drag communes, underground queer literature networks and Gay Days in public parks, the GLF urged the queer community to unite around a simple set of demands. Self-made pamphlets, zines and newsletters were the DIY vehicles that helped forge solidarity of thought, galvanising citizens who refused to remain silent and ultimately propelling forward the movement for the emancipation of queer people. These vehicles called for an end to discrimination against homosexuals in employment and sex education, and confronted the unequal age of consent and the pathologisation of sexual and gender difference by the medical establishment.

Andrew then faced the audience quietly and named a long list of those who 'were with us and aren't now', particularly GLF activists lost to HIV/AIDS or hepatitis. The crowd went completely silent as he began to describe the 'liberated 1960s' for the heterosexual community as 'a nightmare of a world' for queers and minorities, full of secrecy and fear.

'Things have changed', he said. 'This event is commemorating the 50th anniversary of partial decriminalisation in 1967. Our aim at GLF has been and will always be "Absolute Freedom for All" – dead or alive – so we demand an apology from the Queen for gay persecution – "pardons?"'

Andrew surveyed the room with a grin and a sassy hand reaching for his hip, suspense hanging in the air, and yelled 'Pah! We'll issue any pardons when we feel like it!'

He left the crowd stunned. As whiskered waiters sashayed through the packed crowd a cheer rose as he invited everyone to pick up a stone – each stone symbolising a lost LGBTQIA+ ancestor – to walk together under the London moonlight and drop them in the River Thames.

As we stepped back into the smoky Soho night air everyone was grateful to be able to touch one another, to hold hands in the street and to talk. The tide was out. We all braved the slippery steps to throw our stones to the river bank shore, where so many sex workers and queers have drowned, vanished, committed suicide or been murdered, to remember those who can speak no longer.

It was time to draw a line in the sand.

Harnessing Grief as a Tool for Transformation: How to Organise a Grief Ritual

1 Welcome in grief as a positive force for change.
2 Balance the head (intellect), heart (emotions), hand (actions).
3 Explore the depths and breadth of grief's alchemical powers.
4 Ask questions – What has been lost? Where can grief take us?
5 Explore how ritual and memorial bring closure.

One of the greatest challenges is our belief that we need leaders. We ourselves have everything we need to create beauty and dignity in this world; let's start by looking in the mirror and at each other. Question everything. Asking questions cultivates curiosity, which leads to change in the mind, the heart, our actions and ultimately the status quo.

Central to this jagged journey towards emancipation from perpetual warfare is love. In order to walk the tight-rope in freeing ourselves from trauma through the practice of love, we must understand that hope is paradoxical. Hope is neither passive waiting, nor is it the unrealistic forcing of circumstances that cannot occur. It is like the crouching tiger, which will jump only when the moment for realisation has come. To hope means to be ready at every moment for that which is not yet born.

With their words and actions, movements like the Stonewall Uprisings, Never Going Underground against Clause 28, AIDS Coalition to Unleash Power (ACT UP) and the Gay Liberation Front (GLF) have helped us move from emotional slavery to liberation. The question now is: how do we interpret these movements in the ongoing struggle for freedom today?

4

Sprawling Anthills Deep Underground

When we develop the capacity to come near to our source of pain, we begin to speak our truth, cherish being different and reclaim our power.

Responses to gay shame, such as drug use, often get to the symptom of everything and the root of nothing. Sometimes I want to live forever and other times I want to pack it all in, but I know I have to raise my spirits and not be too hard on myself. The road is long and the struggle continues.

In Britain, youth drug abuse is significantly higher than in most of Europe. Every addiction and consequential imprisonment and death holds a mirror to the face of an establishment so devoid of meaningful transformation that illicit drug users are set to rise 25 per cent by 2050.

Add economic austerity, institutionalised stigma and mass isolation to this toxic mix and, across the West, more than 10,000 suicides and up to a million cases of depression have been diagnosed during this 'Great Recession'.

As a teenager at the height of the 'free party' era, thousands of us danced together every weekend to challenge the aftermath of Thatcher's promotion of an individualistic society which built the framework for today's austerity programme. As I began to inhabit my London hometown streets, hedonistic weekend adventures were our life source – increasingly, drink and drugs were too. As the years flew by, for many friends scurrying their way through life, addiction became the way to falsely meet unmet needs and pacify life's pain. Without attention, this disease has too often ended with mental healthcare, prison or death as souls begin to flicker and fade. I know, I'm complicit. The self-loathing I feel has often prompted my customary response, to pick up the phone to my dealer and call for more sedatives.

Mature clarity can now distinguish the drug-taking times of empowered hedonism from reckless hopelessness, as I take a stroll down memory pain and dig underneath the surface, crawling around for a way out. We need to see this disease of sorrow as beyond one of mere criminality to a symptom of the root of society's ills – for this I love the term 'Sonder' and have it engraved on a necklace at all times.

Sonder n. the realization that each random passerby is living a life as vivid and complex as your own – populated with their own ambitions, friends, routines, worries and inherited craziness – an epic story that continues invisibly around you like an anthill sprawling deep underground, with elaborate passageways to thousands of other lives that you'll never know existed, in which you might appear only once, as an extra sipping coffee in the background, as a blur of traffic passing on the highway, as a lighted window at dusk. (*The Dictionary of Obscure Sorrows*)[1]

The only way to stop pain in its tracks is digging at its roots and exposing the structures which enforce it. This can help shift these patterns, where the internal light suddenly shines brightly and the 'Ah-ha' moments of clarity begin to find their way through. I remember when it happened for me.

During my twenties I was a community activist and youth worker with Plane Stupid, a climate change activist collective organising with communities living under flight paths affected by higher than average rates of pollution. In 2008, a letter plonked on my doormat. I had won a community-development award for this campaigning work trying to tackle climate change and associated public health concerns. The patron of the award was former Prime Minister Gordon Brown and the invite was to 10 Downing Street!

'This is pretty ridiculous. I won an award for supporting communities to challenge the expansion of runways, from a

Prime Minister who wants to expand them all. No no no, I can't be accepting this. This is too hypocritical', I thought.

I didn't know what to do, so I spoke to my friend Tracy, one of the residents under the flightpath and asked her, 'What can we do to highlight this hypocrisy?'

Tracy grinned 'I know – why don't we write a speech and when it's your turn to shake his hand, you superglue yourself to him and then read it out – come on, it might get all over the news!'

'Great idea Tracy', I yelped.

'No no no. Dan, don't superglue yourself to the Prime Minister, I was only kidding!'

Too late – the idea had taken hold. The awards ceremony was fast approaching and the day before the action I was in the park with my friends from Plane Stupid and I was pretty nervous to say the least.

Leo said, 'You know Dan, this is a solo action. In a lot of actions that we do there are a group of us. The press might pry into your life and if so, they will be all over you. So – is there anything that you don't want out in the public?'

'No, no. It's all cool. Ohhhh shit. Oh, um, actually Leo there is something . . ..'

'What is it?' Leo quizzed.

'I mean, I . . . Oh I don't know if they can go into your medical records. But there is something that I just really really really do not want out . . . it's the HIV', I mumbled.

This was the moment of shifting the pain, the first seismic shift since 'Shafted?' – I couldn't carry on by just going to the hospital and getting my tests, especially if I was going to be a public nuisance.

That evening, standing in the queue in the Prime Minister's home at 10 Downing Street reception halls, I squeezed the pack of glue that was attached to my leg through a hole in my trouser pocket, and went for Gordon Brown's sleeve.

'Don't move Mr Prime Minister – I've stuck myself to your arm to say that you can run away from my hand, eventually, but you can't run away from climate change', I said, to laughter from the crowd as he nervously smiled and eventually pincered my hand off his arm.

It was the biggest news story in the world that day – CNN, BBC, the lot. The next day I visited my Nan who was in hospital at the time. She was sitting upright in bed with all the newspaper clippings on top of her, shouting and boasting to all the other old dears in hospital in her shrill excited Polish-Yiddish accent. 'Look at my grandson! What is your grandson doing? Look at my grandson! All over the papers! Oy vey!' she shrieked as she planted a huge kiss on my cheek. 'I'm so proud – you make me so proud! We are all so proud of you!' Bless her, I couldn't bear to tell her that, in her excitement, she had missed out the part about the superglue and thought I was in the papers just for winning the award – G*d bless her soul.

After the press died down it was back to dealing – or not dealing – with my whirlwind of emotions and thoughts about being public with my HIV+ status. The cat was running out of the bag. Disclosing my HIV+ status really started hitting home. So I started going out partying loads. Well, more than usual.

Soon after, I hooked up with this guy Adam. We were kissing, softly kissing. Suddenly I got worried, 'No, no. We need to go to the hospital.' 'Right now', I yelled.

Imagine, one moment you're having the most intimate, beautiful time with someone, the next you're going with them to a packed hospital in the middle of a Saturday night. I felt I needed Post-Exposure Prophylaxis or PEP, a pill you take up to 72 hours after a possible exposure or infection. I had the most horrible, gut-wrenching feeling in my stomach. I felt like a leper. I just wanted to shut up shop and never to have sex or even bother going down that route ever again. I went from being merrily sexually free to suddenly thinking, 'I just don't want to have this feeling in my stomach, I don't want to be standing around here on a Saturday night'. Even though I knew that I had been honest with this guy, I just thought, 'I don't want to put anyone at risk and I never ever want to go through this again'.

Shame is the most unproductive emotion. Homosexual shame is a particularly cruel emotion. Debilitating, scornful, paralysing.

Gay shame and toxic shame hand-in-hand, getting married and waltzing down into the cauldron of fire, is an all too familiar pattern.

I smoke like a chimney, drink buckfast like a gulping fish and sniff enough ketamine to sedate the entire line-up at the Royal Ascot horse race. So I started taking more drugs. You know when you're taking drugs and partying for the hedonism and for the fun of it. Now I was getting totally mashed because I didn't want to think about HIV+ any more. I didn't want to have pills rattling around my pocket for the rest of my life as a daily reminder that I have HIV, that I am different. I didn't know what to do. I ran all the way back to hospital to get my regular tests and to carry on running on the hamster wheel, going around and around and around. Going to the hospital to do your test then ten days later going back for results. Spending any extra pennies on vitamins, going to the gym, good food, orange juice and all the many things that doctors say you have to do to look after yourself when I didn't have any money anyway. Everything was going round and round in my head. I became dizzy. Everything in life became about HIV.

When I wake up in the morning, there's three pink neon letters in front of me – H.I.V. Whilst sitting in my flat, it's cold – it must be the HIV. I'm tired – I think it's gotta be the HIV. I go out, and have a shit night – it's got to be the HIV. It began to drag me down to the ground and I just didn't want to think about it anymore.

Matt, a guy I met at a party rang: 'I heard you got HIV+, are you sure Dan?' he said.

'Why?' I asked back, on edge.

'Well, you really don't look like you have HIV', he muffled.

'Matt, should I wear a leather jacket and look a bit dour-faced like Mark Fowler? Should I wheeze a bit more and walk around and look a bit pasty like the pictures you saw in the 80s? Should I dance around like Freddie Mercury? What stereotypes do people with HIV need to fulfil for you?' I was not in the mood to suffer fools.

What image or what stereotypes do people with HIV, or anyone who is 'othered' by society, need to live up to to make things easier for the dominator culture, I wondered?

So I ended up going to my best pal Paddy's birthday party.

'Paddy we are going to have the wildest night ever. I've got four bottles of buckfast, five bottles of whisky, 4 grams of K, loads of acid, nipple clamps, spanking paddles. We are going to have the best night EVER!'

'Alright Dan, er, OK.'

I ended up a few hours later in the toilet, racking up a massive line of K. Bigger than an elephant could handle. I couldn't even see the K, I was crying so much. I was think-ing to myself, 'Dan, Dan, you can't ignore this. You can't live in denial and think you can just take as many drugs as you like. You know the pain is still going to be there. You're not daft. You're not dumb. Don't think you can just stuff your face with sedatives and it will vanish into thin air.' Half an hour later I went upstairs after picking myself up from the toilet floor. My friends Oscar and Olivia saw me and straight away said 'There's something wrong with you. There is something wrong.'

'No, I'm fine, no I'm fine.' As best mates can do, Oscar grabbed my legs and Olivia got me in a headlock and they dragged me onto the bedroom floor. 'You're clearly not alright, we've seen for months that something's up', Olivia says. 'No. I'm not alright', I whimpered, and then Oscar continued, 'That's alright. You don't need to be alright because we love you anyway.'

Curled up in foetal position on that bedroom floor was the first time that I felt I was cracking. Through the love of all these people I'm slowly learning how to deal with myself. This is why I am alive today. Later that week I knew I needed to see my old wise-hearted friend Amy who had known about my diagnosis for quite a while.

'I don't really know how to deal with this. I'm just getting too fucked. Taking too many drugs. Drinking too much. I don't want to think about this demon growing inside of me.'

She paused, looked at me and questioned, 'This demon that is growing inside of you . . . Well, what have you named it? Dan, what is it called?'

'Eh? You what? What have I named it?'

'You've got to name it. It's a living organism inside of you. You can't think you can just stuff it with drugs, suffocate it with smoke and ignore its needs and think everything will be ok.'

At the seemingly absurd suggestion to 'make friends' with the HIV whom I despised, I belly-laughed, from deep inside, and said, 'Well . . . Dot Cotton then', the oldest character appearing alongside Mark Fowler in *EastEnders*, 'because she refuses to die too'.

Upon reflection, I began to see her point. HIV is a stress-related illness as prolonged stress depresses the immune system. Only through humanising our challenges can we begin to overcome. Learning to live without stress was a challenge I knew I had to face, a golden ticket for my very survival, but I knew it wasn't going to be easy.

So I decided it was time to speak to my Mum and Dad. I couldn't tell them. I literally wanted to vanish, to die and let the ground swallow me up, right there and then. My mind, heart, guts and my whole insides felt like they were crumbling. I was just sitting there mute around the table with my sister on my left, my Mum on the right and my Dad opposite. 'Er, it's nice of you to come to us Dan, what's the special occasion?' my Mum said. I thought I was going to be sick. I needed to change the subject. 'It's just really nice to see you. You look well, Ma. How's work?' My sister Naomi quietly looked at me and smiled supportively but the voice in my head screamed 'just fucking say it!' She had prepped me on the conversation a few weeks before. For six years now she was the only one in the biological family who knew, it was time to relieve her of the burden. It wasn't fair.

'Er, this food is delicious. Is this Nan's chicken soup?'

'Just fucking say it', Naomi whispered a bit louder.

'Erm, er, there's something I've got to tell you.'

'Well, what is it Dan?' Mum said with increasing curiosity.

'Well, you know, I went for a check up recently, for an STD test.'

I was staring at the door, ready to lunge at any minute.

'Well, the tests came out positive.'

Sounds so nice, doesn't it?

'Positive? Positive for what?' My Dad said.

"Er. Positive for HIV. I'm HIV Positive."

I barely looked up and when I did, I saw my Dad's face vividly shatter and crumble. My Mum, after a minute, came up and put her arms around me.

'How long have you known?'

'Er, six years . . . Sorry I didn't tell you before. I just needed time to work it out in my head.'

How the deep need for a mother's love never dies. My world terrifies her. I can't blame her. When I was mincing around the kitchen table as a child she heard on the radio that gays were a plague, and saw pictures of tombstones on the TV.

A little Jewish girl seriously traumatised by what her parents went through in the Nazi Holocaust, she was dragged backwards through life's hedge where only listening to traditional Yiddish Klezmer music rife with woes was what she could grab and hold onto, a hedge spiked with thorns she couldn't avoid. Thorns of war, thorns of religious fundamentalism and thorns from thousands of screaming voices from a gas chamber choking her with fear. That life-hedge was too much and I am a thorn too much – a thorn that took her back to the roots of a poisoned soil. A soil that demanded order, convention and playing by the rules.

The only productive way forward is to understand the legacy she was passed. The cold-hearted destruction, the underground caves of hiding out of which her parents crawled in Nazi Germany made her distrust everyone, especially someone who would rock the boat and raise the attention of the authorities – they were too used to that. She's never known genuine intimacy, the sharing of each other's reality, of the honesty and care that is essential for a human to grow. She was never allowed, she doesn't know any different, so how can she pass it on? Life was about clutching on to what remained and living in fear of everything else.

The relationship between trauma, power and love then slowly began to become clearer for me – as the writer bell hooks says: 'Sometimes people try to destroy you, precisely because they recognize your power – not because they don't see it, but because they see it and they don't want it to exist.'[2] In her book *All About Love* she also platforms the work of Erich Fromm, who defines love as 'the will to extend one's self for the purpose of nurturing one's own or another's spiritual growth'. Explaining further, he continues, 'Love is as love does. Love is an act of will – namely, both an intention and an action.'[3]

Spending many years silently grappling with stigma, I began to internalise the violence, resulting in low self-worth, suicidal tendencies and drug addiction. If I didn't want to die due to the violent culture I was perpetuating, it was time to make a choice and change the story. For myself and the wider world.

It's dark because you are trying too hard. Lightly child, lightly. Learn to do everything lightly. Yes, feel lightly even though you're feeling deeply. Just lightly let things happen and lightly cope with them. So throw away your baggage and go forward. There are quicksands all about you, sucking at your feet, trying to suck you down into fear and self-pity and despair. That's why you must walk so lightly. Lightly my darling, on tiptoes and no luggage, not even a sponge bag, completely unencumbered. (Aldous Huxley)[4]

5

Leave the Gay
Donkeys Alone

Taking ownership of the notion of 'pride' requires carving out time to understand who we are, what's been stolen from us and how we can reclaim it. The skills we have to contribute to society gradually become clear and blossom into our strengths. Fundamentally, this then helps us step up to the challenges of our time each in our own unique and beautiful ways.

'Activism' means acting upon what you care about. It has just been lauded as a dirty word by the establishment who try to manipulate us by guiding our actions. Activism is about cultivating curiosity and knowledge about ourselves and the world at large. Powerful systems everywhere maintain the status quo of environmental, social, racial and economic oppression by wielding their age-old weapon that makes us believe there is nothing we can do – that we are too little, insignificant and daft to challenge them. Once we begin to realise this the mist begins to clear and the apparatus of the elite is laid bare for us all to dissect, challenge and transform.

In 2019 nations, institutions, organisations and movements around the world began celebrating five decades since the Stonewall uprisings, which lead to the birth of the GLF, who paved the way for the first Pride march in the UK in 1972. While the commemorations are growing, year on year, as the dust from the street protests continue to settle and people continue to bloom and speak their souls, the need for questioning is still very much alive. Amidst the carnival of corporate rainbow-flag branding, school trips to the Stonewall Inn, Hollywood-style film productions and politicians speeches referencing the Universal Declaration of Human Rights, what does this anniversary mean for those who started Pride? And what does continued memorialisation of the 'official breakthroughs' against modern-day criminalisation such as at Stonewall mean to people who still live within homophobic cultures?

Today we live in an age of 'where next?' Hyper-gentrified turbo-capitalism where multinational corporations are hellbent on profit-making at the expense of destroying environmental, economic, spiritual and social resilience. They rely on ordinary people not being able to be mindful of the present so they can pull the wool over our eyes whilst we hunger for the next installation of whatever consumerist agenda we are fooled to believe we need. Within this blizzard the major difficulty is to stand still and focus on the breadth and depth of social queerstory in order to sow the seeds for collective liberation in the here and now. Cultural theorist Mark Fisher's work explores the relationship cultural amnesia has with public time, such as celebrity dancing and Saturday night TV spectacles, which have powerful parallels with Pride. The machinery of capitalist institutions sell the public the notion of 'Pride', capture it on the noisy day it takes place and sell it back to us the rest of the year. It is a closed-loop, that loses the origins and essence of what Pride was about in the first place. In his fascinating essay 'Is It Still Possible to Forget?' Mark Fisher sheds light on 'This frenzied activity of recording and image-generating – to call images that will only ever appear on social media "photographs" is a misleading archaism – that erases the very present it aims to capture'.[1]

Freedom is a buzzword used by some to imprison others and by others to liberate. What does it mean to be free? Economist and social theorist Karl Marx considered all emancipation 'a reduction of the human world and relationships to man himself'.[2] The work of 'popular education' or 'peoples' education' is widely seen as a methodology to achieve this, based upon building critical consciousness to achieve an in-depth understanding of the world. The concepts 'Transformation starts with yourself', 'breaking through a culture of silence' and 'breaking down the barriers of blame and scapegoating' are critical tools to encourage people to think for themselves to create possible solutions. If I met Freire in a gay bar today I am sure he would have a field day at Pride.

Leaders in transformative community education Anne Hope and Sally Timmell founded the global Training for Transformation (TfT) movement out of their direct involvement in Anti-Apartheid activism in the 1970s. Along with Steve Biko from the Black Consciousness Movement they together generated a leadership programme which led to hundreds of trainings in South Africa that alchemised collectively the awareness and the will of the people, lifting their spirits to rebel against the regime. Through recommendations from ACT UP activists I was lucky to train at their school near Cape Town. The TfT methodology, full of riches including Biko's wisdom and Freire's teaching, has been the sharpening of my curiosity and understanding on how to transform the world ever since. As Anne and Sally crystallise in the handbooks, 'Development is a process in which a community of people strives to make it possible for all its members to satisfy their fundamental human needs and to enhance the quality of their lives'.[3] This unity and clarity in the struggle for liberation has much to teach about conflict, transformation, truth and reconciliation.

At the height of Apartheid, the white supremacist regime enforced tryanny through state shootings, mass incercarations and forced assimilation into 'white' education. The Black Consciousness Movement pioneered the thinking that before we can expect to have physical liberation from the oppressors we have, first and foremost, to have psychological liberation. This was when, just before he was brutally murdered at the hands of the police, Biko said 'the most potent weapon in the hands of the oppressor is the mind of the oppressed'.[4] This lesson speaks volumes to the intimate powers of the human imagination to overcome psychological imprisonment today.

Biko's words have inspired me ever since scampering off stage, along with the giant penis-shaped 'Shafted?' human cannonball, after revealing my HIV+ status. My heart has been racing and my mind on fire as to how we can continue to empower ourselves to speak our truth. So when, in 2014, the UK Independence Party (UKIP), a right-wing, anti-immigration, populist political party that has energised Euro-sceptics and contributed successfully to BREXIT, were all over the news, it was time to apply these learnings.

A journalist asked the then UKIP leader Nigel Farage, 'Who should be allowed to migrate to Britain, Nigel?' Nigel swiftly responded, 'People who do not have HIV, to be frank. That's a good start.' Apparently that wasn't low enough as he continued, unabashedly, 'We cannot afford to have people with life-threatening diseases coming into the UK'.[5]

Attendance at ACT UP London's meetings skyrocketed and this time there was standing room only, with some stalwarts and lots of new faces.

'We've had enough of HIV-phobia and Farage and his cronies at UKIP's foul bigotry, let's plan an action. Something stinks, but it hasn't come from abroad, it's coming straight out of Farage's mouth', yelled ACT UP activist Patrick with a glint in his eye. The room cheered him as he sat on his hands in excitement.

It wasn't just that Farage was spewing hateful, xenophobic opinions – that's nothing new. This time he was offering outright lies which directly harmed the lives of those, like me, who are living with HIV. This stigma creates silencing and results in the 'Second Silence', the first major mainstream cultural silence being in the AIDS epoch of the 1980s and 1990s. The 'Second Silence' today consists of the three contemporary compounding problems of budget cuts, rising transmission levels in certain demographics and the general belief that the HIV/ AIDS epidemic was resolved in the 1980s.[6]

'We've had enough of their crap and we want to give it back to them for a change', Patrick continued, taking note of the raised hands of those keen to get stuck in.

Long-term ACT UPper Mike then raised his hand and said, 'Democracy is more than voting every so often and so to achieve it, it must include direct action and civil disobedience. Why hasn't anyone in power been bold enough to call out Farage for his dangerous misinformation?' This is where we came into our queer power heritage.

So later that month a few of us decided to give Nigel Farage a gift. After all, the man has given us all so much crap in recent months, it only seemed right to return the favour. On a dazzling Winter's morning, early on 'World AIDS Day', 1 December 2014, it was time to commemorate and celebrate. So we took half a tonne of horse manure in a van at 5am in the morning to Croydon, South London to dump it on UKIP's headquarters doorway.

Strapping a banner to their garage which read in rainbow paint 'What goes around comes around, stop spreading filth, solidarity on World AIDS Day', whilst putting a beautiful silk red ribbon on the manure, was enough to make me forget how the freezing temperature was making my naked legs turn blue. My PVC hotpants and a kiss from Dan for the photos made up for it. A few days later, the press headlines blazed: 'UKIP kicked out of London offices after HIV activists dump horse s**t outside', whilst the local UKIP party chairman announced that the protest 'was the last straw' for their office owners, and UKIP will have to find a new home.[7]

It was more than we at ACT UP could ever have hoped for.

It is still rare for us to openly discuss the impacts of sexual bigotry and HIV stigma on our common social psyche. Dumping the bullshit brought it out onto the public stage.

Through this 'poo power action' we had carved out a place in our minds for people living with HIV or any stigmatised condition, because once you enter it, you simply expect sadness and despair. It's the kind of sadness associated with disasters and ticking time bombs, so it is crucial that we stand our ground and communicate our private pain with firm public action. This helps us to remain intimate with the world and cherish one of life's great medicines: the healing potion of collective action.

Engage in Creative Civil Disobedience: How to Organise a Poo-Power Action

1 Who deserves pooping? Find your priority target.
2 Create a recipe for the perfect action, including your message, aesthetics and dream team.
3 Speak to a lawyer to get to know your pooping rights.
4 Find your friendly poo supplier who has a penchant for targeting politicians and freedom fighting.
5 Wear gloves.

When the press attention had died down after the UKIP poo dump, I found myself sitting back at the Joiners with a handful of other activists planning what to do next. Unfortunately we weren't short of options. Not content with targeting HIV+ migrants, UKIP had their sights set on some of the other most vulnerable communities in need of love and support.

In the news a few days later, Farage attempted to blame immigration for traffic on the M4. When accused of 'pointing at immigrants and the disabled and holding his nose' on prime-time political commentary TV show *Question Time* he responded that he has 'never' criticised people with disabilities.[8] But the UKIP manifesto policy document that was deleted from their website tells a different story. The party claimed that 75 per cent of incapacity benefit claimants 'are fit and healthy' and 'a parasitic underclass of scroungers' who are 'an unreasonable tax burden on the working population'.[9]

Farage also didn't like hearing so many foreign languages on his train journey 'because that's not what Britain should be about'.[10] One UKIP candidate called gay people 'fascist perverts'.[11] Another candidate in Merthyr Tydfil even made a bizarre speech claiming that a gay donkey had tried to rape his horse.[12] The news stories continued with UKIP wanting to privatise the NHS,[13] instigate a ban on all new migrants[14] and end environmental regulation standards.[15]

'After all the bigoted statements they've made, it's about time we all stood up for ourselves because absolutely no-one should feel frightened by UKIP', said Ray, an artist, activist and young mother-to-be. Ray was fuming because of the misogyny coming from Farage's mouth when he said 'breastfeeding mothers should face the wall'. We decided we wouldn't let Farage get away with it.

Sitting in the corner reading about the latest football scores, Saph piped up, 'Nigel is a believer in hard borders, alternative truths and imperial nostalgia. He spends his days campaigning for control of all things British and marginalising vulnerable minorities. We need to stick up for ourselves and I do think there is strength behind that. You know what Martin Luther King Junior said though, "words will never kill me".'

So that night a few of us sat around a phone reading a series of UKIP's latest inflammatory stories, to hatch a plan.

'Ah-ha!' Even though Nigel was renting a £13,000-a-month Chelsea townhouse while being driven about in Range Rovers by his £5,000-a-month body-guard[16] he was boasting that he was a 'man of the people' whilst drinking a pint of ale in his local pub.[17] Bingo!

We Googled 'The George and Dragon' in Kent, picked up the phone and booked the function room in Farage's 'local' for 'my Mums birthday'. A week later a few of us headed down to do a reconnaissance. Lucky we did because it turns out that there are two pubs called 'The George and Dragon' in Nigel Farage's town – it could have easily gone wrong if we hadn't checked. Inspired by the emergence of art and theatrical dissidence during the Weimar era in pre-Second World War Berlin, when ordinary people crea-tively responded to rising fascism, we decided to put on a cabaret of our own. By showcasing the beauty and diversity of our global community we wanted to make sure history never repeats itself.

Over the next two months multiple different groups dreaming of a world beyond bigotry came to practise their satirical responses to UKIP. Ray introduced the dress rehearsals with a message: 'They think we will run and hide and be sad and depressed but we celebrate our diversity. We will take our diversity to the heart of where Farage exists to show him he has nothing to be scared about. We will not succumb to their prejudice. We will create the world we want to live in. A world beyond UKIP. A world full of Pride.'

The buses were booked, our multicoloured 'bigotry' pinata was made by a Mexican migrant solidarity group and the Polish, Chinese and Arabic table signs made for our language classes.

The day before, I was sitting in the park in the sunshine and I finally had a moment of calm and peace, but not for long. 'There's no donkey's for hire in the region', Dan's voice down the phone startled me. He had given up his day off work to call local donkey sancturies so we could respond to UKIP's 'gay donkey' scandal. Probably unneccessary and definitely not fair on the donkey, we now had to make a last minute gay donkey costume.

Finally the day had come. It's 10.30am on a Saturday morning and we are gathering in the pub meeting point before getting on the bus. Tired but dazzled with all the people full of adrenalin I'm racking through the check-list in my mind to make sure I hadn't forgotten anything. I had.

'Whose up for being a volunteer to be in the gay donkey costume? We need front and rear', I asked hopefully.

Luckily people were keen. One hundred activists piled onto two coaches all dressed up in their costumes to exaggerate the type of cultural differences and stereotypes UKIP exacerbate, to open our show 'The Beyond UKIP Cabaret'. Onlookers couldn't make out if it was a political cabaret, fancy dress party or both.

After greeting the pub landlord and a quick set up in the function room we were ready to start. The cabaret opened with Nazi Holocaust survivor Ruth Barnett who came to Britain aged four on the Kinderstransport. She read from her recent book *Jews and Gypsies*, which underlines how the Holocaust didn't happen overnight. It is about how oppression and fascism creeps up by targeting and blaming communities.[18]

Next up was Zita Holbourne, a member of Black Activists Rising Against the Cuts (Barac), who recited her poem 'Multiculturalism'.[19]

Multiculturalism cannot fail to succeed

It's not in the gift of a politician to proceed

With its termination

It's not your creation

It's in our blood and in our bones

You can't create multicultural free zones

It's on our airwaves and in our streets.

The energy in the room grew as queer go-go dancers shook their hips to 'Its Raining Men' in response to UKIP's allegation that bad weather could be blamed on the introduction of gay marriage. A traffic jam of queer migrant groups in cardboard cut-out cars made a ring outside the pub because that's what migrants do, they 'swarm our communities' and cause traffic jams. A group of mothers had their boobs out, defying Nigel who asked a breastfeeding woman to cover up, saying that mothers should 'perhaps sit in the corner' when they breastfeed, and the pub tables were busy with classes in foreign languages, which Farage had blamed for the downfall of 'Great Britain'. It was a day to remember.

Saph had just finished hosting the cabaret and we sat for a well-deserved pint. She took a gulp, smiled and said, 'Today is about a "no fucks to give" attitude to bigots. Friendships across different struggles have been created and creativity sparked. It is art-in-action and sows the seed for more defiant, courageous creative actions ahead', and finished her drink.

Dressed in a beautiful traditional Palestinian 'thobe' dress and panting after finishing her group 'Dabke' dance at the front of the room, Ewa Jasiewicz, a long-term Palestine solidarity, anti-war activist and trade union organiser, came and joined us. For years I'd been in awe. Ewa always brought the best out in people. Her visions and intuitions you could not ignore. Her challenges were constructive but brutally honest.

Ewa's analysis as ever was red hot as she said 'The politics of experience, which incorporates identity and how people identify and are identified by others, in complex ways, needs naming. Where the politics of identity might say "who are you?", the politics of experience say "what's made you who you are?".' She pauses and takes a moment to absorb the room around her, someone reciting the Koran next to a table with four people sitting there including a Holocaust survivor, a Palestinian dancer, a Roma teacher and a breastfeeding mother, all learning Chinese together.

Ewa smiles and continues, 'This is a deeper conversation, a listening where identity can sometimes be about looking more than listening. If we can't come to accept each other, if we can't have queers, HIV-positive people, Muslims, Jews, Christians and people of any beliefs or none, migrants or any lived experiences Dabke dancing together, in a pub, then it's not my revolution', and trailed off as her eyeline caught sight of the 'gay' donkey sat lonely in the corner.

After the donkey got back on all fours and weaved its way through the bar receiving pats and wiggling its bum, it made its way for the toilets. Ewa continued, 'this cabaret-action may not intervene in Britain's growing inequality at an economic level, despite the Polish language class designed to overcome divisions in the workplace starting with the basics "Hello – Czesc!" and "What's

your name?" followed by "Down with zero-hours contracts!" and "Let's unionise". These classes show that
today's racism has its roots in economic competition and
exploitation, that it's a symptom of oppression under
capitalism. Fellow workers aren't the enemy. The fight
has always needed to go back to the bosses and those
exploiting the situation, and not for just a bigger slice of
the ever melting pie, and votes in one direction or the
other, but for the whole bakery, once and for all. Farage
and his party don't offer that.'

As our cabaret continued throughout the afternoon
the atmosphere at the George and Dragon was calm, and
in the words of the pub landlord, 'everyone was very well
behaved'. Locals got involved with the talks, participated
in the classes and attended the HIV anti-stigma class, run
by Luca, an ACT UP artist wearing a bunny costume with
huge floppy white ears. We were all having a great old time,
but there was someone missing. One of the pub punters
told us that Nigel was sitting in another pub, across the
road. Apparently he had other plans, unfortunately, and
didn't join in. It was time to confront our nemesis.

So we took our all-singing, all-dancing conga line
featuring a glistening array of ethnicities, sexualities, abilities and fabulous outfits singing Sister Sledge's 'We Are
Family' over the road to him. Pub cabaret had become
street theatre. He was standing with one woman at the
bar, gripping a pint glass to his face looking hostile. Not

interested in engaging with us, he turned on his heels in his 1980s-style pin-striped polyester suit and soon drove off in a hurry. An hour later we saw headlines on the news about his kids 'going missing'. Strange, as at no point did anyone see him with any kids. The conga line came and left and the master of 'spin' left on his own.

As everyone joined in the final Dabke dancing we were ready to devour a huge rainbow-coloured 'Pride' cake lovingly baked for the cabaret by a movement of HIV-positive Nigerian women. Elated, it was time to clear up and go home.

The very next day I received at least 100 abusive messages and phone calls, including death threats. 'You are backwards thinking', 'anti-success', 'an energy sapping piece of low life pond scum', 'you and your friends are the world's biggest losers of life', 'you will ALWAYS be in the minority' and 'locked in a cage like the animal that you are'. Charming. Some attacked me for being gay and others ironically called me a Nazi.

Later that evening a video was posted onto the Facebook page of Britain First, 'a patriotic political party that will put our own people first' which campaigns viciously against multiculturalism and what it sees as the Islamisation of the United Kingdom. Britain First advocates the preservation of traditional British culture. Its leader, Paul Golding, proclaimed that they were 'to give these traitors their comeuppance'.

A tirade of hate mail followed, some horrific, some scary and even some strange veiled 'come ons' by UKIP LGBT+ members asking me on a date. I'm always up for getting out of my comfort zone so thanks, but no thanks.

The next week we were having our debrief at a charity HQ in Old Street when around ten members of Britain First, dressed in green and black stormed the building entrance. Saph was at the door and they barged through.

'Britain First fighting back', shouted the activists on the other side of our meeting door as we clasped it shut. Thumping the glass they chanted 'UKIP on the ballot box, Britain First on the streets!' clearly exposing the realities and the connections of the growing far-right. Britain First leader Paul Golding even led the chants while making Churchill-style 'peace' signs.

A stream of further comments in my inbox that night. 'Mr Glass you got what you deserved and there will be a lot more to come; so if I was you I would take your batty banging friends and hide up each others arseholes.'

It seemed we had touched a nerve. I'm not sure this is what Freire had in mind to stop war and injustice, when he said 'humanise the oppressor' but it's a reminder to get out of your comfort zone to try and fight for humanity at large – however gay the donkeys are.

How to Organise a Politician's Pub Invasion

1 Find a common enemy as an easy concept to mobilise around.
2 Welcome creativity through creating political parodies.
3 Find a key date in the political calendar to intervene.
4 Raise funds for logistics to get everyone there in an easy, accessible way such as coach hire.
5 Have way more fun than them (the oppressors).

PART 2
POWER

6

The Golden Egg

It is easy to get to the symptom of everything and the root of nothing. Globally, Pride is now the biggest cultural event in the world attracting millions of people in over 100 cities. 'Stonewall50 – World Pride' in New York City in June 2019 attracted 5 million people alone.[1] Yet, if Pride is to be an effective tool for full LGBTQIA+ freedom, it must not get complacent. It must get to its root – the etymology of radical – to become the force in society it can be.

It's summer 2019 here in boiling hot London and Pride begins in one month. Every high street bank, travel company, furniture store and food brand are waving rainbow flags outside the stores. It's easy for ordinary queer people to get drowned out.

I am sitting with Tam outside the queer venue by Hackney canal she manages. Tam is such a powerhouse behind so many queer freedom projects, I think there must be five of her. That, or she mustn't sleep. Tam runs places and events across London that create a platform for marginalised queer activists, artists and audiences to own and create spaces for understanding, liberation and building queer utopia.

'I do what I've always done, I stay visible, gender-queer and radical. Queers are that bird, singing of freedom that can't be heard, because society is so heteronormative. Everyday is a protest against white supremacy, patriarchy and capitalism. As my friend and pioneering lesbian activist Aderonke Apata says, "I'm not free until everyone is free, we aren't saved till all of us are safe". We don't have queer freedom. In some countries gays have the same rights as other capitalists, but intersex people don't, trans people don't, queers are marginalised, we aren't accepted by some gays. So for me it's really about not stopping with my rights, not resting in my "freedom", never taking the easy path. Even from our cages we can make a difference if we sing loud and long.'

Chuckling, she continued 'queer visibility is part of a wider psychic connection we queers have, collective queer unconscious is what she calls the "queer third eye". This is an energy, a concept, it's all-seeing, it links us to our queer ancestors, right back to when our alien family seeded us on earth. This, I'm beginning to understand, is what gives us the power to laugh, which in turn helps us to act.'

Tam mesmerised me as she persisted to pump my heart with joy.

'Why do you think so many queers have such a good sense of humour? It's like, you've shut down, Why do you think Stuart from the GLF is hilarious? So fucking shut down because of everything that has happened to him. The only thing that's left is to joke about everything. And actually nothing is a joke; it's terrible. It's the only way to cope – that's one way to look at it. We're all fucked. I also think that when I was a kid and it's probably the same for you, a lot of the things that you're told don't really resonate straight up because you're different and you know you're different. And then it starts to become bullshit. And most of what we've been told is bullshit. But, physiologically if you are laughing you feel better. Just "ha ha ha" at each other and we feel better.'

I couldn't agree more. The legacy of queer 'joie de vivre' is beautiful.

In 2011, Tam and friend Ginger Johnson, an ascendant drag queen, became part of a disparate group that came together to create a cohesive campaign in less than a week. They called it 'Affordable Pride'. On the street outside Tam's venue, it tapped into the original spirit of Pride as a protest for marginalised people. 'People were putting up art, posters, slogans all around the little back streets, and as the buzz grew the revellers came pouring in. It was so queer that 500 people took over the whole street. There was a place for everyone. Affordable Pride is the exact reason why Pride is fucked and that's why the spirit of it still lives on.

'Queers had come from all over London, trying to find somewhere friendly, personable and affordable. They started at 2pm to be there for anyone who felt that they couldn't go to the official parade. First to arrive was legendary GLFer Lavinia Co-op, from radical GLF drag theatre group Bloolips,[2] doing Alexander Technique for free whilst Tam gave free reiki. Ginger made a pinata, a papier maché head (filled with bad ideas) of the far-right LGBTQIA+ Milo Yiannopoulos.[3] They did people's puppetry as Ginger prepared the show with a whole gaggle of queens and performers that she had asked Lavinia to be involved in.'

So Lavinia whipped up slap and went right out there on the street and screamed out, 'Can You Spare Any Change for a Dying Queen' by Jimmy Camicia of New York City's the Hot Peaches, a monologue built around the Stonewall uprising and Marsha P. Johnson.

'It was very real for me, doing it on the street and getting people's attention', said Lavinia. 'How did you feel?' I ask Tam.

'It was a genuinely intersectional and affordable day and that's why it felt so fucking amazing. I think my favourite banner representing the corporatisation of Pride was "LGBTQIA£+".'

Scratch beneath the shiny official Pride in London propaganda and you will find incredible stories like this. A courageous, radical and contentious liberation struggle that continues to resist the sell-off of queer culture and holds Pride accountable to its 13th October 1970 roots on that day. In a room at the London School of Economics, the course of history changed forever, as the GLF initiated an anarchic, witty and assertive campaign that permanently changed the face of Britain. Stuart, Andrew, Nettie and Ted were there when GLFer John Chesterman polished off the legendary original GLF statement.

We believe that apathy and fear are the barriers that imprison people

From an incalculable landscape of self awareness

That they are the elements of truth

That every person has the right to develop and extend their

Character and explore their sexuality through relationships

With any other human being, without moral, social or political pressure.

That no relationship formed by such pressure, or not freely entered into,

Can be valid, creative or rewarding.

To you, the others, we say we are not against you, but

the prejudice that warps your life, and ours

It is not love that distorts, but hate.

On your behalf, and ours, we demand:

The same right to public expressions of love and affection as society grants

To expressions of hate and scorn.

The right to believe, without harm to others, in public and private

In any way we choose, In any manner or style, with Any words and gestures, to wear

Whatever clothes we like or to Go naked, to draw or write or

Read or publish any material or Information we wish, at any

Time and in any place.

An end to the sexual propaganda that disturbs the innocence of

Children, conditions their image of human relationships and implants

Guilt and nurturers shame for any sexual feelings outside an artificial polarity.

An end to the centuries of oppression and prejudice that have

Driven homosexuals from their homes, families and employment, have

forced them to cynicism, subterfuge and self-hatred and

have led them, so often, to imprisonment or to death.

In the name of the tens of thousands who wore the badge of

Homosexuality in the gas chambers and concentration camps, who

Have no children to remember, and whom your histories forget.

We DEMAND honour, identity and liberation.[4]

These regular gatherings of tens, sometimes hundreds of people were called 'Think Ins' or 'consciousness raising' groups. They were and still are 'expressions of freedom' that derive from the real interests and struggles of ordinary people. They also challenge the effect that the corporate, cultural and psychological monopolisation of Pride has had on their daily revolutionary potential. The work of Guy Debord in *Society of the Spectacle* resonates here in that the spectacle in this instance, 'Pride', absorbs everything, similarly to capital, so it is hard to avoid it.[5] As soon as the struggle for LGBTQIA+ freedom reaches a certain point of coverage, it will then be appropriated to co-opt, commodify and endorse capitalism's products.

'Co-option' is a word that has rung like alarm bells in my ears ever since reading Stuart's book, meeting the GLF and re-engaging with modern-day Pride. In 2015, I entered the Pride landscape not as a youngster desperately needing sanctuary from homophobia, but as a conscious adult knowing that without constant vigilance, hard-fought battles for queer freedom will be sold to the highest bidder. The barbaric tentacles of the British capitalist system knows few limits, and today, 'Pride' is firmly in its sight.

Reflecting on her involvement since the early GLF days Nettie said 'Today they want us to try and join the establishment, buy a big house, and support our military and forget social change. If you don't comply with all that, you're much more likely to be vulnerable, you're much more likely to be exposed to homophobic abuse, you're much more likely to suffer under multiple and overlapping vulnerabilities. Any institution, corporation or pillar of the military-industrial complex that the PiL [Pride in London] board desire to be part of Pride – for sentimental or strategic reasons or both – are more important than the dreams and desires of the people who started it.'

The Pride in London Board, who are responsible for 'delivery of the Pride event and its strategic direction', is made up of mainly business bodies. The Board's Chair, Michael Salter was the Political Head of Broadcasting at 10 Downing Street, and Boris Johnson, as former Mayor of

London, gave the Pride committee £100,000 as a donation from the Conservative Party.[6] Money comes with strings attached, and these strings obviously led all the way back to 10 Downing Street, to the man now in charge of Pride.

Over the last 50 years the shift in corporations aligning themselves with Pride has been seismic. Fifty years ago and throughout the AIDS epidemic it wasn't profitable to be seen to associate with such a stigmatised community. Now that the LGBTQI+ community is seen to be more palatable, which comes as a result of back-breaking work by campaigners, the companies are becoming much more comfortable to align themselves with Pride. There is a great deal of money to be made. In 2015 huge corporations infamous for giant sums of tax avoidance, like Citibank, Barclays and Starbucks, were pushed to the front of the parade into Section A, while trade unions were relegated to Section C.[7] This directly impacts LGBTQIA+ people surviving in austerity Britain. The decline of vital services in the wake of austerity cuts are the collateral damage of companies' avoidance of corporation tax.

That same year, UKIP were invited to join, despite a deep and entrenched history of homophobia in the party. Not a great start, especially with attacks such as when UKIP member Roger Helmer said 'homophobia is a "propaganda device" that describes something which simply does not exist'[8] and when UKIP councillor Geoffrey Caton said of Liverpool Gay Pride, 'Being an arse bandit is nothing to be proud of'.[9]

For ACT UP, UKIP's acceptance at Pride in 2015 was the nail in the coffin and an emergency activist call was sent out. Controversy was at boiling point and even though Pride in London eventually rejected UKIP's application, it was too late. Our rage was compounded a few days later when it was announced that Barclays Bank would lead the march, relegating trade unions and community groups to the back.

Harnessing the alchemy of grief either over an individual loved one or wholescale movement for freedom is nothing new to ACT UP. Being genuinely accountable to everyone in danger and creating an alternative platform, in life and death, is key. As a display of creative rage, political funerals have always been integral to the success of the movement that captured the public's imagination. For example, David Wojnarowicz, a trailblazing ACT UP artist, helped mobilise for the 'Ashes Action' in 1992. The flyer said 'In an act of grief and rage and love, we will deposit (our loved ones') ashes on the White House lawn. Join us to protest twelve years of genocidal AIDS policy.' In the run-up to the action he said,

> I imagine what it would be like if, each time a lover, friend or stranger died of this disease, their friends, lovers or neighbors would take the dead body and drive with it in a car a hundred miles an hour to Washington D.C. and blast through the gates of the White House and come to a screeching halt before the entrance and dump their lifeless form on the front steps.[10]

David didn't make it to the action himself because he died three months earlier due to complications related to AIDS.

So, in tribute, a week later my kitchen floor was covered in masking tape, paint was somehow splattered all over the kettle and a new group of queer rabble rousers were becoming acquainted. We struggled to hold cardboard boxes together in order to tape them into a coffin shape and collapsed in stitches as it looked more like a squashed slug. Others were piercing the foam R.I.P. Pride letters with fake flowers picked up cheaply that morning from Bethnal Green Market, whilst the rest of us smoked ciggies and laughed in the sunshine at my dusty basement home in Whitechapel.

I love the process, the wonkiness, the surprise and the rambunctious nature of actions in the making. You put a call-out into the world in order to mobilise around an issue and soon you've made new friends for life. Systems of power tell you 'everything's ok', 'you don't understand' or 'leave it to us'. Instead, deep in your gut you know that (a) they're lying (b) they're tricking you, and that if you and a ragtag army don't intervene then the fundamental freedoms that our ancestors fought for will be completely hollowed out. Pride's promotional video from 2016 was called 'no filter'. In 2017, the theme was 'love is here'. It's a nice idea, but it's wrong. Love isn't here. Rising homophobia and fascism are here. It is Orwellian doublespeak: if we say love is here, then it will be and the story then serves its purpose.

As ACT UP New York artist, activist and author Sarah Schulman says

> The story of how gay people who were despised, had no rights, and carried the burden of a terrible disease came together to force the country to change against its will, is apparently too implicating to tell. Fake tales of individual heterosexuals heroically overcoming their prejudices to rescue helpless dying men with AIDS was a lot more appealing to the powers that be, but not at all true.[11]

Our demand for the protest? That the organisation of Pride becomes democratic – that decision-making power should be taken away from the current unrepresentative, largely corporate board and replaced by an LGBTQIA+ assembly who gets to decide the theme and direction in the future.

Getting dressed in a Soho park in black jackets and rainbow feather boas, the time had come. It was the morning of Pride. Passersby looked confused as 30 funeral mourners waved rainbow flags. We put the coffin on our shoulders, walked to Oxford Circus and snuck under the security gates and upstaged Barclays at the front of Pride.

As we marched at the front of Pride the opening speech was given by Coroner Nancy Stonewall-Bummer who looked like the most spectacular drag-priest I had ever seen.

> Dearly beloved, we gather here today to mark the death of Pride in London. We mourn the loss of the

true meaning of pride, the loss of politics, solidarity, protest, vision and rebellion. It is with our deepest sadness that we invite you to Pride in London's Funeral. All of Pride's friends and family are warmly invited to attend. After years of London LGBTQIA+ Pride deteriorating condition, the United Kingdom Independence Party, a usually manageable fungal infection, dealt the fatal blow to Pride's health. Pride tried to struggle back but it was too little too late.

Coroner Stonewall-Bummer let everyone pause for breath and then continued,

Ferocious but delicate, Pride couldn't resist the invasion of UKIP. On Tuesday 2nd June at 11.45 am local specialists were alerted to the news that 'UKIP have entered into Pride because they are a legal entity and have paid'. At 12 noon, Pride was announced dead at the gay-scene.

At the end of the intervention, after passing thousands of people, mostly bemused and often cheering, we caught sight of a guy in a 'UKIP LGBT' T-shirt. 'You're just a party pooper, you don't know how to have fun', he screamed at us. He was quickly put in his place as Mica, holding the coffin defiantly, yelled back 'Trust us we do, we just don't want to dance with the devil'.

The message was clear and it grabbed the attention but I still left feeling torn. The LGBTQIA+ community is vast and heterogeneous, shot through with divisions and disparities, to the extent that it's not always 'us vs. them' but often 'us vs. us'. More often than not, the most difficult community challenge is your own.

How to Organise a Political Funeral i.e. R.I.P. Pride

1 Now is the time for method acting. Remind yourself that 'this is not a show' and be genuine with your emotions.
2 Learn from other political funeral protests. Watch United in Anger about the history of the radical HIV+ activist coalitions across class and race utilising defiant creative action tactics that created a zeitgeist for change.
3 Write a eulogy and create your own death appreciation process – every society and culture has their own.
4 Create your own key demands for justice as well as learn from previous generations who have helped bring us here.
5 Invade!

Stories of the invasion spread around the media and within hours of getting home I was approached through Facebook by someone I knew vaguely in London's LGBTQIA+

community. He asked if I would like a coffee. Little did I know this would turn out to be one of the most hilarious interactions of my life.

The following week, we met and he told me he was one of the convenors for the London Pride Advisory Committee and had seen the reports about the R.I.P. Pride funeral challenging UKIP.

'Dan, I'm glad that UKIP were there. Everyone should be welcome to come on Pride.' 'We want to be inclusive so protest isn't helpful.' And, hilariously, 'it would be really good IF YOU STOPPED PROTESTING'.

Oh my, pick your targets.

He went on to report that the Pride organising committee has announced news of Royal Air Force jets wanting to fly over Pride the following year.

The corporatisation and now the militarisation of Pride was becoming clearer, with BAE Systems, an arms trading company, marching as part of the parade. Questioning the significance, morality and necessity of military jets flying over Pride I was told 'they are just entertainment and it is great that all corporate and military LGBT+ representatives come to Pride'.

I appreciated him reaching out to me to understand the issues at hand. What I don't appreciate is trying to be silenced. His final failed persuasions were 'Pride is not a protest anymore – there is no need for it to be', and just when I thought it couldn't get any worse: 'We must eradicate any protest. Can you cooperate Dan?'

Obviously his attempt fell flat. While he was a nice guy, this was largely beside the point. It was his investment in maintaining mechanisms of power that was so problematic.

The R.I.P. Pride funeral led to an ongoing campaign against these contradictions – the wider military-corporate takeover of Pride. In light of the news of the upcoming military fly-over of Pride, those involved and new people with whom the interventions resonated, created a 'No Pride in War' vigil outside City Hall, where Pride in London Corporation are contracted, to remember all those killed at the hands of military institutions.

There are so many horrendous institutions capitalising on Pride that it's hard to know where to start. Since 2016, we set our sights on kicking BAE Systems out of Pride. BAE Systems is one of the world's largest arms companies and so depends on the existence of war that inflicts death, injury and exile on many. The firm sells weapons to countries with poor human rights records such as Israel in its colonial occupation of Palestine, and Saudi Arabia who have targeted civilians numerous times while 'intervening' in Yemen, including in hospitals, and also appears to have passed weapons on to various local factions. Their intervention has also caused a famine in Yemen which has claimed the lives of up to 85,000 children as of October 2018.[12] So focusing on BAE Systems seemed like a good place to start.

Inspired by the GLF, this new queer activist collective called 'No Pride in War' decided it was time to email the

Pride Community Advisory Board – or CAB – that was set up by Pride in London as an independent advisory and scrutiny body.

> We are people who believe in Pride, and how it marks the anniversary of the Stonewall Uprisings. It is a contradiction of Pride's own values, built on principled confrontations with overzealous police to essentially celebrate policing and war. The Royal Air Force, and companies like BAE Systems, cannot be allowed to use Pride to appear queer-friendly, as though the human suffering that they cause is irrelevant.

Eventually we received a response from the current chair of the CAB,

> I'm sure our views are similar to concern around war and arms but as we try to be the most inclusive Pride, every organisation is reviewed for entry to the parade by the CAB and just because the company may have a policy that we find difficult to agree with that's no reason for its LGBTQIA+ employees not to be part of the Parade.

R.I.P. Pride had sown a seed and we started to organise for the GLF 50th birthday in 2020 and plans began to deepen. Every month since the close of 2018, founding

GLF activists and a new generation of queers hungry for systemic change began collectively plotting in a basement back in the London School of Economics – the very place where the GLF in the UK began. The topic of this month's 'Think In' discussion was 'reclaiming Pride'.

'Pride's great success is that it follows directly out of GLF's key demand to COME OUT', Andrew embraced the packed room.

'Even now, it gives a little bit of the flavour of the first London Pride in 1972. For many spectators and some participants, it's their first coming out with all the nervousness and anxiety and the inhibitions of being public about our sexuality and making our inner gender our outer gender. I love the spectators along the roads behind the railing who come from everywhere in Britain and Ireland and from around the world and have next to no money and give us vivid smiles and even say thank you to those of us on the march.' Andrew trailed off and regained himself, startled.

'But I'm saddened by the laboriousness of the Central London march today. The long waits, the impossibility of it all if you have any spinal or leg or bladder problems. Why do we have to accept limits by the public services committee advising the Mayor of London? I hear Westminster Council takes from us an average of car-parking fines they would have levied in the West End on the day if there hadn't been a Pride march, a cost that the voluntary company holding the franchise today meets by corporate sponsorship.'

'Andrew, what gives you hope today, 50 years later?' asked a young fresh-faced woman in a bright pink puffer jacket.

Andrew smiled and responded, 'Above all there is a huge latent part of the general population which is queer and doesn't say so but more and more people are coming out in their heads and they like to know of Pride Month. I sit on the tube or bus to get there on the day and there are people aboard who are as queer as coots just sitting there smiling.'

Once Andrew finished, up stood Stuart.

'My name is Stuart Feather, I'm a Nancy boy, I'm a radical drag queen. I'm in opposition to society. Yes. And I was part of the GLF which ran from 1970 to 1975.'

I was in awe.

'Pride in London have captured the golden egg. Present day Pride is completely unrecognisable from how it was in 1972. It's been captured by the former UK Prime Minister David Cameron's office in 10 Downing Street. It's become a business model, a community interest company which doesn't have to publish how or where its money has gone.

Pride today doesn't want to work with us, the GLF who started Pride. They don't want us to tell them what we'd like to, they don't want to know that in 2020 it'll be 50 years since the founding of Gay Liberation. They don't want to know that in 2022 it'll be the 50th anniversary of the first pride. They don't want the mass of gay people to know their queer history. They are simply there to make a lot of money for themselves.'

Stuart paused for breath, regained his composure and continued.

'I'm angry and frustrated of course that it should have come to this, but it's also exciting and interesting because it's a challenge and I think it's a challenge we must face and overcome. It's quite easy – we've done it for 40 odd years already. The first pride was a protest and it was also a party in the park afterwards. That's how it was and it was the second demonstration in which gay people, we called ourselves gay people in those days, gay men and gay women, in which lesbians and gays went to Trafalgar Square and held a demonstration there which was also a kind of party. Then we went and had a party in the park and did a lot of kissing under the noses of the police, who rapidly disappeared, and enjoyed ourselves in the park playing games and things.'

If only everyone at Pride in London today got this memo. As Stuart reminds us, the ultimate goal of the GLF wasn't the ability to march from A to B, chaperoned by police, corporations and establishments who instigate and maintain institutional homophobia, but complete and absolute freedom to exist on our own terms.

Queer identity has become such a huge brand that I couldn't fault anyone for thinking Pride in London started in Marks & Spencer, who have just released their 'Pride sandwich', or even in the boardrooms of Listerine, who now proudly sell 'Rainbow mouthwash'.

If we understand these manoeuvres within the context of global capitalism – a for-profit, commercial, money market economy – the purpose of sandwiches, mouthwash and so on becomes clear. They exemplify the ideology that any marginalised community must be brought in line with the norm, the military-industrial complex. These capitalist development indicators are economic growth, technological progress, industrialism, infrastructural development and economic growth. Walter Rodney in the seminal book *How Europe Underdeveloped Africa* explores this further, 'there was a period when the capitalist system increased the well-being of significant numbers of people as a by-product of seeking out profits for a few, but today the quests for profits comes into sharp conflict with people's demands that their material and social needs should be fulfilled'.[13] In light of this, serious questions need to be asked of Pride in London and the corporation behind it. The money made goes to the wealthiest council in Britain – Kensington and Chelsea[14] – which also is home to the Grenfell Tower, where in 2017 the building's combustible cladding resulted in the worst residential fire since the Second World War, murdering 72 people and leaving hundreds homeless, with blame often attributed to corporate negligence and institutional government inaction. Is something sinister going on with their involvement in Pride too? If so, how did it become that way? How much profit is made? And fundamentally, what values are lost in the process?

A market-based model of development fails to account for the social indicators crucial to fundamental human needs, such as independence, affection, wellbeing or, heaven forbid, some semblance of dignity. We are led to believe that macro-level economic growth and the accumulation of wealth will trickle down and provide for our human needs, yet turbo-capitalist economies are the very places with the lowest quality of life. As Cathy McCormack writes in 'The Price of Economic Barbarianism: An Uncomfortable Truth',

> A global market economy which the bankers and the politicians still keep referring to as being 'free' but in reality has enslaved our humanity in a race towards human, social, economic and environmental destruction – and where the wealth in this country has not been trickling down from the rich but gushing up from the poor.[15]

'Development' or progress at Pride in London is something that is done on us, the poor and all marginalised people, whilst we are told it is in our best interests. Perpetuating an insidious culture of aid and dependency the public are told to dig deep to help out those in 'need' of support – those poor groups in need of charity, which entrenches deep individual and collective low self-esteem. This cycle of dependency, which, if left unbroken, always keeps the majority of the world's people, the poor and stigmatised, in chains. That is why 'pinkwashing', the marketing and political strategies aimed at selling products through a smoke-screen of gay friendliness, is so rife today.

Young, articulate and radical visionaries, Erkan and Levi are lovers who met on the R.I.P. Pride protest and came forward to speak next in the discussion, hungry to explore how to reclaim Pride.

'Every aspect of my being is Political and Pride pacifies that. The things I've been through. The place I was born. The class I was born into. Being gay. Having been to jail. Been through the social care system. Inherently it makes everything about my existence political. I think naturally as two queer People of Colour trying to exist and form a relationship in this day and age is naturally political', said Levi quietly but knowingly.

Erkan continued, 'I was a completely different person before being part of R.I.P. Pride. Literally. That day. It sounds stupid, but that day was the beginning of a new era for me. I never realised but the others on the action were my queer family who I now have around me, or as I like to call it, "our house". But I think that what Pride stands for today is an assimilationist project and a way for corporations to relinquish their guilt. It's a diversity hire. These corporations don't care about us; they want to use us to be like, "Hey, look guys, we're ethical!" – insert brochure with smiley queer man. Yes of course we want everyone in all institutions to be explicitly LGBTQIA+, but that's not the way towards equality.'

Every conversation and sharing of tactics between the Pride founders and the new generation of ordinary people demanding a life of integrity is fiery, like a gem that people have been waiting for a lifetime to be found, but the building janitors were knocking on the door and it was time to go home.

'Come to mine tomorrow, we are not finished yet!' said Stuart. So the next morning, I'm mincing through the clean bright white building fronts and wide tree-lined streets of Notting Hill. Stuart originally lived there as part of the 1970s GLF communes when the area was a hub of street life, carnivals and revolutionary movements, before the Conservative elitist politicians moved in. Stuart has been Queen of the Notting Hill streets ever since.

Apprentice engineer by day and radical drag queen by night, in the 1960s Stuart was outed by two senior apprentices on the factory floor. The moment the penny dropped that action could be taken was when a GLF activist asked 'How do we behave as homosexuals at work?' Stuart's attitude towards his whole persona at work flashed across his mind. The levels of dishonesty, falsehood and cover-ups he engaged in, in order to just be himself – or not – were becoming clear. Stuart felt he was deceiving his colleagues (they likely knew he was gay) and more importantly, deceiving himself. Angry that he had been pushed into this position, he decided to come out and everything else began to fall into place.

This 'ah-ha' moment drove him to become an activist. Stuart didn't want to erase or pacify himself whatsoever in order to remain hidden. His resolve, compounded by the injustices that he experienced as a teenager in coming out, inspired him to go along to his first GLF meeting. This is how he described it to me.

'It was very exciting. We had consciousness-raising groups, and we talked to each other about our experiences and what had happened to us. And I began to build up a picture really, so I wanted to carry on with the GLF.'

Sitting straight in his glamorous spearmint green arm-chair surrounded by beautiful portraits of fellow activists and lovers he painted himself, Stuart looked spectacular. He swiftly turned to me and said with a surprising sense of urgency, 'If you speak to anybody, any of the survivors who are still with us in GLF, they would all say that it turned their life around completely, and it did. And when I look back at it now and I can put it in perspective, there was a sexual revolution.'

'Where did it all begin?' I ask, eager to learn how such a fire was started.

'1969 was Stonewall, which was the model of a fight-back by homosexuals – unheard of, you couldn't have even dreamt the idea up. Today there's not a country in the world that isn't aware of gay people and lesbians, what-ever their attitude but it's there and there to fight for. So I was swept up in that, yes, and delighted to have been so because it opened my mind to what was going on in the world.'

Two years later, in 1972, the first ever Pride march was held by the GLF, a socialist-oriented ecosystem of criminals, deviants and revolutionaries. Leading the charge was the GLF working group of under 21s to confront the partiality of the 1967 Sexual Offences Act. The supposed liberating legislation still criminalised a huge swathe of the queer population, anyone under 21 and anyone older than 21 who had sex with them, like those still punished by the unequal age of consent for homosexuals.

Iconic GLF slogans on badges and literature were touted and used as hilarious comebacks as a form of identification amongst the queer community, such as 'Hello I'm gay, can I help you?', 'How dare you presume I'm heterosexual' and 'We are the people your parents warned you about'.

Radical, antagonistic and grounded in real policy change this was a far cry from the Barclays-sponsoring, M&S-sandwich-saturated, militarised Pride scene that we have today. In order to extract capital from gays and lesbians the commercialisation of LGBTQI+ culture hadn't yet distinguished between the palatable types of sexual difference, the 'straight gays' as Stuart defines them, and the queer militants and dissidents not wanting their culture to be bought off. Here, the privileging of heteronormative ideals, of marriage, monogamy and 'keeping up with the neighbours' brings the concept of 'homonormativity' to life, and the GLF didn't want to be part of it.

Amongst many iconic protests was the first real GLF street theatre protest where a group of women had disrupted the 1970 Miss World contest in the Albert Hall. It was live on TV, seen by the nation and the police came and arrested them. The BBC transmitter had been blown up the night before by the 'Angry Brigade', a revolutionary movement against state oppression. So a street theatre demonstration began outside Bow Street Magistrate Court where GLFers enacted a parody 'Miss Trial' competition, when four of the Angry Brigade defendants first appeared on trial. This was the first time Stuart got into drag.

'I was knocked over by its power really, of confusion, and the way it was like a magnet that drew people in and I thought that was just wonderful for getting attention to oneself and to the movement as a whole. So that was fun', Stuart finished with a smile blooming across his face.

Stuart went on to become part of Bloolips, the legendary radical street theatre drag troupe along with Lavinia Co-Op, Ivan Carwright, Bette Bourne, Paul Shaw and others. Bloolips blazed a trail through the world of theatre and queer politics by continuing to hijack the earnestness of 1970s gay theatre with early shows like 'Lust in Space' and 'The Ugly Duckling'. They turned the theatre into a wild, satirical celebration of queerness littered with anthems called, for instance, 'Let's Scream Our Tits Off'.

I asked Stuart what gives him hope today. He chuckled, 'Gay people. Lesbians and gays. That's what gives me hope. Because we are different. We have been oppressed by the nuclear family and everything that stems from it. We stand outside it and can see all too clearly, its hatreds, phobias and taboos. We have developed our own ways of relating to each other in order to survive outside that model. We can have our spouse and other lovers without a drama. We've all been fucked up by our families and society so we understand the difficulties of being our authentic selves, despite the implanted voice that puts us down.'

His words were like sparks directly into my soul as he continued, 'It means we have a better way of life than most heterosexuals. If we allow it to happen, more love and understanding in our lives for our fellow human beings grows because it is a universal love beyond the limits of blood and race. We have a trust and respect for each other that has never needed to be enforced by laws, and we have lived together as couples in defiance of the law, bravely, without rings and certificates. And it doesn't take a leap of the imagination to look at other people chosen as society's hate figures and see how they've suffered and empathise with their position whether it's transphobia, racism or migrants or all those othered peoples who are being degraded in the world today. We understand their plight and can be moved enough to go out there and show them solidarity in the hope that they will understand our values.

'You know Dan, the point of queer activism is to get people protesting against the conditions they're living under, yes ... and, well, activism is the only cure for apathy, and apathy is what governments rely on to get their way. The world has moved on from mass democracy to managed democracy. So, the message is turn around, enjoy a healthy body and a sane mind by resisting degradation through radical agitation. Agitate the root cause – agitate the nuclear family.'

At the end of the evening I floated back to East London high on Stuart's wisdom.

The following month at the next GLF 'Think In' I asked Ted and Nettie the same.

'Absolute Freedom for all! That's what gives me hope!' Nettie banged her fists on the table. 'When we started I was doing GLF all the time, pretty well. You know, on Monday I'd go to the action group, on Tuesday I'd go to the Red Lesbian Brigade, on Wednesday I'd go to the general meeting, on Thursday I'd go to Camden GLF, on Friday I'd go to the Women's Group, Saturday we'd have a demonstration, and Sunday I'd go to the counter-psychiatry group', she beamed.

Ted chimed in, smiling, 'One of the funniest events I've been involved with was GLF's direct actions against Pan Books' publication of "Dr" David Reuben's rubbish book *Everything You Wanted to Know about Sex but Were Afraid to Ask*. Amongst its myriad of nonsense, the book stated that typical gay sexuality involved inserting light-bulbs and cucumbers anally. So we created a 14-foot-long cardboard cucumber and a large inflatable plastic light

bulb. Carrying these items through the streets with placards giving specific instructions, we marched to and into
Pan Books' offices, suggesting they partake of these sexual
practices themselves. I'll never forget the faces of the management and staff.'

Even though the GLF demanded a world where we
would be a 'Queer Nation', half a century on LGBTQIA+
inequality is still rife. Complete LGBTQIA+ liberation is
part of a matrix, for housing rights, universal healthcare,
economic freedom, and so complete liberation will not be
met without state resistance. However, the GLF teaches us
to have hope.

Hope in turn generates a mentality of fearlessness
against personal and political limitations. Years of negative
isolation, oppression and poor mental health caused by
systemic inequality which, if left unattended, then results
in what postcolonial political philosopher Franz Fanon
calls 'colonisation of the soul' as marginalised peoples'
fundamental needs continue to be ignored because of their
refusal, or inability to be conditioned.[16]

Queer culture – at its most raw – is the profound experience of being queer and alive in a world set against us.
Our queer ancestors, radical or not, remind us to pierce
through the fog of collective amnesia that has been struc-
turally utilised to manipulate us into inaction and remind
us how much we still have to fight for and never to be pac-
ified. The 50th anniversaries since the Stonewall uprisings
in 1969, the Gay Liberation Front in 1970 and the first

Pride protest in 1972 are great moments to celebrate progress. However, rather than a linear, forward movement, this 'progress' often tends to look like two ships sailing in opposite directions.

The corporate-funded, militarised Pride in London boat sails into the sunset with a tiny section of our community. On the other ship *SOS – None of Us Are Free until We All Are* (everyone else, including Pride's founders) struggles to get a life-ring thrown overboard.

The critical moment that led to this was in 2004 when Pride changed from a 'Protest' to a 'Parade', costing £100,000 extra each year to hold and infrastructurally becoming a Community Interest Company (CIC) – that is, a company with an interest in monetising a particular section of the community and abandoning the rest. Today, the capital still has no permanent queer museum, community centre or arts centre, AIDS memorial or comprehensive LGBTQIA+ housing programme. Without grassroots projects intervening in the status quo, like The Outside Project who have reclaimed an abandoned fire station in North London to support the growing LGBTQIA+ homeless whilst holding exhibitions, workshops, cabarets and skillshares, our queerstory is in danger of being forgotten.[17]

As the years plough on, more and more members of the LGBTQIA+ community become frustrated with what London Pride has come to represent. Other Pride in London business models could have been adopted, but a CIC is unique in being able to hide all financial dealings behind a City of London-designed financial statement where only summary figures are given rather than income, expenditure and drawings that state what monies are spent and where. From its beginnings PiL declined to offer financial transparency to its own constituents – the community it exploits. All of Pride's expenses are now lumped under one nebulous sum, rendering the origins and direction of its capital ambiguous. Pride claims to represent the gay community, yet from the outset of their corporate life, they have failed to display any transparency whatsoever.

As Stuart told me in his flat 'The privatisation of space is nothing new. Both physical and psychological, it has been a colonising strategy for centuries. It's a typical Tory thing – they've had only the one idea since the fourteenth century. It was smash and grab then and its smash and grab now.'

Known then as the 'enclosures' it's now known under the neoliberal term of privatisation. It's rare to find treasure without murder, rape and pillage, to acquire capital or acquire treasure – it's theft. Rich critiques contribute to the commodification and privatisation of radical queer culture. The neoliberal penetration of the money-market economy that 'accommodates' radical movements is resonant with David Harvey's concept of accumulation by dispossession[18] or Silvia Federici on primitive accumulation.[19] However, hope for continued radical change should not be abandoned. Alan Sears in 'Queer Anti-Capitalism:

What's Left of Lesbian and Gay Liberation?' explores the ongoing movements arising out of the spaces that the capital restructuring of queer life leaves and reminds us to continue to scrutinise 'Pride' from a range of perspectives, including but not limited to its financial dealings.[20]

The concept of 'homonationalism' too can help us unpack the reality of Pride, of which Britain is a potent illustration. Homonationalism describes the process of LGBTQIA+ identity being endorsed by national and military projects invested in maintaining and legitimising the political and cultural status quo. One such example can be seen in the practices of weapons manufacturer, BAE Systems, who fly the Red Arrows fighter jets over Pride alongside the Royal Air Force.

The branding of 'LGBTQIA+' swiftly becomes a pink gloss on Britain's nationalist military projects. It becomes a colonial product to be exported to other countries. Bombing for LGBTQIA+ visibility becomes part of the imperial horror show just as the West bomb for women's emancipation in the Middle East, and they are all inextricably linked. Through this branding, Pride and the presence of the military legitimises Britain's existence as a Western, liberal entity. It is classic 'othering', the regressive 'other' where everyone is sexually perverse, restricted, oppressed and waiting for Britain to liberate them from their shackles of oppression. It's the binarisation of creating a good and bad using LGBTQIA+ identity to justify it at its core.

Since the R.I.P. Pride protest Levi and Erkan have flourished into well-respected radical queer artists and thinkers and so it's lovely to catch up with them for a cup of tea and reminisce at their Tottenham home. 'When we managed to get rid of UKIP off of Pride I realised that protest works. Dragging the coffin to the front of the march was brilliant. People are mobilising and gradually Pride is returning to its radical past. Then when in 2016, Pride became militarised, with stiff men in red coats marching left-right-left; defence company BAE Systems sponsoring the event and the Red Arrows doing a flyover ... I knew homonationalism was alive and well.'

Erkan continued, 'In fact, there's really nothing to be lost through taking action – almost literally – given the warfare so much of the global queer community exist within. So once the personal fear of death is overcome, which is a highly irrational thing in itself, then queer activists against the militarisation of Pride are paving the way for "No Pride in War" to become true.' Once again, here, Steve Biko's words come to the forefront of my mind: 'You are either alive and proud or you are dead, and when you're dead you can't care anyway.'[21]

Without meetings revolution wouldn't happen. As Stuart told me, 'If we are really feeling the effects of feudalism in this country again that's leading us into a disaster', then we have to dig deeper. So at the November 2018 'Think In' we – the remaining founders of Pride and newer recruits to the GLF – decided to call Pride in London Corporation and demand a meeting.

As the planning meeting drew to a close Stuart ended with a rallying cry, 'There is always an alternative. We have one. Please help us end this charade.'

Andrew spoke up.

'Exactly! It's not even called a march anymore. Well, first of all, there aren't as many people today on the parade as there used to be. Before this present group who are organising it now, back in the 1970s we had 100,000 people coming on a gay pride march. We had over 100,000, we had 120,000, we had 130,000, but now it's restricted and they make all sorts of excuses and they're banning individuals for just joining the parade. Now people even have to pay for a wristband to join it. They even brought BAE Systems – the weapons company – with a mobile cinema onto the Pride parade this year with a film on loop. Every now and again, it even had a war plane casually rolling across the screen.'

The room gasps.

'A totally up to date modern warplane. A big picture, about 15 feet by 10 foot, for people watching our march to see.' Andrew finished and let out a big breath.

Then Sue, a new GLF member said, 'Are we asking for what Pride in London want to hear or what we actually want and need. They are just a corporation with a contract and we have it in our capacity to kick them out if we wish.'

The GLF activists were staunch in their mission. The original aims of the GLF rocked the world and I knew these would too. Sick and tired of rainbow supermarket sandwiches they wanted their golden egg back and insist on its political orientation.

'One last thing!' Ted said excitedly 'Remind them [Pride in London Corporation] that Stonewall was not a riot, it was an uprising that led to where we are today.'

Later that night we sent this:

Dear Pride in London.

We are nearing the 2020 50th anniversary of the founding of GLF and urge

A NEW AGREEMENT ABOUT PRIDE EVENTS FOR A NEW WORLD AGE

1 Pride is free – Pride organisers who want ticketed events must arrange free Pride marches as well. No one should be denied entry to Pride because they don't have enough money.

2 Pride is always a protest as well as a celebration. We've a whole world yet to change and we've hardly begun.

3 LGBTQIA+ community groups actively engaged in grassroots LGBTQIA+ empowerment programmes, or key allies such as the miners in the 1980s, always to head Pride Marches.

4 Arms dealers and other corporations who trade with nations in violation of the U.N. International Charter on Human Rights are never again to be allowed to sponsor or have floats at Pride Marches. Individual LGBTQIA+ employees of such corporations are welcome as always, but not marching in groups in corporate logos.

5 The target is to be vehicle-free: no diesel-powered vehicles unless for mobility or safety reasons.

6 Full accessibility and reminders to LGBTQIA+ friendly venues near the March that full accessibility is the target.

7 GLF to lead Pride in London in 2020.

Yours, the Gay Liberation Front

The GLF knew not to wait for approval but still were keen to hear PiL's thoughts on the agreement nonetheless. On a crisp Sunday morning in March 2019 – we sat around an East London corporate HQ overlooking the Thames with Alison, Pride in London's co-chair.

After the agreements were vocalised it was time for specific questions. Nettie didn't waste precious time: 'Why were the Red Arrows (military jets) allowed to fly over Pride?', only to be told that whilst those flying the Red Arrows weren't necessarily LGBTQIA+, the military – its history and its present – should be celebrated.

Unperturbed, Nettie continued: 'And why are Tesco and supermarkets allowed to be at the forefront of Pride and LGBTQIA+ community action groups at the back?'

Because Tesco provide Pride with sandwiches, we were told, without any hint of sarcasm.

Well that's that then. Apparently.

As we left the building, and before speeding off into the night towards the station, Andrew turned and said to me angrily, 'The Ministry of Defence's arms sales marketing involvement in Pride still remains unacknowledged by its co-chairs. So long as BAE are allowed on Pride Parades in selling mode the Red Arrows too are unacceptable. If they choose to fly over in a vulgar pinkwashing exercise we can try all we can to stop them, but we definitely don't have to invite them or thank them.'

Usually a big cuddly bear, I'd never seen Andrew so enraged.

Was the earth made to preserve a few covetous, proud men to live at ease, and for them to bag and barn up the treasures of the Earth from others, that these may beg or starve in a fruitful land; or was it made to preserve all her children? (Gerrard Winstanley)[22]

7

Coming Into

As soon as you fall out from the clouds of 'normality' and into the sea of 'deviance' you become exposed to the dynamics of power and begin to understand what it means to be in solidarity with others. That is the moment we become radicals. So how can we flip the script and start 'coming into' our powerful queer heritage rather than 'coming out' into a world where we feel powerless?

A new year arrived along with a resurgence of GLF energy too.

'Welcome everyone! It's the 50th anniversary of the Stonewall uprisings and I'm delighted right now that in 2019, nearly 50 years later, after the GLF started, that we're still having "Think Ins" at the London School of Economics with lots of new-generation activists.'

Andrew continued embracing the packed room full of many new faces, 'What we were trying to achieve was to change ourselves – there were other people that were very energetic and capable of changing laws. Sod it with changing the heterosexual mind, we said in 1970, let's change OUR OWN MINDS ABOUT OURSELVES! There has been much progress and so much left untold. Through our actions against religious homophobia GLF even helped abolish "the Blasphemy Law" that banned speaking out against God in Britain since Medieval times. If it still existed, the revived American-style Evangelical Christianity today and other fundamentalists would be using that law now', Andrew whooped.

No matter how tired or busy they are, these remaining founders of Pride come to every 'Think In' without fail, cracking jokes about occupying PiL in their wheelchairs. Their commitment is unwavering.

Directing his attention to the younger activists in the room, Andrew took a breath.

'Be like trees and breathe out the oxygen of self-respect and the world will change. We were about changing our sense of self so that we would be Proud, stand for ourselves, take no advice and take no conversions or transformations.

'Those of us who were white, a majority in GLF, learnt what we had in common with crushed people of colour and what we could learn from their 500-year rebellion in the Americas. Those of us who were cis-male, learnt what we could from crushed women and THEIR rebellions, above all the Suffragettes. Activism isn't for everyone and no-one should put themselves down if they give it a miss.

For those who can't help but be activists, activism changes them as people, it makes friendships, it creates lovers and it also changes the outside world because activism has changed us', Andrew explained.

'Art colleges such as Hornsey in North London rose in rebellion against teaching methods in 1968. The GLF ran for three years at full tilt from 1970 to 1973. What inspired me was the other people at GLF. It was like a university with a student staff, which was one of the ideals of the 1960s among all young people, not just gay ones. It really was in effect an open university for kings, queens, intersex, trans, single mothers and the generally fed-up. We had people coming from every kind of background and who were of every kind of appearance – especially in the later stages radical drag – unlike the ferociously conformist Universities like Oxford, Cambridge, St Andrews and Trinity, Dublin of those days', Andrew beamed.

Dialogue in community such as at the 'Think Ins' is far deeper and more primal than language and must be able to capture the subliminal, magical language of the human spirit that notes on a flip-chart never can. Critical perspectives and explorations into the mechanics of institutional war and homophobia were given space to breathe. How Thatcher's 'inalienable right to be gay' statement still haunts many of the GLF activists and the sexual freedom protest songs sung at marches over the decades still soothe their soul, and so we raise a toast to Tom Robinson for the Queer Power anthem 'Sing If You're Glad to Be Gay!'

The British Police are the best in the world,

I don't believe one of these stories I've heard

'Bout them raiding our pubs for no reason at all

Lining the customers up by the wall

Picking out people and knocking them down

Resisting arrest as they're kicked on the ground

Searching their houses and calling them queer

I don't believe that sort of thing happens here

Sing if you're glad to be gay

Sing if you're happy that way[1]

The revolutionary roots of the GLF were crystal clear to the original activists but eye-opening to the younger people in the room, as Andrew shared the letter by the revolutionary Black Panther Party for Self-Defense founder Huey Newton in August 1970. It was called 'A Letter to the Revolutionary Brothers and Sisters about Women's Liberation and Gay Liberation', that controversially pledged the Panthers to support Gay liberation.

We should be willing to discuss the insecurities that many people have about homosexuality. When I say 'insecurities', I mean the fear that they are some kind of threat to our manhood. I can understand this fear. Because of the long conditioning process which builds insecurity in the American male, homosexuality might produce certain hang-ups in us. We should be careful about using those terms that might turn our friends off. The terms 'faggot' and 'punk' should be deleted from our vocabulary, and especially we should not attach names normally designed for homosexuals to men who are enemies of the people, such as [Richard] Nixon or [John] Mitchell. Homosexuals are not enemies of the people. We should try to form a working coalition with the gay liberation and women's liberation groups. We must always handle social forces in the most appropriate manner.[2]

In September later that year, the Black Panther Party sponsored the People's Revolutionary Convention in Philadelphia. Sylvia Rivera, who two years earlier changed herstory as part of the Stonewall uprisings along with Marsha P. Johnson and a leaderless, racially mixed movement of street queens, fags and dykes, met there with Huey Newton. They agreed that such groups as GLF and Street Transvestite Action Revolutionaries (STAR) were all revolutionary peoples and must unite.

LSE students Aubrey Walter and Bob Mellors, who were travelling in the US at the time, attended. Upon returning to London and inspired to act, Aubrey said 'I came back to the UK and it all seemed flat. Bob had gone back to college at the LSE and we spoke on the phone. Bob booked a room and we held a meeting.' These initiatives led directly to the formation of the GLF meetings in London later that year.[3]

These origins of the GLF bring power to the root of the word 'education', that is 'e-ducere', literally, to lead forth, or to bring out something which is potentially present. This catalyses 'Conscientisation', which refers to a critical positioning (action) in the face of a reality, understood from a continuous process of reflection and questioning (conscience). Through engaging simultaneously with the three territories of 'head' or intellectual arguments, 'heart' or emotional engagement and 'hand' the action-oriented potential of such injustice – powerful dialogue can begin to blossom. If you are too stuck in the head you will be an 'armchair activist', too stuck in the heart you won't get out of bed in the morning as it's all too depressing, and too stuck in the hand and you will be knee-jerk and reactionary. By asking ourselves which of the three comes most naturally to us, we recognise our innate 'go-to' space. I know the territory of the heart grips me as I too often find myself staring at the wall listening to Billy Holiday and Lena Horne's saddest songs. The trick is that all territories need to be in balance, where we can connect to an even deeper realm of emergence, the field of future possibility. This then, ultimately, enables us to 'come into' rather than 'out of' our radical queer heritage. In other words, we become subjects of our own change.

Sitting with younger GLF activists after the 'Think In', we reflected on everything we were trying to absorb. I met Dani and Ashley through ACT UP and felt lucky to be deepening our queer understanding as part of the GLF together. 'What do the beginnings of Pride mean to you?' I ask.

'There's something magical about the Stonewall 50th and the 50th anniversary of Pride. For once, there seems to be a real desire to acknowledge where we've come from. Acknowledging the anniversary, offers us an opportunity to connect with our queerstory and understand we're a part of something much bigger. As a young gay man I found myself completely lost in the world. I felt like a drifting island and so I started researching LGBTQIA+ queerstory as a means of anchoring myself to something bigger. In doing so, I learned of all those who came before me and the battles they'd fought for their liberation and the liberation of others and began to understand the responsibility we have to fight for each other', shared Ashley.

'I had no idea that was Andrew', said Dani about their experience in joining the 'Think Ins', 'and they actually were there and the next thing I know is that we are doing a queer tour of Marylebone together and creating a GLF tribute show. Now I am glad to say Andrew is designing my next tattoo. It is in honour of the first generation GLF activists when they were held up in court. When the magistrate asked them to take off their hats, they yelled "NO!" until the magistrate lost his temper, yelling back "why not?" only to be told in response "Because it goes with the shoes". Such sass!'

Instilling in me the importance of 'anchors' to ground us in our learning journey, the GLF inspired me to visit my friend, liberation educator and activist Alastair McIntosh, and through our conversation the poignancy of the GLF spaces became clear.

'The fundamental purpose is to allow people to unravel from the cold stigmatised outside and simply be. To provide a space where people can centre down at deeper and deeper levels, and I know it's a cliché, but quite literally to find themselves. To shift from the ego level and the persona, the mask level of functioning, and let go of the masks. Even starting to let go of ego identity, and just settling down into who it is that they are comfortable to be. That's the spaces where love starts to open up.'

Alastair looks at me, waits for me to nod and after taking a moment to absorb this, he continues.

'What's important is what next. If you're forced to be deviant along one parameter then it opens up along other parameters too – the potential for deviance relative to the consensus in straight mainstream society. That's the time when focus shifts on what you're moving into. If your only focus is what your getting out of it, then you're always looking back. When you start to focus on what you are getting *into*, that opens up profound questions about the nature of humanity and how we use our lives.'

As Alastair finished, his words shifted and opened my mind like a blast of fresh air. He then handed me a book.

'Have you read this?'

In his book *Walking Each Other Home*, spiritual teacher Ram Dass wrote:

> We're all going to the same place, and we're all on a path. Sometimes our paths converge. Sometimes they separate, and we can hardly see each other, much less hear each other. But on the good days, we're walking on the same path, close together, and we're walking each other home.[4]

'He also said "Treat everyone you meet like God in drag"', Alastair chuckled, and we hugged as I left to go home.

There is no other way to learn about the transformation that brings meaning and love in our community, except by practising it.

Listening to the Pride founders at the 'Think Ins' made me ponder. Their method of coping with suffering itself is a politicising declaration, to overcome the hauntology and work through it in some alchemical way. Every day that they are still here is a blessing as they have so much to share – if they haven't already left the building, having died because of the AIDS epidemic or are suffering from mental, physical or spiritual exhaustion from decades of queer resistance. For some, Alzheimer's and dementia are stealing their powers, so the poignancy and the urgency of our mission to cherish our difference escalates.

Literally, our difference is rooted in the essence of 'queer', which simply means 'weird', which is why so many refrain from embracing it. The act of not conforming to the norm, whether you choose to or not and whether you embrace it or reject it, guides all of us in our relationship to empathise with ourselves and others.

My first 'I am different' memory occurred in my primary school hall when I was about six years old. It was coming up to Christmas and my teacher didn't know what to do with this strange Jewish kid at a Christian School. I remember the moment so vividly when she brought out the nativity play script to dish out the roles:

'Natasha, you will be the angel. Sharlene, Soraya, James, you will be the three wise men . . .'

As she continued and I was waiting for my part we came to the end and I asked 'Miss who am I?'

All the key roles were taken. Even the part of the sheep. What else could there be? I wondered, rejected and waiting.

'Ah yes, Daniel, we made a part specifically for you . . . The Stranger in the Barn.'

Destiny sealed. The rest, you could say, is queerstory.

Being 'othered' can provide a deeper understanding of conformity, disobedience, witnessing, power, love, discernment, faith, conviction and purpose to be courageous during our short time on this planet.

Common to all these perspectives is the relevance of speaking the truth above all else. Gandhi called it *sat-yagraha* – a Sanskrit word that means 'truth force', which he saw at the heart of *ahimsa*, or nonviolence. 'It is better to die on your feet than to live on your knees!' said Mexican peasant revolutionary leader Emiliano Zapata.[5] Civil rights activist and Muslim Minister Malcolm X said, 'we need more light about each other. Light creates understanding, understanding creates love, love creates patience, and patience creates unity.'[6] These philosophies were all part of the context that gave rise to GLF. Born out of the aftermath of global uprisings against colonialism, patriarchy and apartheid, GLFer's had witnessed poverty, racism, police brutality, state violence, imprisonment and the mental and physical turmoil that ensued.

Some crimes against 'the other' are so heinous that nothing will ever rectify them. All we can do is attempt to understand their causes and do everything in our power to prevent them from happening to anyone, ever again. To grasp the meaning of the impact of Section 28, concentration camps, an atomic weapon explosion at Hiroshima, the mindset which created the Buggery Act centuries ago or current homophobic legislation like the 'Kill the Gays' Bill in Uganda[7] would take more than one lifetime. You would have to hear every story and take in the memories of how the vanished repeat themselves in the minds of their loved ones and others like them across the world. These are traceless traces of queerstory, the crying in the dark or the sound of feet on a certain staircase or the dull aching pain of constant invalidation. The never-ending stories of hopelessness. Echoes resounding for years in the experience of each human who for generations holds this private life of war.

Suffering is not highly respected today in queer culture; often there is not the physical or psychological space within the pressure cooker of our existence. So much of our culture considers the pain of suffering the province of losers, something to be avoided or a punishment for making mistakes in life. Those affected by trauma are then doubly damaged by being silenced on a subject considered taboo.

If our destiny as different – as queers – had sent us down a different road, would there have been no suicide, no genocide, no trauma? Is there a way we can see the world for all its goodness instead, as a way of healing from this pain? We are the generation who can deal with trauma differently – but how?

The importance of love is thrown into our orbit through advertising, religion and every key societal pillar, often trying to sell us something. Yet the failure of love is apparent. War, domestic violence, rape culture, misogyny and patriarchy prove that love can't keep us together. This bleak picture in no way alters the nature of our longing to love, but first we have to know what 'love' means.

Love's meaning has preoccupied humankind throughout time and across the world and has been the catalyst for many movements for revolutionary change. Today in austerity Britain, political and economic solutions are readily advocated for social change in our culture; love doesn't appear within political manifestos. This situation cannot be faced merely from an intellectual focus but requires a more complex vision. We can empathise, connect and commune with someone right in front of us. Building the roadmap for love in community is needed now more than ever. We have a choice.

Foucault's history of sexuality, which explores the patriarchal production of sex and its function in establishments of power, resonates here – how the mechanics of patriarchal power controls the sexual body through the micro-politics of everyday life and oppresses anyone who falls out of the narrow confines of the nuclear family life. Becoming unemployed, homeless or a target of police by confronting patriarchy or homophobia in the workplace, standing up to homophobic landlords, protesting against entrenched religious bigotry or the growing militarisation of Pride exposes the sinister tactics of structural violence in the state.

Today we have to be ever more vigilant.

So, how can sharing trauma become a tool for greater development, a subversive act of soul activism that declares a people's refusal to live numb and small? How is this 'sense of living connection' being maintained and perpetuated even as the founders of Pride leave our midst?

'Calling out b*llshit' is a fantastic way to start.

On the night that singer Aretha Franklin died, an opportunity arose to do just that.

The media spotlight is an important place where we have to stand up for ourselves. Throughout all these actions and campaigns there are usually a lot of media requests. Many of these are supportive but it's important to get out of your echo chamber. This specific request booted me right out of the chamber door. My fellow 'Queer Tours of London – A Mince through Time' guide, Dan de la Motte and I found ourselves in a pit of hell-fire as we tried to defend our right to exist as queers on the radio show DEJAVU FM, let alone our right to respect.

The show's brief was 'a debate on gay rights', but we found ourselves debating with a hardcore homophobic pastor. Within minutes we were called Neanderthals, paedophiles and blamed for the moral corruption of children. Just when I thought it couldn't get more intense we were held up and targeted as sneaking criminals who in our spare time spread gayness through infecting chicken burgers with pheromones. An angry caller said that we are pushing our agenda on schoolchildren

'They're trying to put oestrogen in children's foods – even in the food industry you have oestrogen that's found in chickens which makes people effeminate – it takes a man and a woman to make a human being! The side effects come out making a man more feminine and a woman behave more masculine – these are the effects of these chemicals.'

Then they asked, 'If it is ok to marry someone of the same sex then surely you can marry a horse?'

FOR REAL.

Even a passerby listening in the reception said, 'It's 2018 For Fucks Sake'.

Dan swivelled in his chair, stared me in the eye and spoke directly into the mic: 'Thanks for asking me that question. We were invited on this show to speak about our activism, but all we've done so far is defend our right to live as human beings. The activism that we do is through tours and campaigns where we remember the queer siblings that went before us and the brave pioneers that ran brave safe spaces who lived in fear of police raids in the face of police entrapment and often faced imprisonment and torture. We do this to remember all marginalised communities to pave the way for something else in the future', he courageously responded.

My self-defence mechanism has always been ripping the piss. It has mostly worked so far but knowing how trauma and vile homophobic abuse runs deep I said, 'Dan, we don't have to do this, we can walk out of here right now [we were doing it for the love – there was no money]', but he continued with intelligence, pride, dignity, integrity, wisdom, love, compassion, vulnerability, eloquence, humour and so much more. I was blown away by him.

We picked up our jackets and with our heads held high Pastor Joe ushered us out as he said, 'Shout out to my wife, we celebrate being heterosexual baby.'

R.E.S.P.E.C.T. Pastor Joe. No more chicken burgers for you.

If the first stage is 'standing up to the bullshit', then next is to challenge the bull-shitters.

Neo-Nazi demonstrations and actions have been on the rise since BREXIT discussions started. The brutal murder of MP Jo Cox brought these dynamics starkly into the headlines.

In early 2016, friends responded to a wider call-out for queers against fascism to challenge a Neo-Nazi demonstration in Dover. So off I minced on the coach, very unprepared for what was to happen next.

It was a cold winter morning and I was anxious as the coach stopped to refuel at a petrol station. It only got worse when the doors of five separate cars burst open and fascists came out to smash up the motorway station restaurant. My nerves went through the roof.

When we arrived at the town square in Dover we were welcomed by a hundred hard-right Neo-Nazis with banners reading '#hitlerwasright' and 'Sieg Heil!' screaming 'White Power WorldWide' and chanting National Front slogans. My boyfriend and friends, along with the bleeding injured couple we were trying to take to an ambulance, shouted 'run!'

I was too near the Neo-Nazis and didn't have a chance to turn back. I tried to run up some steps to a house but no luck. A huge, white middle-aged man saw me clutching my 'Jews against Fascism' sticker on my bomber jacket and screamed to the others 'got one!' As his friends came to his aid and he swung the first of many punches to my eye, I remember being pushed to the floor and thinking 'Oh My Days . . . This is so so so . . . 1980s . . .'.

I'm wearing a flea-market bomber jacket, white Reebok classics and a dodgy baseball hat, and the Nazis are still sporting Harrington Jackets and Kappa tracksuits. If I dug deep enough in my jeans pocket I'd probably even find a Christmas voucher for more sovereign rings from Elizabeth Duke in Argos.

After the bruises had gone down and I was ready to face the world again, I went to the launch of a new queer community centre project. Later, as I walked to the bus stop in front of Dalston Kingsland station, after mincing the night away at local queer bar Dalston Superstore, to my surprise, from behind the bus stop two guys jumped out and punched me. The pain in my chest was unbeliev-able. I grabbed onto a lamppost and regained composure. Looking at their tense faces I thought maybe they were jealous of my new calypso melon shirt (I am, and I own it!) or even they fancied me. Either way it was hilarious see-ing them getting rinsed by the morning tube workers after I knocked one of them out. Clearly they underestimated how much buckfast one human can drink or how much strength queer-community-power can pump someone up.

Thanks fate. The moral of the story is, if we are commit-ted to lifelong social transformation, don't fight yourself, there's plenty of people and systems of power that will try to do it for you. Laugh at yourself, learn, fight back and crack on. There's incredible people all around shifting the tide towards truth and justice.

SOLIDARITY FOREVER.

How to Build a Movement

1 Incorporate 'Action–Reflection cycles' – the understanding that 50 per cent of our efficacy in social transformation comes from reflection as well as action. I know I spend about 10 per cent of my time throwing myself at walls – it is a constant learning process.

2 Explore the revolution outside your comfort zone and create the world you are striving for in the here and now.

3 Celebrate how far we have come and agitate for where we need to go.

4 Question what needs you and your community have to meet (and explore what pathologies arise when these needs are not met).

5 Explore how independence, generosity, responsibility and owning your emotions can bring courage to continue the struggle ahead. These four elements make up the 'wheel of courage' – the basic needs for positive human development.

8

Janine

Entrenched systems of power premised upon fear and hierarchy will always try to extinguish any threats to their existence. Police infiltration, dirty press tactics and corporate spin are just some of the strategies used against the alternatives we embody, that are gaining traction. The corporate and neoliberal takeover of queer identity relies upon the LGBTQIA+ community being genuinely powerless and isolated to resist.

Rat, squealer, snitch, tout and snout – there is an endlessly rich list of names for informers. There have been as many as 200 names dating back to the seventeenth century. Today in Britain, however, the biggest gang of grasses has the sanitary name of Counter Terrorism Intelligence Unit (CTIU), and is barely known by the general public. It exists to 'prevent or respond to incidents of terrorism and domestic extremism to investigate and prosecute those involved' that increasingly classifies civil rights activists as 'domestic extremists' and deploys its full surveillance and interference. The message is quite clear.[1]

Good-looking undercover police officers, known as the 'pretty police', aiming to entice men into sexual activity before they arrest them, is one of the oldest tricks in the establishment's book. During the 1980s, criminal prosecution was bestowed upon thousands of men for consensual gay behaviour – a level of institutionalised police and judicial discrimination greater than any other European Community member at the time.[2] The presumption that life for queers was an escalator of improvements since the partial decriminalisation of homosexuality in 1967 is thwarted by the fact that in 1989, convictions for 'gross indecency', a consensual, gay-only offence, were more than three-and-a-half times higher than in 1966, the year before decriminalisation began.

Whilst thousands of queers' lives and careers were ruined for the simple act of winking or flirting, gay-bashing and other seriously violent crimes went unsolved as police spent their time creating spy-houses across from public parks with infrared cameras, camouflaged shelters and a rejuvenated programme of 'pretty police officers'.

Out from the toilets and into the streets, the trailblazing queer activist movement 'OutRage!' was formed.[3] Unwilling to accept anything less than full legal citizenship rights and protection they organised defiant theatrical protests that empowered the community. They launched a tantalising programme of guerrilla-style hit-and-run protests including invading police stations, photographing undercover 'pretty police', displaying warning signs to frustrate entrapment operations, demolishing hidden cameras, invading public appearances by the Metropolitan Police Commissioner and my favourite, a 'wink-in' to protest against laws that prohibited men from winking, meeting and exchanging numbers.

Within a year, the police agreed to five of OutRage!'s key demands for a non-homophobic policing policy. Within three years, the number of men convicted of gross indecency fell by two-thirds, saving thousands of gay men from arrest and a criminal record.

However, these tactics of repression are not new. The Black Panther Party and radical feminist movements of the 1960s that gave rise to the GLF were notoriously infiltrated and under intense surveillance by COINTELPRO, short for 'Counterintelligence Program'. These were a series of covert, and at times illegal, projects conducted by the United States Federal Bureau of Investigation (FBI) aimed at surveilling, infiltrating, discrediting and disrupting domestic political organisations.[4] The GLF are fully aware of the levels of police suppression of their liberty that the state are happy to sink to as it was police harassment which catalysed the Stonewall uprisings to begin with.

Today the tables are turning as the public demand accountability and GLF activists are leading the charge for an apology for those convicted under homophobic laws.

Further resistance includes recent movements like Police Spies Out of Our Lives, a campaign and support group working to achieve an end to the sexual and psychological abuse of campaigners and others by undercover police officers, who have taken the police to the High Court through a 'Spycops' operation demanding the depth and breadth of institutional police violence be exposed.[5] Long-term embedded police infiltrators in a wide range of civil rights movements for social, environmental, economic and racial justice are being outed and social movements now have the technology to turn the tables on the police and surreptitiously record them back. The Home Office is facing public pressure to release a report called 'Left Wing Activism and Extremism in the UK', which has been prepared by its Extremism Analysis Unit (EAU) and is still refusing to do so.[6] No doubt many of us who are part of the resurgence of GLF and ACT UP protests are on this secret list.

I know I am.

After the attention had died down since supergluing the Prime Minister I was delighted to receive an invitation from activist groups in the US to share skills on campaigning. This could be my opportunity to meet the ACT UP and Gay Liberation American networks in person – a dream! Or not.

Standing in the US embassy visa queue minding my own business, outside a car door swings open. Out steps a tall man in intimidating shades from a giant blacked-out

SUV, he scans the queue and stops at me and says 'Are you Dan Glass?'

Everyone in the queue looks at me wondering what the hell I have done.

'Yes it is me', I said.

'Hi, I'm Eric Jackson from the CIA, I would like a few words', as he pulls me from the queue and takes me into a side-room and asks, 'I just want to know what you'd do if you met Obama [the current President]'.

Oh wow, gathering myself I respond, 'Er I'm not going to superglue myself to him if that's what you are asking'.

'Well actually yes.'

'As an activist – whether on LGBTQIA+ rights, health-care, climate change – whatever, you have to be original, I'm not some kind of superglue addict and either way I think he has more important things to do than greet me at the airport', and off he left.

The unexpected interventions got even more scandalous and salacious when a journalist hid in a rose bush by a motorway restaurant in Glasgow's West End to take photographs. At the time, in my spare hours I was working for Cavendish Knights,[7] a non-sexual male escort agency, under the pseudonym of 'Danny Devine' (I don't know how I got away with it) accompanying well-heeled ladies to business conferences and lunches as a buffer against sleazy men. It was good work as I like talking to people and it helped me pay back my many thousands of pounds of student debt whilst studying in Glasgow. Escorting is a reputable business, which has featured in such venerable journalistic outlets as . . . the *Daily Mail*.

So I met up with 'Janine', who described herself as a recent divorcee. She wanted me to accompany her to educational conferences abroad, in Madrid, Brussels or South Africa. I was happy to, but wasn't prepared to whimsically fly, especially within Europe because of aviation emissions. We discussed sending me by Eurostar and the difficulties of getting to Jo'burg without flying because of the mammoth pollution it creates. Although she hinted a couple of times, I made it perfectly clear: I won't be joining the Mile High Club. Not for love, and certainly not for money.

A week later she called me back, no longer as client 'Janine', but now a journalist, for the *Daily Mail*. They were running an exposé on me. I told her I was worried, we both knew I'd refused to fly, but the *Mail* is more renowned for 'creative' stories about celebrities and immigrants than adherence to fact or reality. She assured me they wouldn't make anything up. I didn't believe her as she'd already lied to me once, so I made sure I recorded the conversation to keep them to account and expose their underhanded tactics. And in true James Bond style I got the recording.

As expected, splashed across the paper was exactly what I feared, a hatchet job about how I was prepared to sod the climate so long as I got paid enough. She'd got her story, but I had my recording . . . and the phone number of some lawyers. Because Janine, when you make things up about people, and print it in the paper, it's called libel, and I get to sue the pants off you. Figuratively, not literally, of course. This was, after all, a non-sexual escorting job.

Plane Stupid climate activism was a critical space to learn tactics to confront and expose power which resonated later in life with the experience of ACT UP and GLF. All injustices are connected and our tactics in response are part of a web of resistance too. I learnt for myself that the right-wing press will do the dirty work of the state to discredit a movement that is inconvenient to them. The importance of interconnection and cooperation between grassroots organisations, learning from predecessors and always stick-ing to your values can never be underestimated. The state's tactics of public discreditation or institutional infiltration wreaks insecurity and generates divided loyalties so the government can reap information on movements for jus-tice that may want to challenge them.

Hidden cameras shared between grassroots revolution-ary groups make the recruitment of informers in political campaigns a hazardous process for covert police units. Clearly taping these types of approaches have a bigger impact in the media as the public can hear for themselves that it has happened and they do not have to rely on the word of the activists. Concealed recording devices pose a problem for the police as the activists have a powerful weapon to expose, and potentially curb, the recruitment of informers from within their midst. Until now, dismissed as paranoid conspiracy by the general public, the media can now hear for themselves the recordings of police interfering with social change movements.

The moral of the story is to keep pushing and document everything as you don't know what will unravel into a massive saga, revealing the innards of the system.

Moreover, in the quest to expose structural injustice we cannot find long-lasting solutions to LGBTQIA+ freedom or indeed any inequality on our doorstep of the global financial crisis, without digging at the root of its origins. As the twenty-first century slips by, we find ourselves grappling with profound social change, mistrust at capitalism's consequences and for many, a deep residue of colonialism still inhabiting our nation's soul as racism, homophobia and fear takes grip.

Not so long ago, the UK was once the most powerful nation on Earth, building its riches off exploiting and colonising over a third of the world. Today the UK is in a triple-dip recession and its superpower has long faded but the connections provide great insight. The oppressed during colonialism were not an unfortunate side effect but an intended consequence of the British Empire gaining global power. The same intentionality stands true for the victims of today's forcibly displaced and marginalised.

Multilateral trading and financial institutions – the International Monetary Fund (IMF), World Trade Organisation (WTO) and World Bank (WB) – are the apparatus upholding the structures of violence that we feel. They create a closed system of domination whereby collusion with governments retains the centre of global power and the centre of ordinary citizenship power through the pharmaceuticals, banks, weapons manufacturers and others. Increased financialisation, security and non-cooperation underpin this neoliberalist model that seeks to transfer control of economic factors to the private sector from the public sector. In the UK this trend towards free-market capitalism and away from government spending, regulation and public ownership was started by Thatcher simultaneously as she unleashed Section 28. This trend continues today, apparent through the institutions present at Pride who pretend to mop up the homophobic mess that is enabled by the very institutions with whom they collude.

The financial district of London remains the home, head office and tax haven for many of these major financial global organisations such as banks, hedge funds, mining and energy companies[8] including ArcelorMittal, BP and of course arms manufacturer BAE Systems and the majority of the top 50 sponsors of Pride. Today the capitalist genie is exposed and out of the bottle and forcefully flowing all over Pride. With head offices connected and local politicians aiding corporate development in many poorer countries to maintain their dependence on them, these corporations are the sponsors of the macro-financial institutions at the helm of the free market capitalist ship. It's a mistake to think that these institutions accidentally or coincidentally support the neoliberal project that has always been at the pumping heart of colonialism. The central characteristics of the neoliberal project are epitomised by free market trade, financial market deregulation, individualisation and the destruction of genuine welfare provision, which now embodies 'Pride'. These corporations are the neoliberal project, its nexus and convergence.

In the shadows of capitalism, neoliberalism dictates the policies of governments and shapes the actions of these key institutions. Neoliberalism not only perpetuates but continues feeding and nourishing the whole support structure of the financial centre. Its underlying purpose is to institutionalise inequity. Today growing financial inequality exposes deep flaws in the approach to economics that has dominated policy-making for generations.

As a community development worker, I am endlessly amazed by the difference between the public and the private face of healthcare and LGBTQIA+ rights, between what the public is told and what's explained in shiny non-governmental organisations' (NGOs) propaganda. Pride is a key arena exposing this under full bright lights, where discrepancy of the growing gap between the grandiose intentions of LGBTQIA+ policy makers and the impacts on the ground change daily before our eyes. Cars get sleeker and the offices even slicker. 'Cut-throat' tactics and 'hostile takeovers' of other smaller groups are not only enabled but lauded as model conduct. These are NGOs, Community Interest Companies (CICs), that make up the model of Pride in London as well as institutions that refuse to discuss politics when they present their proposals to the very government ministers who have historically voted against our freedoms. Disconnecting the economics from the politics causes individuals and communities to not be able to meet their needs, leading to human tragedies of inequality. It is like separating a calf from its mother. It only spells danger.

Can we put a price tag on the increasing number of LGBTQIA+ or HIV/AIDS+ suicides? And what is the economic cost of loneliness? You can't quantify human tragedy. Capitalist economics does not account for qualitative value so everything, every feeling, every experience, every relationship becomes an opportunity to sell to the highest bidder. Not only do these corporations at the front of Pride destroy the planetary resources which all humans depend upon, the consumerism and materialism they advocate relies heavily on the nuclear family unit as the primary consumption model, obediently consuming products made in sweatshop slavery in countries where queer freedom is denied.

This is why critical community activism that decolonises our mind and actions becomes a crucially important tool for awareness building among the oppressed as it unveils the forces protecting power. It helps us to understand the hegemonic gridlock behind marginalisation and exposes a dynamic process where the awareness of the oppressed is articulated and provides a platform to act in the context of our own communities, take our queerstory into our own hands and move forward.

9

As Soon as this Pub Closes

We put up a fight and cost the developers money,
time and their reputation and, basically, we were a
pain in the arse. We didn't know what was going
to happen, but we still gave it everything to challenge their superiority complex. (Amy, Friends of
the Joiners Arms)

When people experience oppression it strips away masks
that otherwise conceal the nature of reality. This is about
oppression and freedom in the broadly economic sense,
as well as the poor spirit. When we experience poverty of
any kind, it strips away a lot of illusions as to who your
friends are and who your false friends are and it brings
you to a deeper solidarity with what is real. This generates strength.

It was the summer of 2017 and I was pounding the pavement to the next Friends of the Joiners Arms (FOTJA) meeting when I bumped into an innocent market researcher on Old Street. They ended up getting more than they had bargained for. Standing next to a freshly painted wall, she was asking about the lager brand Pilsner Urquell's new wall 'art' to publicise their drinks, and whether this was appealing. They had painted over some incredibly beautiful feminist graffiti. I wasn't in the mood to suffer fools gladly and spoke my mind about the continual prioritisation of corporations over what people in London actually need, spaces for community nourishment rather than getting sold crap we don't need. After 30 minutes of gabbing away about Queer Power and the anti-gentrification fight back, I'm pleased to say she signed up to join the Friends of the Joiners Arms campaign mailing list.

So glasses off to let the sunshine in, head up and onwards!

At Friends of the Joiners Arms campaign meetings every month we – faggots, dykes, ravers – continued to plot after the Joiners was shut down in 2015. Amy, a mainstay since the beginning of the campaign, remembers fondly when they first properly met the landlord, David Pollard at the end of a cheeky mid-week dance. Amy ended up staying after the bar closed, chatting, drinking and talking about how to save the pub. That's when David started singing 'As soon as this pub closes, the revolution starts!' That is when the campaign started, to restore the iconic symbol of queer counterculture to its former rebellious glory, but also to create London's only fully cooperative, LGBTQIA+ community-led pub.

Everyone at the regular meetings takes pleasure in queering the process as much as the outcome. By this I mean that the plan is to create an explosive space for the queer imagination to inspire a new generation to question authority and respond to the emotional passivity effect that gentrification has on queer spaces. One such moment was in that summer, when FOTJA activists found themselves face to face with the property developers. As Oli shared, 'We were sitting in Tower Hamlets Town Hall at a round table and in comes a property tycoon. It felt like a moment of queerness in a sense of how absurd this situation [was], where this guy was a "self made" fucking cocky bastard, and he's having to sit on a Monday night with us, at 9pm, in a room, and actually have to listen to us and Dan [my boyfriend] strutting about being super queer and camp with his red earring. This challenges the closure and what that looks like.' Claps and giggling erupted across the room.

London's soaring rent costs have choked many LGBTQIA+ venues into submission, allowing speculative property developers to buy these spaces from under their feet. This only further strangles the capacity for transforma- tive queer social change given how coopted and assmiliated so much of the gay community has been during this process. If we stand any chance of stopping the implacable spread of gentrification, it will involve a level of cooperation and dedication not seen in the LGBTQIA+ community since the early Pride marches. This is exactly why the Joiners campaign is part of a wider, budding movement to protect queer venues from the pressures of London's overheated property market. It is rare for London's LGBTQIA+ spaces to be owned by the communities that use them. Most, if not all, LGBTQIA+ spaces are rented or leased from property owners, so they're particularly vulnerable to the effects of the market. Closures and threats to these venues are generally recognised as the result of external pressures, rather than any failing of the venues themselves. A prominent study by Urban Lab at University College London states 'The most cited reasons for closure are large developments, lack of safeguarding of dedicated venues in existing planning systems, sale or change of use of property by landlords and rising business rates and rents.'[1]

Saph is busy. Not only is she an FOTJA activist but also a DJ with 'ResisdanceLdn', a diverse group of women and non-binary people taking hold of the tech and decks, smashing the patriarchy and supporting under-funded radical grassroots organisations. I ask her how the closure of spaces affects her.

'I'm proud that we are gay. Like, it is harder – a lot of my friends, we struggle with money, we struggle with our mental health but I have never really fitted in to be honest with you, I'm kind of used to it. And I'm happy that I don't want to be the status quo, I don't wanna try and keep up with the neighbours or anything like that. Gentrification in general isn't just an abstract, physical thing. You've got working-class families being moved away from their families, schools, communities – it is displacement. Displacement is never a good thing. London will soon just become a soulless city, and every time some of my friends move out, they move into a different zone. Everyone's moving further and further out of London.'

When we take to the streets or inhabit our queer spaces we inhabit our community – historically, culturally, emotionally, physically, psychologically, spiritually. When we step out onto the streets we ask the questions, 'Who are we?' 'Where are we from?' 'Who persecuted us?' 'How have we resisted?' To be able to expose our vulnerabilities, desires and passions within and beyond four walls as queer is absolutely necessary, essential in fact. It allows us to breathe.

Peter, a determined and resilient long-term FOTJA activist, continued 'At the root of the problem is money, the fact that rents are increasing. The bigger issue that we came up against early on was how does our campaign relate to other campaigns like housing-rights movements like Focus E15, where a group of mothers in East London fought back to resist eviction from their emergency accommodation.[2] I think it's interesting to see how the tide is turning in those battles.'

Not everyone agrees. Some argue that legislative equality and growing acceptance of gay culture in Britain mean there's no longer any need for dedicated LGBTQIA+

spaces. They say the closures are simply a result of supply and demand, changing tastes and a move away from ghettoisation. Yet with every queer venue that closes, a new campaign rises and with every new threat, the resistance grows. Though each movement is as diverse as the bars they're fighting for, the ultimate goal for queer visibility is the same.

A formidable combination of wit, affection and vision and a tour de force in her commitment to the 'work-hard-play-hard lifestyle', Oli doesn't take prisoners. I ask her 'what motivates you?'

'We are usually in non-queer spaces, like most freakin' hours of the day, and people say "Oh, you can get married now . . . so why do you still need a gay bar?" Like, as if we would have even come close to having gay marriage if we didn't have queer spaces to start with, where we can come together and talk and organise how to fight for things.' Oli laughs and puffs on her cigarette into the night.

The next-door chicken shop smell drifts through the street, stifling the warm summer air and causing my stomach to rumble so loudly we both chuckle. We had been in the meeting for hours.

'Oli, what should we be fighting for?' I ask

Without hesitating she looks at me with deep conviction and says, 'One of the aims of queer activism should be to make spaces and time, and the city of London, more accessible and more inclusive. And what I mean by these things are not just buzzwords, but actually thinking about the needs of the most vulnerable members of our queer community – which is also an inclusive community that extends far beyond what the acronym "LGBTQIA+" allows us to say and do sometimes. One of the things I've learned from being involved in queer activism in London and especially in relation to the Friends of the Joiners Arms campaign, is that often you do things and you don't know who's gonna take them up or what's gonna happen and what they're gonna look like in the future and you might not even be around to see that happen. But that doesn't mean it's not worth it, and actually, there's incredible queer potential in that act of unlocking possibilities and doors and sort of seeing where they take you. For me that's what queer utopia looks like.'

It is moments like these conversations that amongst the continuous campaigning, our fondness for each other as friends in the struggle is renewed.

In August 2017 the big day to protect our queer utopia had arrived. We were at Tower Hamlets Town Hall to reject the developers plans, as they do not go far enough to ensure viability of replacement 'queer space'. Friends of the Joiners Arms had requested to make a representation on behalf of the community. Amy, the current campaign chair, who helps organise 'drag king' cabarets in any spare time she had, was given an opportunity to speak to the councillors, developers and the public on the campaign's behalf. Like David and Goliath, but much more fabulous. It was time to demand the space be wholeheartedly queer and much more than a Gay Starbucks that they wanted to sell back to us.

On the day of the hearing in the heart of the summer, it was just our bad luck that it was raining cats and dogs. FOTJA activists, old and new, arrived nonetheless, including Dwayne. It was his first involvement in the campaign. He had just finished writing a dissertation on 'gentrification of cities and displacement of communities' and with just £10 in his pocket he knew he had to be there.

Arriving in a sharp suit with short spiked up hair Amy has an unstoppable zest for life. Listening to 'Dancing in the Dark' by Bruce Springsteen she puts down her 'Don't rip the heart out of East London' placard and takes out her headphones. It was time for Amy's speech.

Councillors, thank you for giving me an opportunity, as a representative of the LGBTQIA+ community of East London, to speak on this proposal.

I'm here today because queer spaces matter to me. These are spaces where I feel safe. In the 13 years that London has been my home, I have been called a dyke by passers-by and been victim to a violent homophobic attack on the street. On nights out in non-queer spaces, I have had pictures taken of me by strangers when I have been dancing with another woman and had my gender brought into question when I walk into female toilets. There are countless other examples I could give you of how I have been made to feel vulnerable, inferior, unsafe, because of who I am, the way I look, and because of the people I love. And I'm not alone. My experiences, and much worse, are echoed by countless others.

I cannot put into words the immense feeling of liberation when I walk into a place like the Joiners Arms. London has lost 58 per cent of its LGBTQIA+ spaces in the past ten years, including 70 per cent of spaces in Tower Hamlets. We desperately need these spaces in order to feel safe and thrive as a community. I'm sure you've seen in the media over the last couple of days, a lot of celebratory remarks about how groundbreaking it is to have the queer character of a venue as a condition for planning approval. And perhaps it is. But we need to recognise: what's proposed is not a viable replacement for East London's most iconic queer venue.

Councillors, you are fully aware of the Trojan Horse tactics employed by developers to gain local authority approval, whereby a pub is promised but fails to materialise. In our view THIS is nothing more than a Trojan Horse draped in a rainbow flag.

We ask you to reject this current proposal in favour of finding a long-term, viable alternative that will truly re-provide the Joiners Arms for our community.

'Trojan Horse draped in a Rainbow Flag.' Genius.

After Amy finished, councillors voted to defer and requested that the developers alter their plans and return to a future committee. We had to fight tooth and nail to the end to win that verdict, so it was a huge, pleasant surprise to us that at the next meeting three months later they voted unanimously to commit developers to grant a 25-year lease for an LGBTQIA+ venue, replicating the late operating hours of the original venue. It was a landmark ruling, as it was the first time a space has been protected on the grounds of its contribution towards LGBTQIA+ culture – and had to be brought back as such.

We can win. Corporate queer-crushing gentrification is not inevitable.

Celebrating over a pint afterwards we were all checking in about how everyone felt after such a victory. Amy looks at the rest of us beaming and says 'I guess we got a lot of love eh? Within the campaign and from the public. I used to joke in the beginning that FOTJA was a self-help group for the Joiners closing. But it keeps me quite sane. When you've been doing this for so long, when you focus, when you're really focused on creating something positive.'

Amy's speech illustrates an embodiment of the courageous queer spirit that has brought us on the rocky road to the present. A deeper queer magic was at play. Of course so many of us are deeply burned by the many systems of power that send us to hell. Our experience of our identity has been oppressive but spiritually we're hungry. We deeply want a search for meaning and ultimately a home. A sense of affirmation with ourselves and with each other but on our own terms. Places like the Joiners Arms provide that.

After Amy had released this cauldron of fire, I needed to understand more about the sense of belonging her speech spoke about, so I went back to Alastair, whose words resonated loud and clear, 'The experience of being marginalised by most pillars of society brings us into territory to form bonds of solidarity that are of a nature to try and work out how to rekindle community. The flame of life that's been sniffed out draws us into responsibility and that little spark ignites in each of us that person and that spark gradually becomes a flame.'

The Friends of the Joiners Arms activists know that the struggle is long so the flame must be maintained and our perspective changed. We know we have to play the long game. Through this commitment to life-long transformation we generate the skills to challenge exploitation not just at the predictable places of power, such as the banks, councils and at 10 Downing Street, but at the everyday, seemingly hidden forms of subtle abuse like property developers that don't meet the needs of most people and even actively keep them away. Challenging the benign images of powerful institutions who rely on our acceptance, we can continue to rise up. As poet and civil rights activist Maya Angelou makes clear in 'Still I Rise', 'Leaving behind nights of terror and fear, I rise. Into a daybreak that's wondrously clear, I rise.'[3]

Whenever I'm feeling a bit lost, I think 'oh, my purpose on the planet is to get behind the Joiners Arms bar when it finally reopens', like a queer Peggy Mitchell (the legendary pub landlady from *EastEnders*); everything else in the meantime just feels like it is a means to that end. I can daydream all I want, but there is no time for that. In Tower Hamlets, where I live, 'social cleansing' through the bulldozing of council homes means that my neighbourhood, of which the Joiners Arms is a part, is a frontline in the battle against gentrification – the fight to save council housing and diverse community spaces against an influx of private interests and corporate buy-outs.

Like many other Nazi Holocaust-surviving immigrants, my grandparents came to London with no money and lots of fear, trauma and a need for community support.

'I feel safe amongst different people', my Nan always said, 'many different kinds of people makes me feel protected.' Multiculturalism was her safety net and she felt that she wouldn't be targeted for her ethnic identity. So, obviously, I have a particular vendetta against those destroying the spaces for queers, migrants and other vulnerable groups' needs in my community here.

Tower Hamlets, the most economically deprived borough in London, is situated in stark contrast right next to London's financial centre, where bankers' daily earnings equate to most in the community's annual wage. It is sandwiched between the Financial Square Mile and Canary Wharf, described by radical historian and author of *Rebel Footprints*,

David Rosenberg as 'being crushed by two ice wharfs'.[4] An increasing number of luxury flats are being built in the area resulting in many homes being snapped up by highly paid city workers. This heavily influences local consumerist habits too.

Gentrification is a specifically oblique form of human rights violation. It's not as easy to distinguish which side we are on as with other more recognisable processes of exploitation. It is much easier to choose which side of the South African Apartheid system we stand on or whether we are for or against the Iraq War and so the battle-lines can be drawn. When the community that gentrification directly impacts don't even know it's happening, it is even easier and far more menacing for the thundering damage to be done.

These patterns of power are the grid that holds gentrification in place and prove that its impact can't be seen in isolation.

So when we at Friends of the Joiners Arms were approached to join other anti-gentrification and housing rights campaigns to protest outside the 'Property Developers Awards'[5] I jumped on board. Paying £3,000 a table, the property industry, property developers, financiers and estate agents get together every year to slap each other on the back at London's swanky Grosvenor House in Park Lane. These are the people making it almost impossible for most of us to keep a roof over our heads in comfort. The rapturous self-congratulatory applause comes at a time when London, along with most of the United Kingdom, is in the midst of a housing crisis. Homelessness levels are at the highest they've ever been and rent prices are skyrocketing more than ever before.[6] It becomes even more vulgar that they feel comfortable celebrating themselves. Are they so unaware of the political climate or just so extremely comfortable in their privilege that they don't have to care?

The award categories themselves beggar belief. Hammerson, a huge British property development firm, were nominated for 'Sustainability Achievement' without, unsurprisingly, any mention of their intended seven-story eyesore at Bishopsgate Goods Yard that flagrantly violates the 50 per cent 'affordable' housing requirement by both Hackney and Tower Hamlets councils, with a mere 10 per cent. Instead the grassroots movements outside created a ceremony celebrating the achievements of housing justice movements and mock awards for the 'social cleansing company of the year', 'Most Effective Avoider of Affordable Housing Provisions' and 'Best Provider of Safe Havens for Foreign Flight Capital' as they walked into the plush hotel entrance carpet. The sheer tone deafness of it all is enough to make a frozen homeless queer youth crack in despair. It was time to push them out of their comfort zone, so off a few of us trotted back to my local city farm to get prepared.

Our mission? To pick up another few bags of glorious revolutionary horse shit, as it's important they get a decent welcome. So many of us have been firefighting and on the defence in this city, whether it's with queer spaces closing, social housing disappearing or domestic violence refuges barely surviving. For once they should know how this feels.

Jane helps every week with Streets Kitchen which, under the banner of 'Solidarity not Charity', provides daily outreaches with food, clothing and information and unites people who want to help, with people who need help.[7] She does this as well as being an activist with FOTJA. Jane came to the demonstration with a giant 'No More Deaths on Our Streets' banner along with the austerity alarm-raising 'March with the Homeless' movement and said, 'We are at the mercy of the housing market, where landlords and letting-agents condemn us to live in unsafe flats among filth and vermin'.

March for the Homeless, Friends of the Joiners Arms and various other housing and squatters' rights groups joined forces and on the day there was a raucous atmosphere.

Standing alongside Jane, Charlotte held a placard reading 'Space for Culture not Property Vultures' and said, 'We're disgusted that property developers are here to pat themselves on the back when they're responsible for tearing up communities, destroying social housing and making people homeless through evictions. They need to understand the impact of their actions. I hope they leave here tonight hanging their heads in shame.'

Standing at the hotel entrance, GLF street theatre legend Lavinia Co-Op looked incredible in a multi-coloured dress and array of beads holding her ground amongst the stampede of men in tuxedos trying to get into the hotel. She raised her placard stating 'Your dinner costs more than my rent', when suddenly a gaggle of drag queens came seemingly out of nowhere. They lunged onto the red carpet and surrounded a giant pile of manure to obstruct the queue of people waiting to get into the hotel to continue 'business as usual'. It was a delight to behold.

A few hours later, just as we were getting ready to leave, at the very top of the building, the faces of three suited men peered over the Grosvenor's top-floor balcony. More like apprehensive schoolboys than luxury property developers, they awkwardly waved and raised their drinks to us down on the pavement. In that snapshot in the evening sunshine this striking image scorched across my mind and illuminated how the London property market functions, the elite nervously laughing up in the tower, knowing that they might come crashing down to Earth at any time. Meanwhile the rest of us are shouting on the street below, hoping for the day the luxury housing market bubble bursts and there is space for all to live, not just a luxury for the few.

Feeling queasy at such stark vulgar displays of ine-quality, I walked sullenly back to Marble Arch tube. Serendipity must have been singing sweetly as I bumped into veteran health-care activist Andria on the way there. Back in the 1980s, when Thatcher's neoliberal policies paved the way for the luxury property developers we have today, Andria was part of many direct actions protests, helping to organise thousands of people to do 'die ins' in Trafalgar Square against the government's inaction when the AIDS epidemic broke out.

Affectionately, she held my arm and said 'The way "us" Brits do harm is with charm and a smiling face. Euch! It truly makes me want to vomit. Some argue that most of our social justice movements are enabled by the well-heeled, but thankfully that is not true. I mean look at us riff-raff! From where I am situated, you know for . . . well, too long really, the urgent thing I had to do daily, was getting a needle and a load of heroin. It soon became obvious to me that heroin was a heavily demonised substance and therefore its users too. Most "normies" see us as crazy, rebellious or undisciplined. But the reality was that the vast majority of us had come from traumatised backgrounds. We were responding to oppression in the family, sexual abuse, violence or childhood illness. So, when I realised that people with HIV were being targeted and discriminated against, I got very angry indeed 'cause all I could see was that sick people were being targeted again. The idea that a group of obviously struggling people were being targeted made me very angry, insanely angry. So I became an AIDS activist, obviously. Through ACT UP, I began to understand that even if I was injecting illegal drugs I still deserved human rights.'

The dynamics on display at the Property Developers awards told a bigger story than the transaction of space. Namely, that in order to burst out of the narrow gulf of inequality the most oppressed must lead the charge. Along with her street mobilisations, Andria utilised the power of the pen while doing her BSc in psychology. She visited

FRONTLINERS which was the coalition for people living with AIDS in the UK.[8] 'I will never forget arriving at the threshold of FRONTLINERS and reading the sign on their door, boldly stating, "Through this door you will not find victims or sufferers. We are people living with AIDS"', Andria finished tearfully.

Soon after, when Andria's life partner died, she set up the John Mordaunt Trust to continue the legacy of her late husband. Their mission is to let drug users just be. To get to the root of the problem and lead the struggle for justice on their own terms.[9] Andria smiled and looked to the sky, 'It was this widow that brought the first woman living with AIDS to address the UN about the failure of the War on Drugs back in 1998', she said, obviously tired, but with a knowing twinkle in her eye.

How to Disrupt an Elite Convention

1 Find out the facts and statistics to spark the action. For example, how much each table at the convention costs and compare that to the financial damage happening on the ground to those marginalised in the community.

2 Zoom out and build a big picture analysis – question and expose both the dystopian reality and the utopian dream.

(continued)

(continued)

3   Do a recce and find the building entry points. 'Reconnaissance' traditionally means a strategic mission to observe the enemy before a strike.

4   Create symbolism in the aesthetics and messaging of the action. Locusts, manure or blood all animate the problem at hand in style!

5   Troubleshoot the action. Ask your action group 'What could go wrong?' and work backwards.

10

Here We Dare to Dream

The bad news is that our society is dominated by a culture of blame rather than questioning. We are conditioned to speculate, judge and consistently fail to see the bigger picture. This results in preventing meaningful social change. The good news is that the LGBTQIA+ community and our allies are not willing to wait. We've had enough.

Institutional homophobia and the consequential cultural amnesia has stopped us from being empowered by queer-stories that have existed in every gaybourhood since time began. 'One in ten people in the UK are lesbian or gay', the Kinsey report, the 'groundbreaking' book on sexual behaviour, says.[1] If you add to that those who are BTQIA then statistically it's much more. How nice it is to be told.

If this is true then every house at some point in queerstory should have a queer story to tell.

During the last throes of the Joiners Arms I remember our conversation so vividly: it was time London Town had a permanent queer home. So on a crisp sunny December morning in 2016 a group of us took to the streets to explore and celebrate our queerstory, by talking to those who started it rather than letting the Establishment pay lip service – or worse – take credit for it. It was time to breathe some life into issues surrounding queer power, sex and spaces, the three arenas we understood as most influential to queer freedom.

Inspired by Stuart from the GLF's creative flair, we made 20 pink filing cabinets and prioritised 20 symbolic places to take them. On them we spray-painted 'Where Is Our home? We Demand a Queer Museum'. After we had set up early in the morning, Stuart, looking iconic, sashayed around the cabinets by the statue of Eros in Piccadilly Circus. Raising his voice to the skies, he stretched his neck and projected to the gathering crowd:

> Why is our history in filing cabinets gathering dust? Since before the Sexual Offences Act we've never been allowed to exist as equals because there hasn't been a place allowed to share our history. Section 28 of the Local Government Act made exhibitions about gay and lesbian life risky grounds for museums, as it banned anything that might

promote homosexuality to schoolchildren. Since then courageous people, programmes and institutions across London have exhibited Bloolips posters, stories of gay women in the Suffragettes, Greenham Common Women's Peace Camp, responses to AIDS and the Black Queer experience – but they are all temporary. We want to bring queer history out into the open and make it accessible to all.

The other sites where we placed the cabinets included Harley Street private medical practices, who previously promoted being gay as a disease, the House of Lords, where the legendary abseiling lesbians protested against the introduction of Section 28, a heavily-policed cruising spot on the Strand which, in the early twentieth century, was known hilariously as the 'Notorious Urinal', and the 1980s 'dykes and faggots residents scheme' to house single people in hard-to-let flats led by a community of punk feminist lesbians, the Deptford Dykes, which was my favourite site. Badass. With hankies flapping out of our pockets, indicating our sexual fetishes from the clandestine 'hankie code', we paraded the cabinets through the alleys of Soho and down to Piccadilly Circus to tip our hats to the 'Dilly Boys' and sex workers who have kept the wheels of sexual London greased for centuries.

Politicians have used their election speeches to make 'London the most lesbian and gay friendly city in the world' and provide a permanent LGBTQIA+ museum like in many other capital cities in the world, yet years later it is nowhere to be seen. Clearly, the queer community are treated tokenistically. We are 'tolerated'. But we don't want or need to be tolerated by a dominating force. Instead we deserve to be totally, wholeheartedly accepted and cherished for all the incredible contributions we have brought to the community of London and the world at large. There can be no progress without justice. We need a queer museum because we deserve one. We are constantly bombarded by a heteronormative society which grips us like a vice and stops us from having the space to figure out as queers who we are, where we can go and how we can belong in the world. Even when *EastEnders* announced it would welcome the first permanent gay bar to Albert Square, I should have been over the moon. But if *EastEnders* were real life the bar would close down after six months due to gentrification.

Museums and archives should speak across generations, sexualities, abilities, races, classes and genders by enabling oppressed people to lead the struggle against the oppression. Museums have the power to help us represent ourselves and to strive for full acknowledgement of our struggles for self-determination. 'Nothing About Us Without Us Is For Us', a mantra with its roots in civil rights movements across the world, most commonly associated today with Disabled people's activism, paints a bigger picture of the systems that oppress all communities that are 'othered' by dominator cultures. Museums, rooted in the colonial project since their inception in the mid-1700s, are a vehicle for that oppression and this is precisely why calling for one is a potent piece of activism.

Reading the newspaper on the tube on the way to the protest that morning the London mayoral office announced they were going to build a private multi-million-pound garden bridge. How lovely! Ultimately, though, the message is clear. The fact that there's not enough money for a building for queer heritage says a lot about the ripple effect of Section 28. Nevertheless the garden bridge project collapsed before it was built, wasting £48 million. Political egos in tatters and property developers' dreams busted were more fuel to add to our rage.

As the morning sunshine rose in Piccadilly Circus and the press started to arrive, Andrew arched his back, fervidly surveyed the scene and with a committed look in his glare stated:

Pardons are for those who harm, not for those who suffer. We want an Apology from the government. In exchange for a British Parliamentary Apology to the tens of thousands of LGBTQIA+ people who suffered in jails and outside them, in the British Empire and here, WE WILL PARDON three men. Our first pardon goes to the one and only King Henry VIII who first took Church law into the English common law and initially legally criminalised us in the 1533 'Buggery Act' which later became one of Empire's most successful exports to all British dominions including the American colonies.

Secondly we will pardon Henry Labouchere MP (1831–1912) who further criminalised us in the 1885 Criminal Law Amendment Act, commonly known as the Labouchere Amendment, making 'gross indecency' a crime in the United Kingdom.[2] He can personally take responsibility for shortening the lives of Oscar Wilde by punishing him with hard labour and the chemical castration that led to the suicide of Alan Turing in 1954, the cryptoanalyst who decoded German messages in World War II saving millions of lives. Last but not least our final pardon from the GLF and friends goes to David Maxwell Fyfe, Home Secretary 1951–1954, who arranged a witch-hunt against British gays in subservience to McCarthyite America, humiliating, among many, the great Shakespearean actor John Gielgud who in 1953 was humiliated and arrested for opportuning. After his conviction he returned to the stage and was embraced with a standing ovation. A notoriety that contributed to the powerful legacy he left for queer arts and heritage today. It is for the People to Pardon and for Parliament to Apologise.

'How did I not know this?' Salma, a young infectiously bubbly artist, reacted taking her gaze from Andrew as shared with the crowd. 'Everyone should have access to dig at the roots of homophobia. Unfortunately for most of us, our families often can't or don't teach us about our queerstory simply because it's not theirs and being generally ignored by mainstream politics and media, young people are left in the dark. Having a reliable queer space is so important for young people if only as a respite from what can often be an unkind and unconcerned world.'

'Thank you Salma, I couldn't agree more and we send out strength to you, the younger generation. You will need it. Today Queer activism means to me fighting for our rights and trying to maintain the rights we've gained. At my age, I suppose, it means passing on the culture that came out of the politics of the GLF and the politics of the GLF itself. The well-intended but misconceived Pardon offers people who are still alive to apply to the Home Office for their bit of paper. This is the same institution that is complicit in suppressing thousands of LGBT+ migrant lives here in the UK', replied Andrew.

'Damn right!' whooped Nadia, a vivacious student with glittery eyebrows, as she swung her hips dancing to 'I'm Coming Out' by Diana Ross on one of the cabinets behind Andrew. 'Growing up as a queer woman of colour, I have enjoyed more privilege than my predecessors, many of whom devoted their lives to claim their identities and their rights. The struggle to free the queer community from the damaging heteronormative world order is nowhere close to finished.'

The music got louder, the glitter face-paint brighter and between young and old a movement had been strengthened.

We had no idea what it would unleash. 'Pink filing cabinets appear around London in protest to get the capital a queer history museum', said the daily *Evening Standard* paper headlines on every seat on the tube that evening. When people on the streets asked what we were doing, we explained to them, 'Our queerstory is locked away in filing cabinets'. Out of that protest, Damien started 'Queerseum', a campaign to agitate the conversation on the importance of queer histories and strengthening the call for a permanent home. 'We need to record radical queerstory because queerness and being queer involves reimagining what politics is and what better source of knowledge and of queerstory than ourselves, rather than formal institutions or whatever we are told in books', he announced to the crowd.

The action was such a success it set the ball rolling for more.

Energised by the action's impact we went back to the art studio in Tam's queer venue to make exact replicas of the blue English Heritage plaques dotted across London's streets honouring 'notable men and women who have lived or worked in them' dominated, unsurprisingly, by white straight males. We wanted to queer up how the establishment chose to recall queerstory – but where to start? Out of a series of meetings there were suddenly too many options.

Eventually we settled on three iconic spaces. 'Black Pride', the UK's only Pride event for people of colour, in Vauxhall Pleasure Gardens, the House of Lords, to celebrate the lesbian abseiling invasion against Section 28, though the plaque was swiftly taken down, and the Admiral Duncan gay pub in Old Compton Street, Soho where three people lost their lives to a Neo Nazi nail bombing in 1999.

To make it happen people chipped in in whatever way they could, as Tam recalled, 'We mobilised the right number of people. So that the arty people like me and Stuart were angrily getting the facts right and using a laser cutter. Then you had all the angry lesbians who were climbing the buildings in the morning at 5am. That was a really good example of a peaceful protest that just went "blap". I got contacted by some New York queer magazine, we all got contacted by different people. So fast so good. You can't replicate that. You can still Google that shit. The Admiral Duncan still has their plaque up, standing proud.'

After a week of criss-crossing London I couldn't wait to get back home.

East End gay gangster Ronnie Kray is the tip of the iceberg of the 'poor' and 'dangerous' label for which my 'no mans land' neighbourhood is known. It's only through meeting the GLF that I have learnt a different story. Gay sailors at the docks, men who lived as women to escape service during the Blitz and the flamboyant cabaret drag scene, strip joints and disco boom that the GLF frequented since the 1970s. All these places are now closed or are not queer spaces any longer but speak to a local queer or King of a certain age, and they will wink and smile.

I could go on all day about how much I love living in the heart of Tower Hamlets – one of Britain's most courageous, freedom-fighting, anti-fascist beautiful London boroughs. How my heart flips when I look at Cable Street from our estate balcony where the anti-Nazi demonstrations of 1936 led to my Nan and Grandad walking these streets after the War. How this makes me feel rooted. How going for a morning run along the Thames every morning feeds my soul. Especially the morning after an action is finished and I mince pass this poem on a Wapping alleyway wall:

When he left me last September he took away my heart. My body and movement suffered, he took away my art. I found another lover who stood with me undercover. Away from despair and pain I ran. Lost in my new future plan. Darkness crept up. My new lover had enough. So now I am free, again to wander and write on East London walls. I support myself, I shall again be strong and tall!

And then underneath it.

I FUCKED my man here.

The poem finishes:

LOVE IS EVERYWHERE.

You just have to look at the walls.

This almost hidden gem spiralled into an epic week of finding queer treasure one week in that summer of 2019. That evening, while reading *Queer London* by Matt Houlbrook I discovered that the local NatWest bank in Whitechapel High Street used to be London's most notorious queer den of inequity 'Miss Muff's Molly House', which was established in 1728.[3] Cycling past on a rainy Monday morning you would never know that here lies a jewel in the crown on the colonised road of our sexual queerstory.

On Tuesday I ran a workshop with LGBTQIA+ homeless youth from across the borough. Inspired by books about the Stonewall uprisings, triggered by a brick thrown at the homophobic police by transgender and homeless rights activist Marsha P. Johnson along-side Sylvia Rivera and the iconic Street Action Trans Revolutionaries (STAR) movement, we started a reading group with the intention to explore how to build queer housing projects. Researching British parallels of feminist, trans, drag and non-binary sexual revolutionaries we found out about the legendary 'Bethnal Green Rouge Acid Drag Commune' on 248 Bethnal Green Road. This building has an incredible queerstory. Bethnal Rouge opened in 1973 as a gay bookshop and commune led by a group of women and radical femme acid queens, a group of gender-nonconformist queers that emerged from the London GLF chapter.[4]

That night I started re-reading *Fingersmith* by Sarah Waters, a historical crime novel set in Victorian London centring on a secretive lesbian love affair.[5] Waking up inspired, the next morning I went for a sunrise mince down Lant Street in Borough to imagine life amongst the thieves in the moonlit underbelly of Queer London. Staring up at the smoky walls I wondered how the modern-day cultural thieves, or 'politicians' some say, behind Section 28 manage to sleep at night knowing that economic inequality is wider today than in the time of Dickens.

Walking back through Wapping I passed a more recent battleground for economic justice. I stood outside the former 'News International HQ' offices where in 1986 Lesbians and Gays Support the Printworkers came together to support workers fighting sacking and victimisation.[6] This was another queer labour rights solidarity movement, like the better known Lesbians and Gays Support the Miners, that we can be proud of, even if inevitably union assets were seized and mass picketing was brutally crushed by Thatcher's police force. Thatcher was, of course, a good friend to News International tycoon owner Robert Murdoch.

Weaving around Shadwell Basin I ran past the Prospect of Whitby pub. This is where the late, great homoerotic poet Wilfred Owen (1893–1918) wrote 'The Ghost of

Shadwell Stair', just before he returned to the First World War front line in France. He was nicknamed 'the ghost' by gay friends Siegfried Sassoon and Robbie Ross because there was a false report that he was dead before he really died. And apparently 'ghost' (we can imagine why, imagine trolling in the London smog) was, for a while, an in-word for gay.

I am the ghost of Shadwell Stair.
Along the wharves by the water-house,
And through the cavernous slaughter-house,
I am the shadow that walks there.

A group of bewildered swans started jerking their heads at me around one of the centuries-old Thames wooden staircases as I continued down the Thames river path past a lesbian couple smooching against a tree and a handsome queen with eyes twinkling in the sun, and then to my final destination. Across the bridge and out of breath I am here to pay homage at Derek Jarman's blue heritage plaque to remember his film *Jubilee*. To dream of anarchy against a governmental system run from the Houses of Parliament further up the river who – yet to apologise for criminal-ising us in the past – are hell bent upon destroying our queer utopia.

Looking down at the murky water it's easy to wonder how much of our queer life has been lost but not so far off, in Russell Square, there's an anchor holding our freedoms in place: Gay's the Word bookshop – the chefs in the holy kitchen of queerdom – who every day dish out knowledge that empowers our community to be proud of our queerstory and bring life to our future.

Remembering LGBTQIA+ queerstory is important because 'It's not taught generally, it's not covered in general books or school. All you're taught is kings and queens and empires', said Jim MacSweeney the manager of Gay's the Word who for over 30 years has weathered the homophobic storms of raids by Her Majesty's Customs and Excise, snatching materials under the pretext they were 'obscene', criminal charges against the staff and vandals smashing in the door.

The next week at the GLF 'Think In' we agreed to develop a programme to celebrate the GLF for the upcoming 50th anniversary in 2020: going back to the buildings they inhabited all those years ago, recreating the events in order to support a new generation of LGBTQIA+ artists, activists, drag queens and kings and everything in between. So off I minced to 248 Bethnal Green Road.

Forty-six years on, unfortunately the building is no longer a legendary drag commune but a Western Union bank and residential flats. Still, you have to try your luck.

Mincing through the Western Union bank door I beelined to the bank clerk where the exchange went like this:

'Er hello my name is Dan, I work at "Queer Tours of London – A Mince through Time". Fifty years ago your building and the terrace above was a legendary drag commune, a haven for the queer community and sanctuary for the legends who overturned homophobic legislation. We would love to hold an event here to commemorate, something like a drag Queen and King banquet or party – but of course we are open to discussion. Are you interested?'

Bank Clerk: 'Er no, we are a bank.'

Me: 'Ok, thanks anyway!'

And I mince back out the door.

On the pavement smoking a ciggie in honour of my defeat I spot someone going into the residential flats on the right-hand side of the bank. Rushing over, 'Er, excuse me, do you have a moment?'

The stoned, hot Brazilian hippy guy going into the flat said, 'Er, yeah sure'.

I produced the same spiel as in the bank, asking if we can have the celebration on his terrace. 'Er yeah sure', he said again.

Taken aback he took my number and I waited all week in anticipation. Unwilling to retreat from the battleground of queer reclamation, along with the surviving drag queens we wrote letters to Western Union with our request in more detail and stuffed them through their letterboxes in the hope of a response. In this short life if you don't ask you don't get, regardless if you never get a response. Western Union Party Poopers.

Us queers are everywhere – it's simply homophobia in all its manifestations that has tried to wipe us out of common knowledge. Who knew that we even had our own language to survive and thrive? Polari was our own secret queer code. A sexy, fun, shady and often catty means of communication that didn't merely serve as a mode of self-protection against the nefarious hands of the law but as a way to express sexuality, flamboyance and a love for other members of our community. Polari had somewhat evolved out of recognition but with rising LGBTQIA+ hate crime it is having a renaissance. And so we are hearing again 'Naff', 'butch', 'fantabulosa', 'camp', 'mince', 'zhoosh', 'khazi', 'scarper', 'cottaging', 'bod', 'beat the face' and 'queen'. While they may have become mainstays in the English language and so arguably lost their status as Polari words, their re-emergence in our conversations reminds us that our community will always sneak through the cracks and how language can be assimilated and then reclaimed.

On a balmy hot summer night later that month, Andrew was leading a queer tour, and while winding through Covent Garden he suddenly jolted to a halt outside Bow Street Magistrates' Court.

'Fifty years ago this is where the GLF Street Theatre began in support of Women's liberation activists who disrupted the archaic and sexist Miss World contest in the Albert Hall', he skips around the street in excitement.

Mesmerised, the group close around Andrew waiting for more.

At the time we were busy organising 'kiss ins' in The Champion pub in Notting Hill Gate against homophobic collusion between the police and landlords of supposedly gay pubs. You could say similarly to the Mafia and the New York City police before the Stonewall Inn was infamously raided in 1969. 'Fat Tony' purchased the Stonewall Inn in 1966, at the time a not-so-popular straight bar and restaurant, and bribed the police to turn a blind eye to them as it was illegal to serve gay customers in what the State Liquor Authority (SLA) considered to be 'disorderly houses'.[7]

Andrew took a moment and savoured the landscape – a mass of tourists shopping, a lonely schoolboy sitting on a wall and a sea of homeless people's tents outside private jewellery stores across the street, a shelter for the dispossessed.

I took part in protests and got carted off pub floors and charged in magistrates' courts after a sit-in. There were some up-sides then. There are far fewer queer spaces now than then and rent was a smaller part of your income in the 1960s. Artists' spaces were easy to find and squats were legal. Everyone smoked cigarettes everywhere, including me. We all smelled of smoke and the buildings were black with soot from the Second World War and I'll tell you, the dentistry was more painful.

As the sunlight dimmed and the turbo-tour unwound I asked Andrew, who at nearly 80 years old is still blazing a trail, 'how do you keep your fire burning?'

He looked at me and smiled. 'If London's trying to look down on you, maybe go to Richmond Park or Hampstead Heath and look down on London.'

Out of the Archive and into the Streets: How to Organise Empowering Street Tours

1 Flip the script – instead of 'coming out' stories ask 'what are we coming into?'
2 Curate the route into a chronological, political, practical and emotional roadmap.
3 Remember it is not what you do but how you do it – make sure to prioritise real-life voices from the heart of the streets.
4 Use the whole journey – between stops is just as important as each stop.
5 Organise an after event – people want to get to know each other.

'Here we Dare to Dream' and 'We Are the Authors in Our Own Reality' are the banners adorning the walls in the red-carpeted Islington Town Hall in North London later that evening. In March 2014 the first gay weddings in Britain took place in this building and five years later a troupe of locals are buzzing around a map of the City armed with post-it notes.

'Welcome everybody! You see the large London map? What are your favourite queer stories that you have never shared or been allowed to tell? Anything which is seemingly small or personal adds to the bigger picture. In this workshop on how to generate queerstory you just have to dig for it. Let the rest speak for itself', says Ali, the queer tour facilitator for the evening.

In the second half of the workshop the community harvested their collective knowledge on issues affecting each other to crystallise them into a tour script. Today the meaningful issues the group are fleshing out include health concerns including HIV, gender reassignment surgery, LGBTQIA+ life and rights in employment and the specific challenges faced by LGBTQIA+ asylum seekers when fleeing persecution.

Throughout the following weeks we train a new team of eager queer tour guides, where, on the first training, Lyndsay mentors the group to curate their first tours.

'Why did you first become a tour guide?' a participant inquires.

'I love the queerstory treasure hunt process because when you learn about something it becomes yours. It becomes less anonymous. You feel part of it because you know it and soon it's like having a relationship with it. For example, you can go to an obscure bit of Bloomsbury.

Virginia Woolf lived here and all sorts of incredible situations that happened in this corner. I feel not only part of my landscape but also inspired to create what queer London needs now. We need to learn our queerstory to honour those who came before us and honour ourselves. It's a really important part of self-respect. It's a birth rite that's been robbed from us.'

The workshops use 'Theatre of the Oppressed' skills to engage people to speak their truth and turn stigma on its head, as Augusto Boal, founder, illuminates:

> The poetics of the oppressed is essentially the poetics of liberation: the spectator no longer delegates power to the characters either to think or to act in his place. The spectator frees himself; he thinks and acts for himself! Theatre is action![8]

Finally we reach my favourite exercise of the tour. Holding two signs – one, a picture of a tub of cottage cheese and the other, a picture of the actor Tom Cruise's face – Lyndsay and I, along with the 20 new queer tour guide trainees, launch into the 'Cottaging versus Cruising' quiz. Whilst standing in a giant laundry bag we ask the group questions on queer crime and resistance.

'This quiz is a winner with all groups when you're out on the streets. Now everyone stand up and form two teams – Cottagers and Cruisers'!

Q – Who said 'Oh look they've come to help with the washing up' in 1984 when the police raided the Royal Vauxhall Tavern (RVT) and three police officers wore gloves on to 'protect' themselves against HIV?
A – British comedian and TV host Lily Savage.

Q – Lime green? Black velvet? Brown corduroy? Sailer lame? Teddy bear? What does the red of this symbolic hankerchief fabric represent?
A – Fisting.

Q – What legislation happened in the House of Lords in 1988 that enacted the most brutal homophobic legislation in modern British history?
A – Section 28.

Q – What was the protest in response?
A – Three incredible lesbian activists abseiled into the House of Lords on a bedsheet.

Q – What did news presenter Sue Lawler say during the invasion of the BBC TV studios by lesbian activists in 1988?
A – 'We have rather been invaded!'[9]

Q – Was Pride in London started by the GLF or Tesco?
A – GLF!

Now for the last question 'Why am I standing in a bag?' The group look perplexed. 'Because that's how cruisers got around the police whilst having fun in the toilet cubicles: one person would stand in a plastic bag, so when police looked under the toilet door they just saw one person.' It's genius. Who knew that Sainsbury's bags were key to our liberation?

Cruising and cottaging culture was born just as much out of need as it was out of want. It's fairly impossible to trace the queerstory of sex acts in public, because so many have done it. However 'cottaging' as a term was popularised in the late 1800s, and became an exclusively gay thing between the 1940s and 1960s. This sexual practice of doing it outdoors, in parks and public loos, is still very much going on today. With the dismantling and removal of so many queer spaces, it is no wonder queer public sex is on the rise once again.

Like 50 years ago, a lack of safe spaces means alternatives are a necessity if you want to get your rightful sexual kicks. From this necessity 'cruising' became a much desired, enjoyable and often super hot sexual practice and so from the need, also grew the want. If you're married, living at home, worried about revealing your sexuality or have a judgemental housemate, it's safer to have fun in the bushes than bring someone back to your bed.

Women's cruising, saunas and cottaging has been subject to even more cultural invisibilisation. Nell, women's queerstory specialist, put it this way.

'It's more difficult to find historical examples of queer women's sexuality, in comparison to men's, because of the usual erasure of women's sexuality, any women's sexuality, throughout his-story, full stop. When we do find representations of queer women's sexuality, it's still often framed by flowery, vague and softly tinted depictions of "forbidden love" and romance. Rarely do we see depictions of queer women having anonymous sex or going out and pursuing sex, for sex's sake.

'There are 101 apps for gay men's cruising sites; women's sites – there are very few. But of course queer women absolutely did and do cruise and cottage.

'In the late noughties there was a women's cruising toilet block in Portsmouth, but it was closed down because it was believed to be an 'opportuning' site. And the only other place our research found for women's cruising was Hampstead Heath pool in London, although I'm told women go there to swim and sunbathe too! There was a dark room setup explicitly for women a few years ago in South London, which was very popular . . . but it was shut down too. Thank heavens for The Clit Club and Chain Reaction in the 1990s, with full-blown sex rooms and BDSM chambers, and for today's 'Sweat' club night, by invite only to women and anyone on the 'trans spectrum'.'

Saunas come in all shapes and sizes. Whilst public baths date back to the sixth century BC and ancient Greeks weren't too shy to engage in homosexual affairs, bathhouses for men to have sex with men date back

600 years. Iconic cruising areas include bathhouses, parks, alleys, theatres and gyms. Lavatories are the most well-known cottaging spaces. In recent history many bathouse owners overlooked homosexual activity, risking prosecution to have been either mindful of earnings and overlooking discreet homosexual activity, wary of profit from the gay clientele.

An emblem of anti-establishment, saunas have been places of escapism from the monotony and fear of a heterosexual world. You could make new friends and lovers or just get some peace whilst watching the city's underground cabaret acts on repeat. Saunas are even where singer Bette Midler began her career. My friend Gethin, a GLF activist and founding member of LGSM, made me smile with his favourite. Stan's sauna in Leeds around 1978 featured Earl Grey tea, cucumber sandwiches and fondant fancies served by a sweet old man, bollock naked except for a frilly pinny whilst wild sex parties continued upstairs.

Next time you stomp down the city's pavement slabs feel the heat from under your feet from another world in the making.

However, in recent years sauna culture has received fairly extensive derision from within the gay community after a spate of drug overdoses. They are looked down on as sleazy, grotty and potentially unsafe embarrassments from a time when gay men were forced to live in the shadows. Why do we need saunas, ask a series of edgy op-eds, when we now have apps like Grindr and Scruff?

Isn't it easy to blame a gay man lying face down on a sauna floor for his own demise. It's much harder to listen and critically question why this happened in the first place.

Will closing down saunas rid society of the consequences of self-destruction and marginalisation? Or will these pathologies pack up and move elsewhere? While basic human needs are the same everywhere, the ways in which we try to satisfy them vary considerably depending on our cultural backgrounds and our standards of living. In order to be fully alive and happy we need to have our basic needs met. Only once we have met our primary needs of food, water, energy and shelter can we hope to meet our secondary needs.

These needs are the freedom to participate in the functions of society, identify ourselves as we choose, create change, protect ourselves and our loved ones, give and receive affection, enable subsistence and plan for the future, own our emotions and understand ourselves, relax, openly love, dream and overcome the material reality of everyday life by imagining a better world. So what happens when society removes our ability to meet these needs?

Through the mist of the steam room I can only hazard a guess as to what's going on inside the minds, hearts and souls of my steam-room mates. Where have they come from? What solace does this sauna provide? What needs are being met here that can't be met outside above the pavement slabs?

Deep down we all know that when we are unable to meet our fundamental human need for connection constructively, we can engage in self-destructive patterns, including dangerous drug use, to hit the spot.

The gay sex app Grindr is a useful tool for some, but it's traditionally mainly great for a certain type of white, financially secure men due to bigoted profiling and stereotypes along the lines of 'No fats, no femmes, no blacks, no Asians'. Saunas offer a sanctuary for people who may not feel safe or able to publicly express their sexuality – people who are poor and unable to access pricey clubs, older men who are victim to an ageist twink-obsessed culture, men subject to racism in our hostile, xenophobic society, and even comfortable middle-class men who may not have come out to their families. Saunas can provide a sanctuary for all of them, enabling touching, kissing, laughing, crying, relaxing, flirting and for some exposing deep vulnerabilities, many for the first time.

That is why numerous campaigns are rising calling for us all to cultivate a society that makes it possible for everyone to satisfy their fundamental needs. Their shared question is simple: in society at large can we collectively break the cycle of tackling the symptoms of everything and the root cause of nothing?

We need to blame the system – not the saunas.

Whether we breathe our last breath outside in this brutal world or on the sauna floor, for many it doesn't matter. Dreaming of equality can only happen when we have time to think and to breathe.

So welcome, have a massage and a fresh towel.

After this mammoth month of actions and trainings I needed some time for queer healing myself which wasn't a protest, workshop or event. I've always been a firm believer that passion, pleasure and fun are critical tools in our toolkit for freedom so off I trotted to Soho where saunas still managed to resist closure. Unfortunately it didn't turn out to be the self-care I needed and, incensed, I returned home and wrote this.

Dear Sauna manager,

It's the Sabbath today and like all good Queer Jews I've just returned from a morning in your gay sauna. You see it's a mitzvah at the end of a working week – blessed by God and written in the Old Testament.*

I've never written a complaint letter in my life but visiting your sauna compelled me like never before to say this:

1   Everything including the steam room, jacuzzi and TV room were furiously filthy and decrepit. London's LGBTQIA+ community deserve better.
2   Luxury flats may have their own jacuzzis but the working folk deserve one too. Queer spaces are closing down. For many in our community they never even existed. This is not because of lack of demand but because of luxury developers hell bent

on hyper-capitalism. Many queers like sex just as much today as we have for millennia – so don't try that one.

3   Other city's saunas I've been to are miles better than London's. Check out Berlin's 'Boileroom' for an example. They are like the Hilton of saunas – you would give Ibis a bad name. 'Boileroom' even sell burgers and chips. Your dribbling water taps smell of cat wee.

4   You advertise 'protect yourself – wear a condom' but how do I protect myself against your mouldy walls?

5   Your gym looks like something out of a 1960s d-rated blue movie. I wouldn't lift a finger in it, let alone try to lift your mis-matching weights.

6   You're painfully inaccessible. In 1995 the Government introduced the 'Disability Discrimination Act'[10] which legislates that you must make efforts to be accessible. That's 25 years old, the same age as the twinks you exploit every Tuesday night.

7   As a tour guide with 'Queer Tours of London' I wouldn't add you to our tourist guide map – only to mark you out with a giant yellow puddle of piss because that is what I saw on your toilet floor.

8   Gay saunas should be a sanctuary – a solution to the anxiety and depression us queers often face – not the cause of it.

As fellow supermodel Kate Moss once said 'Never Complain. Never Explain.'[11] I defy her to say that after a visit to Sweatbox.

Thank you for the refund. Rant over.

Yours sincerely,

Dan Glass

*(because I said so)

I'm glad to say that two years later massive refurbishment took place.

It's not just older queers who face discrimination in today's LGBTQIA+ culture. The next morning I got a message about a series of events Queer Tours had planned at The Glory – the dazzling new home away from home for East London's queer and drag community.

'Dan, good to see you've organised the event tonight but I am sad to see that I can't get there because there are steps at The Glory. Access and equality for all and all that!'

Fuck. Cornered.

That was my good friend Josh. Josh is a PhD student looking at neo-colonialism and criminalisation of same-sex activity. He is a Disability equality trainer and works with many universities and art festivals to look at the best way of interacting with Disabled people. He wrote a very open piece about his sex life for *The Guardian*.[12]

Josh's activism is based around the social model of Disability. This means that Josh believes that he is only Disabled by his environment. He very much acknowledges he has an impairment, cerebral palsy in his case, but he views disability as synonymous with oppression. This is why he taught me that you should always say 'Disabled people' rather than 'people with Disabilities'. I now realise that if we recognise Disability as the lack of resources by the state to cater for one's impairment, we can see Disability in a way that one can see homophobia or misogyny, completely invented by society, and based on stigma and discrimination. Josh isn't Disabled inherently because of cerebral palsy, but rather because of society.

'You're absolutely fucking right I'm so sorry darling. But I know sorry means jackshit. Actions speak louder than words – old habits die hard', I responded sheepishly.

Too late to cancel I knew that this was the last time 'Queer Tours' could hold events at the Glory before engaging in how we can democratise the space. Like most of London's new venues it was small and in a building with a basement unfit for disability freedoms. Unless you had £10,000 lying about to refurbish.

In 1995 the government introduced the Disability Discrimination Act, which meant all businesses over a certain size must make reasonable adjustments so that Disabled people can access the building. Superseded by the Equality Act 2010 this thankfully got rid of the exemption for small businesses. However, there is still a reasonable adjustment duty which unfortunately gives businesses many defences for not making adjustments, such as cost. Also if a building is listed or has historical significance it can also find a way around becoming accessible.

Josh continued, 'Very few gay bars properly consider access. Not many have level access, lower counters or accessible toilets. Speaking as a wheelchair user this is my personal experience as someone with a mobility impairment, there are many other different impairment categories to make a space fully accessible.'

The following weekend I met with LGBTQIA+ Disability-rights activists in the sunshine of a leafy and sexually charged Soho Square to make placards. We are a few streets away from the most iconic queer street in London Town, the supposed sanctuary of the community that is Old Compton Street. Before we took off to ask bar managers about their access we placed the placards on the ground and move around them proudly.

How can I be proud of my LGBTQIA+ identity at Pride in London if I can't even get to the bar to celebrate?

How can I mince, flirt and meet others if there is not even one LGBTQIA+ bar or club that is fully accessible to the LGBTQIA+ Disabled community?

How can I be proud of my impairments if I'm discriminated to come on Pride?

And my favourite

I'd shag in your toilets if only I could get in.

Before we set off we stop outside 37 Wardour Street, the site of the former Shim Sham Club, named after the Harlem Tap Dance. After it opened in the mid-1930s it shortly became a queer-friendly, predominantly Black, jazz club and a meeting place for anti-fascists, pan-Africanists and socialists that was described by complainants as a 'den of vice and iniquity'. Underneath the growing glitzy shop fronts Soho has always been a haven for 'the other' – Josh started his brief for the group.

'We know that capitalism promotes homophobia. Bars focusing on income rather than equality and accessibility means more marginalised groups such as those who are Disabled are oppressed even more. Oppression from the state is filtered through austerity from those who do not have the desire to fight for equality. Austerity does not help those who are Disabled like us. It paints the picture of Disabled people as needy rather than seeing them as individuals with entire personalities and ultimately the capitalist nature of Pride doesn't help anyone anymore either.' And off we set down the street to see the bar managers for answers as we all chanted 'We demand equality over profit' and 'Access 4 All'!

Some of the managers we met were brilliant after we discussed with them their legal obligations to be accessible. They apologised, listened and committed to action by getting ramps, toilet radar keys, braille signs and more. Others were not so great. We bumped into the notorious owner of London's gay superclubs 'G.A.Y.' and 'Heaven',

Jeremy Joseph, and his tiny dog. We asked him if he is going to change accessibility and get a ramp so that people with disabilities could get access into the 'Heaven' nightclub. Access. Into. Heaven. The raw irony didn't go over our heads.

He said that 'If the back door is good enough for Adele [the singer] it should be good enough for you. There is really no need to protest.'

Bigoted comment inside a bigoted comment, like a Russian doll of oppression, we didn't quite expect this level of malice.

Thankfully, if Soho wasn't going to be the queer utopia we were looking for we had other options. London is a cruisy city, with many choices, each with unique characteristics and niche markets. So off we went to George Michael's choice, Hampstead Heath, known as 'the daddy of all cruising' grounds. Forest bonfires in the winter and jam-packed swimming ponds in the summer, every day there can be hundreds of queers here looking for friends or, quite likely, sex in the bushes. 'Erratic George Michael's New Shame' were the headlines in *The Daily Mail* paper,[13] printed to try to humiliate him after he said 'Fuck off! This is my culture' to a photographer in the bushes. What a legend.

A few weeks prior to our visit to Hampstead Heath, at Christmas, George Michael died and we were working out our best to pay our respects.[14] Behind the scenes our George supported many HIV/AIDS organisations and movements for LGBTQIA+ sexual freedom including the first one that had supported me after my diagnosis and that had made me feel human again. So what were we to do? Josh and I minced off to Hampstead Heath to investigate.

PART 3

SPACE

11

Sex Litter

George Michael Wants You – 20th anniversary 'Outside' Special! – Done with the sofa? Done with the hall? Done with societally enforced standards of sexuality which don't conform with your reality? On 8th April 1998 in a Miami public toilet, so was George Michael. Back by popular demand on this 20th anniversary, bring your friends, learn the lyrics to 'Outside', wear whatever makes you feel fabulous and 'Let's Go Outside'. See you in the bushes.

The party invite went out far and wide and die-hard George fans, cruising fans, families with picnics, AIDS activists and more were getting their outfits prepared. When the day arrived people skipped through the woods, hung bunting and minced hard. Josh's smile was growing from ear to ear. There were no bigots here. Stuart danced alongside a bunch of topless young queers. Dame, dressed in an ass-less rubber playsuit, strung different coloured handkerchiefs through his jockstrap, while Nell gently wiped the rubber down as he lay getting ready for later on Hampstead's famous 'Fuck Tree'.

'Even in the tightest sweaty restrictive rubber I feel absolutely free to breath queer liberty here upon the Hampstead breeze', said Dame beaming. He continued, 'Queer life is a beautiful, powerful, necessary, gentle, caring culture and it's ours. The criminalisation of it only serves to perpetuate myths of homosexuals and those with a sexual appetite for something outside the four walls of a bedroom as predatory, soliciting, dangerous and not as people who want engagement in a community activity that is as important to us as a Sunday Roast with all the family is to my wonderful Irish Mum. In a society that wants to criminalise your every desire and upbraid any means of alternative pleasure, seeking and finding it is still a radical act. So, Let's Go Outside.'

Lyndsay was hanging off a tree branch tantalising the wind with her tongue. 'As someone who has healed from an eating disorder it helps me to think about what I do to my body and what my body does . . . there's a lot of agency there . . . If we are dancing and dressing our bodies up titillating each other . . . and exciting each other with the colours and the sparkle and the why the fuck not', she radiated.

As the day went on, the crowd swelled. The meeting point, complete with volunteer-stewards in high-vis vests and fabulous get-up, was Jack Straw's Castle on the top of the hill at the forest entrance that leads to Andrew's favourite incredible viewpoints looking down on London. This is where people with shifty eyes and hungry souls gravitated before being directed down into the glistening trees, with 'Out of the Closet and into the Woods' signs – made at home the night before on cheap star-shaped UV cardboard – helping folk to get there.

New friends were made and impromptu speeches given and a dog walker in a bright cashmere jumper minced past the edge of the party with a bemused look on her face. My friend Tommy was pleasing the crowd doing a handstand wearing only a white jockstrap. When he spotted the dog walker he stood back up and picked up his giant red tray of lube and condoms to hand out and said, 'Everyone is welcome here, come on in', and invited her to the stage.

'Oh, I knew George; what a lovely man. He used to walk his dog here and we used to bump into each other from time to time. I welcome you to our glorious home in Hampstead Heath, have a fabulous time – everyone just make sure you pick up your sex-litter', she said in a high-pitched excited voice.

'SEX – LITTER' – now that is a concept that should join the dictionary and invade our dreams.

As the day went on and the crowds of human diversity intermingled I saw a solo man with silver hair. Wearing a half-unbuttoned light-blue shirt, upturned smiling eyes and cats whiskers wrinkles that could tell a thousand stories he minced through the bushes like he was on the catwalk at Paris fashion week, whilst he daintily did up his flies.

He looked around the crowd like a meerkat on a Sub-Saharan savannah plain. As he scanned the crowd and read the banners, the pennies dropped. A wild smile raced across his tanned face.

Within minutes he had his arms in the air, shrieking 'let's go!' as he skipped through the queue waiting to get on stage.

'Oh how delightful! A celebration of sexual freedom! Well I've been frequenting these bushes in Hampstead for 30 years now and indeed all across London's finest toilets, parks and backstreets – and it's about time we celebrated it!'

As the bright daytime sun faded and the wind whispered through the tall oak trees we had some uninvited guests. The cops. Or the actual cops to be clear.

Normally with the police I'm too full of rage to try to be eloquent and have healthy dialogue. I can't find the words to engage with a murderous, bloody pain-inducing stigmatising system that's wrapped up in British jovial stereotypes to get my message across.

This time I was smugly confident. The party set-up was perfect and we knew our legal rights. It's not illegal to be naked unless someone is offended, and our rubber police outfits could in no way constitute police impersonation either. We had the upper hand.

Strewn across the party blankets were fake police batons, cops hats, medallions and outfits. In the corner of the party in a large bush behind the fuck tree you could see fake cop hats bobbing amongst the leaves as a loud giggling threesome took place.

They sheepishly approached the dancing crowd looking for someone to speak to.

'Ello ello officers and how can we help you today?' I said.

'Well we are just here to make sure everything is OK', they winced.

'It's fucking fabulous officers – want to join the fun?' squawked Dame wiggling his bum in his jockstrap in the trees behind them.

'There'll be no following orders here you NAUGHTY BOY!' a woman shouted from the picnic blankets. Startled but unable to hide their smiles, off the police trotted and so the party continued into the night.

A few hours later I bumped into two Hasidic Jews wide-eyed and cowering from the side of the bushes. 'Hello, are you ok?' No response just still stunned eyes. I repeated myself to no avail, so pointing to my 'CHOOSE LOVE' tight T-shirt and tropical Wham!-style calypso swimming trunks I said, 'Remember George Michael?'

'Er yes, yes we do', looking totally bamboozled. 'What is this?' they quietly said.

'This is a party to celebrate cottaging, cruising, sexual freedom and our George. George Michael.'

'Oh . . . what's that about?'

'Well there's lots of people here from all walks of life who have faced many obstacles. Through fears and social repression we come together to celebrate sexual freedom. It's a family affair – come and say hello.'

Cautiously I wrapped my arm around one of their shoulders whilst the other walked in tow through the bushes, beelining for the 'This Is My Culture' banner twinkling in the late spring Saturday sun.

'Welcome home.'

Knowing all too well that 'their culture' is one I knew from the bottom of my gut, a combination of terror and beauty welling up inside, I counted my blessings that I managed to break free.

I wondered if they could tell. I doubt my outfit gave it away.

'Well enjoy the party!' I said, as we parted and they went off to join the crowds.

The families lunching on picnic blankets, young ravers hogging the decks ecstatic at being able to party freely, a lesbian couple smooching on their backs on the famous 'fuck tree' and the gaggle of queens, twinks and bears all pounding their feet under the 'This Is My Culture' banner.

As if the day couldn't get any more surreal. Ted from the GLF then sat on the ground under the fading sunlight and breeze in the trees. In a tight green T-shirt and khaki shorts, looking as handsome as in the photos of the first Pride, he sat cross-legged next to a giant banner emblazoned with 'Out of the Closet and into the Streets' and took the mic.

The crowd gathered around.

Thank you for having me and the GLF represented today. My family, friends and colleagues and I have always sought equality for all people, whatever their culture, race, gender or ages. During the 1950s and 60s, when my parents were campaigning in the National Association for the Advancement of Coloured People (NAACP) led by Martin Luther King, they heard speeches from one of its other leaders, the openly gay Bayard Rustin. They heard the call on August 15th 1970 by Huey P. Newton [Commander of the Black Panther Party] to join forces with the Women's and Gay Liberation movements.

Captivated everyone inched closer, forming a horseshoe around him in the heart of the woods. Ted continued.

Several experiences led to me being involved in LGBTQIA+ campaigning. As a Black Gay teenager in the 1960s homosexuality was genuinely 'the love that dare not speak its name'. There were no 'out and proud' role models. If ever it was mentioned it was in terms of sickness, crime or evil perversion. Gay life was extremely restricted and of necessity, furtive. Sex was deeply disapproved of and highly illegal, with severe penalties.

A lonely, furtive life yawned before me.

My queer icons were and still are Bayard Rustin for his courage and great achievements. As a proud Black gay man he simultaneously contributed very significantly to the Black Civil Rights along with Martin Luther King. Also Barbara Gittings, who founded the first lesbian organisation in the USA, The Daughters of Bilitis in 1955 and of course James Baldwin for writing important literature on the gay and the Black experience. Also Harry Hay who founded the homophile Mattachine Society in 1950. They all could have adopted the furtive closeted lifestyle of most queer people at the time but they publicly, bravely challenged homophobia in the face of intense hostility and minimal support.

In 1969 when I was 19 years old I was living in Blackheath in South London and read a newspaper article flippantly and dismissively reporting on the Stonewall uprising. I did cartwheels all around the living room. But Stonewall happened in New York, thousands of miles away. Then in 1970, at the Odeon cinema, Leicester Square, I watched the first ever Hollywood film about gay men, *The Boys in the Band*. It argued that the only real problem for gay men was self-contempt. 'We hate ourselves so much' was the mantra with one of the characters even stating 'Show me a happy homosexual and I'll show you a gay corpse'. On leaving this dubious movie I encountered a group of people leafletting in protest against its misrepresentation of gay life. They were members of the newly founded GLF. I took several leaflets and a few days later I attended my first GLF meeting at Middle Earth in Covent Garden, becoming an active member.

Ted paused, scanned the crowd and smiled.

My sex life involved occasional trips to the two gay pubs I knew at the time, the Vauxhall Tavern and my favourite, The Coleherne in Earls Court, though neither of them was particularly welcoming to Black Gays. Within a year, by late 1971, I'd moved into one of GLF's three communes in London. These were set up to enable LGBTQIA+ people to form our own families, facilitate public campaigning and encourage a lifestyle of being open about being queer (although that word was not being used positively at that time). I took photos of the very first ever queer demonstration through central London, which was organised by GLF's Youth Group and took place on 28th August, 1971.

Most people believe the NAACP focused solely on race issues but their debates and campaigns were far wider, covering social issues entrenched by class, wealth, nationality and gender, even sexuality. A theme which ran throughout their campaigns was 'until all of us a free, none of us are free'. This also became a driving principle for GLF. Through the NAACP my mother learned, and passed on to me, the knowledge that there are people of every culture who will fight for freedom. Once this is recognised it's comparatively easy to work with others towards that goal. This is what I've always tried to do. When faced by a hostile environment, together with supporting colleagues such as GLF, I do what the Feminist, Black and LGBTQIA+ communities have done to achieve progress. Firstly by working together, we recognise and publicise the specific oppressions we face. Then make it clear we will not tolerate, and will in fact, overcome them.

Iconic. The speakers ramp up for 'Outside' one last time.

Back to nature, just human nature
Getting on back to
I think I'm done with the sofa
I think I'm done with the hall
I think I'm done with the kitchen table, baby.

As the GLF activists mantra teaches us 'Out of the Closet and into the Streets'. Indeed.
And long may it continue.

How to Organise a 'Let's Go Outside' Woods Party

1 Harness a political and cultural hook such as celebrating George Michael's life and his commitment to sexual freedom on the day he was arrested for cottaging.
2 Catalyse the cultural memes like the lyrics 'Let's go outside' from George Michael's song 'Outside' that capture the public imagination.
3 Know your 'sex rights' from cruising laws to public displays of affection (PDA).
4 Make it cross-generational and protect your sacred space by working with legal observers such as Green and Black Cross1 who work in the spirit of mutual aid to support social and environmental struggles within the UK.
5 Welcome the 'absurd'. Dress up as those who oppress you, such as the police, and have way more fun than them when they turn up at a sexual freedom party.

There is no way to repress pleasure and expect liberation, satisfaction, or joy. (Adrienne Maree Brown)[2]

12

Over Our Dead Bodies

You lot need to refuse to be defined by an external box created by a capitalist idea of what you should be like. You need to throw out the boxes and definitions and celebrate your own uniqueness instead of conforming to the limiting ideas fed to you by a brainwashing social media and enforced corporate doctrine. Try and evolve, go on, I dare you. (Lanah Pellay, pop star and HIV+ advocate, performing on top of the BANG BUS)

The roadmap to a collaborative society from an authoritarian society can spin like a spider's web, glistening in the morning light. Self-care, dialogue and active listening are at the heart of the map to get us there. Like the

interconnected ecology of an enchanted forest, queer community building provides the forks and shovels that lace the divine into nurturing a collaborative society, away from the violent one we currently inhabit.

Today the legacy of humanity rests on a knife-edge with humanitarian and environmental crises exploding throughout the world. The wisdom of Dr Jonas Salk speaks here in his work 'Are We Being Good Ancestors?' where he says,

> In our work, in our policies, in our choices, in the alternatives that we open and those that we close, are we being good ancestors? Our actions, our lives have consequences, and we must realize that it is incumbent upon us to ask if the consequences we're bringing about are desirable.

> If we don't change the story then humanity's legacy will be of behaviours that uphold structures of domination. This idea continues to affirm that there is no alternative. Many societal structures uphold authority-based societies including theories of human nature, education, socialization and human behaviour. Every human society is built around a particular 'story', 'meme' or 'narrative' of what human beings are like and what life is about. In order for the story to change, we must intervene in its making. It is time to re-write the book.[1]

In the years since my HIV+ diagnosis I began to notice a real difference in the atmosphere when I went to get my regular blood tests. I knew the stress the NHS was under. It was all over the news headlines and now it became acutely real. The AIDS unit in the hospital I go to has been running since the height of the first crisis in the 1980s. Usually it is a really calm and a nice, serene environment to go to, essential for people living with stress-related conditions. At my next appointment I went in and there was a noticeable level of panic in the air. 'Something's not right', screamed the look in the receptionist's eyes. Many more people were there than normal with drastically fewer staff.

'What is going on?' I asked the nurse when my turn came to get my blood tests done.

She was a nurse that I hadn't met before. She was a student nurse, she must have been about 21 years old. 'Yeah, a lot of the social workers have been cut, a lot of the support workers have been cut, too, and some of the doctors in the hospital have to face voluntary redundancy.'

Why, just when so many living with HIV are without support, when there is an increase in diagnosis amongst many demographics and when many sexually transmitted diseases (STDs) are on the rise are sexual health services being cut to the bone? Why did spending on sexual health, advice and promotion fall by 35 per cent in 2018 alone?[2]

Whilst all these thoughts had been running through my mind she quietly said, 'Dan, you are gonna have to come back for your other blood test in a couple of days'.

Why? I normally get my CD4 and my viral load – the indicators of the health of the immune system and the progression of HIV in the body – in one go. I was already worried about paying the rent and taking another morning off work. 'Why do I have to come back?'

'I don't know, it's a change in bureaucracy. You're going to have to come back in', and she put the needle into my arm. It missed my vein resulting in excruciating pain and felt like a physical example of the stress that's going on in wider society being jabbed deep into my arm.

'Aaarrrggghhh! Ouch! What is going on? Something has to be done!'

We all have lightbulb moments, when the sky begins to clear.

I yelled internally. It was a real wake-up call. The whole harsh reality got me right there under my skin.

Homophobia and HIVphobia are made worse with the austerity cuts as victims of a recession are those who rely on public services. The first danger facing people living with HIV, and all marginalised people, particularly those who rely on tailored healthcare rather than a 'one size fits all' approach, is the privatisation of the NHS. The second is the negative impact on a person's mental health that comes as a consequence of stigmatisation, which means HIV+ people need focused and holistic free mental health support.

The invention of antiretroviral drugs in 1996 stopped HIV/AIDS being a death sentence, but for many today it is still a life sentence.[3] In 2012 the former UK Prime Minister Theresa May made her strategy to create in Britain a 'hostile environment' for illegal migration explicit.[4] As a result, in particular social demographics, transmissions have increased steadily over the past decade. Particular rises are amongst migrants who are too fearful of going to the doctor's in case they may be deported, and women of colour, sex workers and intravenous drug users.

As of the beginning of 2020, 103,000 people are living with HIV in the UK. One in six don't know they're HIV-positive.[5] A major new breakthrough is Pre-Exposure Prophylaxis, or PrEP, a revolutionary pill that is up to 99 per cent effective in preventing the transmission of HIV if taken daily.[6] Previous to Theresa May, the Prime Minister David Cameron refused to release PrEP for fear that the right-wing media would be up in arms that he is kowtowing to the LGBTQIA+ community.[7] Pure state-sanctioned homophobia at its finest. Currently the government still refuses to roll out PrEP nationwide, even after multiple test cases have proved it works, provoking the anger of HIV campaigners, clinicians and anyone who believes that access to healthcare is a right.

I came home from the hospital with my vein still throbbing and remembered Thierry's advice to 'ACT UP' and 'Fight Back'. So, with a big pizza in bed, straight away I re-watched *United in Anger* and *How to Survive a Plague*, a queerstory of fearless HIV+ activism in the US. Peter Staley's story was one of the central stories in the film as he helped fight government inaction and pharmaceutical greed in the first AIDS plague of the 1980s and 1990s.

Learn about your icons, dream about them and email them. If they are still alive – the worst they can do is ignore you or say no.

I'm a big fan of contacting idols and trailblazers without whom I wouldn't be here today.

Peter was certainly one of them, who in 'Lessons from the AIDS Movement' said 'I think it's a great way to live, to fight for yourself, to fight for your friends, to fight for a community of individuals who are sharing your experience and to fight for dignity and a better life, and there will be a tipping point. There will be victories and they will be joyous.'[8]

'You can't fancy a man twice your age', said Patrick. A wild source of mischief with a golden heart, Patrick is the queer comrade that dreams are made of.

'Yeah I fucking can. Particularly if it is Peter Staley.'

Diagnosed with HIV+ in 1985 Peter swiftly joined ACT UP New York and has been a full-time AIDS activist ever since. Pharmaceutical office invasions and disruptions of the New York Stock Exchange floor led to lowering the price of drug AZT and through the founding of Treatment Action Group (TAG) he was part of an action covering homophobic Senator Jesse Helms' home with a giant condom.[9] As part of his and many others' activism, hundreds of thousands lost the battle but ultimately they won the war. Without him and his comrades we might not have

Antiretrovirals (ARVs), the drugs used to prevent a retro-virus such as HIV from replicating. Indeed the system that is hell-bent on making money for the elite might not have been forced to provide medication for the masses and the AIDS genocide that had already claimed thousands of lives would have blazed on.

'AIDS genocide' is, of course, a bold use of language. Genocide is defined as 'the deliberate killing of a large group of people, especially those of a particular nation or ethnic group'. That is why I always stipulate 'Nazi' before Holocaust as there are other Holocausts and other genocides, each unique and that should never be dimin-ished, trivialised or relativised. Now 80 years old, ACT UP founder Larry Kramer's famous blistering speech on AIDS stated, 'I believe genocide is being inflicted upon gay peo-ple'.[10] His life-time work points out that the American government, through sins of omission or commission, allowed the extermination of my homosexual population to continue unabated. Today, after millions of people have died, the gravity of genocide speaks volumes.

Fresh from my own hell of a series of hospital horrors witnessing the breakdown of services, the forced pay-off of nurses and the replacement of doctors by never-ending telephone triages, I knew what had to be done.

'Fuck the "Second Silence" Patrick, I'm calling Peter Staley.'

'Yeah I'm actually going to Ukraine soon, I can stop off by the UK', Peter said. Game on.

So five months later in a Dalston gay bar I met one of my heroines. After watching *How to Survive A Plague* and a mesmerising Q+A, Peter sparked a fire in the hearts and minds of those in the cramped bar, young and old, and we began to put together a campaign plan. Fast forward a few weeks and along with a coalition of HIV clinicians, charities, advocacy groups and activists we turned up on Dean Street in Soho. This is the busiest sexual health centre in London which can't prescribe PrEP at the level required. Our action involved creating an orderly queue. A 'queue to nowhere' to animate the relentless mind-numbing approach of the government refusing to release the medication needed.

The energy catalysed the next confrontational protest where a week later we stormed the NHS head office in Elephant and Castle banging pots and pans chanting 'No more AIDS deaths give PrEP now!' and 'How many more transmissions before you start listening?' Chants of 'Act Up, Fight Back, Fight AIDS' ricocheted off NHS England headquarters while employees awkwardly sidled past the assembled crowd.

Then off to the Department of Health in Whitehall. All the demonstrators were asked to deck out in blue, the colour of PrEP, and scrawled blue chalk graffiti over the pavements of Westminster as speakers lambasted NHS England's refusal to get behind the most valuable new tool in the fight against HIV in two decades.

Seventeen protesters stood on stools bearing an array of placards demanding immediate access to PrEP whilst

ACT UP activist Alex roused the crowds booming into the megaphone 'What do we want? Prep! When do we want it? Now!' A flame-haired nurse with a boisterous spirit and laugh to match, Collette had worked overnight to create the props. Whilst allocating the placards to the growing crowds she shared 'these represent the 17 people a day who will be diagnosed with HIV in the UK until NHS England accept responsibility and finally tackle the epidemic head on'.

This was the summer of 2015. Tall, handsome and cheeky, Alex had returned to London after working in New York as a photographer's assistant and go-go dancer. Alex had first been given PrEP in New York.

'I got back to the UK and I was like, shit I haven't got PrEP anymore and I need PrEP now. I was looking online for who is fighting for PrEP right now and reading up on my AIDS queerstory because I still didn't know anything about AIDS at this point. The only people who I found that had mentioned PrEP publicly that I could see were ACT UP because of the PrEP demo outside 56 Dean Street called "the queue to nowhere". So I thought, right, I'll go to a meeting then.'

Alex continued 'I went in feeling awkward and guilty that I was walking in late (as always), I didn't know anyone in the room and I also had no idea what people were talking about. "Hi everyone!" I said to a group of strangers and ten minutes later I was helping write action plans on the board.'

'There I met Greg, who was equally as determined to get PrEP, and hatched a plan. We knew that online "buyers' clubs" helped communities deprived of medication through government inaction or pharmaceutical greed to get the medication they need so we went back to mine and started researching', he recalled frantically.

One month later, Alex found himself naked with four other ACT UP activists with 'G.R.E.E.D.' written in giant black paint letters on their backs shining through a giant window onto the streets of London. This was Gilead HQ, the pharmaceutical giant behind the life-saving medication PrEP. My favourite role on actions is that of the 'decoy', to distract the authorities, in this instance, looking after the naked activists clothes and distracting the security guard whilst others adorned the window with signs reading 'DROP THE PRICE'.

The monthly cost of producing the pill is estimated at £15 and unbranded alternatives available online cost around £44 per month, while Gilead's version costs a staggering £400 per month. The protest was part of a global day of action coordinated by a coalition of over 25 health advocacy groups from six continents. Demonstrations were held outside the offices of Pfizer, Gilead, Roche, the Tufts Center for the Study of Drug Development and the Pharmaceutical Research and Manufacturers of America (PhRMA), demanding an end to unfair medicine pricing, corporate tax inversion and deception about research and development costs.[11]

Alex and Greg went on to set up I Want PrEP Now to support people needing access to PrEP where the government failed.[12] Alongside healthcare workers they courageously refused to toe the government line and two years later, this resulted in a 90 per cent reduction in HIV+ diagnosis amongst gay white men at Dean Street Clinic in London, showing what can be achieved on a grander scale. The Scottish government has since rolled out a free PrEP programme for all who may be at risk of HIV in the UK regardless of gender, ethnicity or sexuality. Meanwhile the British government, in collusion with the pharmaceuticals, stalls to make more money, on the grounds that people aren't going to wait to continue the fight to stop HIV and AIDS in its tracks. After such an epic tragic journey it seems like they are winning.

Five years later and after countless media appearances pushing for PrEP Alex reflects on this time: 'You know, the huge decrease in new HIV diagnosis – partly because of I Want Prep Now – would never have happened without the meetings because at the meetings people can say "I've got this outrageous idea for a protest. Lets fucking do it." You make the best connections in meetings. It's all very well going to the protest and doing all the glamorous part but meetings are actually the most inspiring part. The action is just the climax. It's the process of getting there that is most productive and most inspiring.'

Next to Alex, Dani stood with the other ACT UP activists who took their kits off in Gilead's HQ. After stopping business as usual we left an hour later, and with striking photos and the clothes back on the activists backs, we headed to the action press room where Dani shared what got them involved in the first place.

'I was not out about my sexuality before joining ACT UP. It was joining ACT UP and learning about the AIDS crisis and the activist communities around it that helped me establish my own sub-community of friends and family, and really quickly. This meant that I can live as a human and actually achieve things and not just spend the whole time feeling that something is missing. Before ACT UP I was still labouring under the information I was a straight cis regular member of society. My gender was different to the one assigned to me at birth. It changed the fact that I realised that I wasn't regular in society because I had absolutely no faith and no interest in what most of society is geared towards wanting that I have been geared to want before that. You go to school, get a job, get a relationship, a house. I was forcing myself into that niche before I discovered queerness and that's why I was so fucking miserable for that whole time in my life, and I was really fucking miserable.'

They continued, physically tired from the action but running on adrenalin, 'Discovering a queer community, which I'd previously never had the opportunity to, completely turned everything around for me and allowed me to start understanding what I really want to get out of life and what was important.'

Whilst marginalised people continue to face rising cuts, we must not let our destiny end up on the scrap-heap of the market economy. These actions, questions and ideas, fused through social and scientific understanding, are essential for intervening in the hegemonic status quo that ultimately will transform our communities' consciousness.

How to Build a Queer Support Network

1   Remember you are not alone in the huge orbit of people transcending traditional notions of 'family'.
2   Acknowledge your own limits. Be kind to yourself.
3   Assess timescales and your own life goals and be ruthless. Ask 'have things shown improvement or is it a lost cause?'
4   Regularly prune your life. Nourish what feeds you and cut out what doesn't.
5   Transform and build new 'containers' or spaces to nurture your community such as civil disobedience actions and theatre shows.

After the action was over and the props packed away it was back to reality.

'Crisis! Crisis! After 70 years of universal health care, is the NHS at a crisis point?' was flashing all over the news in 2018, but where did it all begin?

I take my HIV medications every morning, Evotaz and Truvada. These two tiny little pills are worth their weight in gold. In fact, they are my lifeline. These systems of support, like the National Health Service (NHS), are the most precious things for so many members of the LGBTQIA+ community and so many others.

A recent Ipsos Mori poll found that the NHS makes more people proud to be British than their royal family or armed forces.[13] Founded in 1948 the British NHS was part of a new post-war social contract that completely transformed British society. It took two world wars and millions of people to die in order for us to get our NHS. Its primary ideal is that good healthcare should be available to all, regardless of wealth. At the time, the then Minister of Health Aneurin Bevan launched it on 5 July 1948 with three core principles:

- that it meet the needs of everyone;
- that it be free at the point of delivery;
- that it be based on clinical need, not ability to pay.

These three principles have guided the development of the NHS over more than half a century and remain.

The founders of the NHS believed that healthcare should be free at the point of use and available to everyone, regardless of their ability to pay for it. We've been given it and we have to fight for it.

'No privatisation of the NHS on my watch', said Matt Hancock, Secretary of State for Health and Social Care, shortly after taking up his post in 2018. At the same time, behind the scenes private providers were offered control of NHS budgets worth billions and departments were being sold off one after the other.[14]

From 2009 to 2013 Simon Stevens worked for the largest health insurance company in the US, United Health. During his time he attempted to use Transatlantic Trade and Investment Partnerships (TTIP) to force state-run health systems, including the NHS, to employ private health firms from the US.[15] Unsurprisingly, after that, in his role as NHS England director, he oversaw billions of pounds of NHS funds going to for-profit companies. These private firms operating within the NHS will often use the NHS logo so patients have no understanding who their services are being provided by. Taxpayer money is funnelled into offshore accounts such as Richard Branson's Virgin Care which pays no corporation tax in the UK as its parent company is registered in the British Virgin Islands.[16]

As a result, since 2015, there have been 30,000 excess deaths due to cuts in health and social care, representing the largest increase in deaths in the post-war period. Accident and Emergency (A&E) is a bellwether for the NHS, a prime indicator of its overall health. Almost all performance targets were missed including ambulance call-out times, and A&E waiting times have been deteriorating across the board, despite unexceptional A&E attendances compared to the same month in previous years.[17]

Before cementing in place a year of ACT UP action plans I met with Jessica Potter, a lung doctor and public health researcher at Queen Mary University of London. Whilst already overworked and under supported, in every spare moment she organises with Docs Not Cops, a campaign group of NHS professionals and patients targeting government fear mongering of marginalised people, who believe health is a right and not a privilege. I asked her about the changes she has seen in her time at the NHS. She promptly responded: 'Health care is a human right but we have more rota gaps than I've ever noticed before. People are under a huge amount of pressure.' She froze for a moment as if a cramped noisy hospital ward had just exploded in her heart. 'When the NHS is understaffed and underfunded in the way it has been by successive governments it becomes really difficult to maintain that good relationship with our patients to provide the best care that we possibly can.' A stack of flyers emblazoned with 'Docs Not Cops – healthcare is a human right' under her arm, it was time for Jessica to head to that evening's demonstration before yet another all-night shift on the ward.

In 2019 the NHS looks after one million people every 36 hours. Between 2016 and 2017 alone contracts given to the private sector grew from 2.4 to 3.1 billion pounds. As I write this and 2019 comes to a close, 70 per cent of NHS contracts have been sold off to private companies.[18]

How did we get into this mess?

The 'Iron Lady', former British Prime Minister Maggie Thatcher, threw the first punch in 1979 when her government published the Ridley Report, proposed by Conservative backbencher Nicholas Ridley.[19] It infamously recommended breaking up the public sector and smashing the trade unions that defended it. As Thatcher went on to say, 'Any set of social and economic arrangements which is not founded on individual responsibility will do nothing but harm. We are all responsible for our own actions.'[20] Ridley himself describes the strategy as a 'long-term strategy of fragmentation', 'a cautious "salami" approach'. Unlike Matt Hancock, their mission was clear.

All political systems redefine and manipulate words for their convenience. In stark contrast to 'individualism' the word 'Economics' is derived from an Ancient Greek word 'Oikonomia' – 'Oikos' (house) and 'Nomos' (custom or law), to mean 'rules of the household' or management of a household. Those of us on the ground left to deal with the destruction of the NHS and its impact have to surgically unpack the political anatomy of the economic framework. At the heart of this there must be an examination of the ways in which institutional structures are formed and the political and economic choices of government and citizens are made.

Thatcher was an eager disciple of economist Adam Smith who laid the foundations for modern economics. Mainstream modern economics advocates that by limiting the role of the state, economics allows the market to be 'supreme' in determining who gets what as it is a self-regulating mechanism. Scarce resources are then allocated through the market to meet the needs and unlimited wants of society. This is done through known factors of production: land, labour, capital and entrepreneurship where surplus market profit is generated through the unequal relationship between the owners and workers of production. What mainstream economics fails to teach us are the relationships of exchange and the incapacity of market economics to put a value on the breadth of human needs. Alternative Human Development Indicators (HDIs) advocate that profit alone cannot paint a picture of the full needs of humankind. Understanding the full scale of human needs demarcates a need for the role of the state where needs are not being met.

This demolition left by Thatcher didn't have much chance to gather dust.

In 1992 the Conservative government carried on what she began by introducing Private Finance Initiatives (PFIs). On the ground this meant that hospitals built by privateers with taxpayer cash ended up costing nearly six times more than they would have cost the public sector. This is exactly how the NHS became saddled with huge debts. Twenty years later, Health Minister Jeremy Hunt, soon after taking office, was so concerned by a delay to the £650m deal to private healthcare company Virgin Care that he asked for assurances from NHS Surrey officials that it would be swiftly signed.[21]

Not long before his departure, Hunt tried to fool Parliament and the public into believing that NHS privatisation 'is not happening' and was 'fake news'.[22]

It is no surprise, then, that at the time Jeremy Hunt was the least popular politician in the UK.[23] He recently saved almost £100,000 in stamp duty on his purchase of seven flats after exploiting a Conservative loophole and conveniently forgetting to declare them to the Tax Office, whilst in the public eye forcing already overworked doctors to work through the weekend.[24] In response to the damage he was causing, junior doctors went on strike and mass protests erupted in 2016. Angry at their contractual changes forcing them to work dangerous hours they were not going to be seen as the ones responsible for threats to healthcare services. They were the symptom, not the root.

Following in the footsteps of Margaret Thatcher, Jeremy Hunt is a close ally with the right-wing Murdoch media empire, but tried to be secretive about it. It didn't go well as in 2010 he was caught ducking behind a tree in order to avoid being seen to be meeting Murdoch, and in the summer of 2018, ACT UP activists wanted to make sure he couldn't hide from us. We tried for weeks to contact him. Surprise, surprise – he didn't answer. One night, we found out that he was to be a keynote speaker at the Institute of Government reflecting on political interference in the NHS, so we decided to question him through platforming the lived reality of us as HIV+ services users, alongside the doctors and nurses we've been speaking to.

'Hello Jeremy we're activists with AIDS Coalition to Unleash Power living with HIV and concerned about the impact of PFIs. We've been trying to get a hold of you for weeks because we're making a documentary about the 70th anniversary of the NHS.

'You say the privatisation of the NHS isn't happening. We've been speaking to hundreds of nurses, doctors and the general public who say the exact opposite. In fact, actually the dismantling and privatisation of the NHS is down to the government and in particular to you. There's no trees to hide behind now. What do you say to that?'

A deadly silence.

'This isn't the opportunity for that', the chairwoman interrupted.

This classic strategy to continue the underhanded privatisation of healthcare relies upon a 'politics of confusion' where public assets are sold off from underneath the public's noses. Incoherent political gestures and 'post-factualisation' are the central components of right-wing strategies to pacify resistance by making out that 'everything is under control'. A hugely pervasive form of social control; political analysts, healthcare professionals, economics and the public discover the facts that have been ignored, but by that time it is too late – as the ACT UP slogan says, 'Silence = Death'.

At the upcoming World AIDS Day we were determined to burst through this silence so I went to speak with my friend Siobhan with a healthy dose of 'Carpe F*cking Diem'.

I adore this woman. We met on a recent 'Brixton Dykes on the Rampage' queer tour and I've been mesmerised

by her ever since. The Director of Greater Hepatitis
C healthcare strategy across Manchester for 20 years,
Siobhan was previously part of the Rebel Dykes in the
1980s, living and organising amongst some of London's
fiercest punk deviants. Creating 2,000-strong lesbian
leather parties, starting BDSM leather clubs, organising
radical feminist crèches and working the system were all
survival skills that the militant lesbian punks learnt before
the perils of Thatcher's Section 28 kicked in. I love the
Rebel Dykes' spirit. Looking back it is easy to romanticise
but today when looking down the Brixton backstreets to
a comparative ghost town full of gentrified markets and
anti-squatting laws, you know a lot of work needs to be
done.

'Why are people so timid these days? So dry? So cautious?' With a guttural Mancunian laugh Siobhan doesn't
suffer fools gladly. 'Thatcher may be dead but she's in all
of us.'

She is right. The dismantling of ordinary people's ability
to resist, compounded by the internalised homophobia and
repression of the queer imagination has worked its sinister
magic. So together we conjured up THE BANG BUS.

13

Homo Hope

THE BANG BUS. HOMO queerstory. HOMO HEDONISM. HOMO HOPE – World AIDS Day Special – an immersive theatrical anti-stigma bus-tour journeying through the decades and places to bring the queerstory of HIV+ in London to life. A raucous, wild, anarchic and soulful queer tribute to the survivors of homophobia, HIV+phobia, Section 28 and AIDS.

'Meet at Soho Square cottage, wear red and whatever makes you feel fabulous', the call out to participants stated. I was running, sweating even in the freezing December morning, from Hyde Park where we'd finished decorating the bus adorned with outfits for the glamorous assistant hosts to wear; I had ten minutes to get to Soho Square. We had kitted the bus out with giant spliffs and long wigs to stereotype the 1970s, studded leather jackets and mohawks of the 1980s and neon UV rave sticks for the

1990s. The 'How Dare You Presume I'm Heterosexual' and 'Hands Off Our NHS' banners along with a 'Tories Don't Die of Ignorance' banner – a subversion of the 1980s Public Health England Campaign tombstones – were ready and hanging off the back of the bus.

We created the BANG BUS to show gratitude for those who gave selflessly through challenging times to demand a permanent HIV/AIDS memorial and to support the many minority communities who face very specific issues that are still neglected. Isolation, depression and internalised homophobia has in some way eaten up our confidence within the worldwide eye of the state-sanctioned homophobic storm. Eventually we arrive to pull together the folks in Soho Square and onto the bus which had now parked outside the former Club Bang on Tottenham Court Road.

The voices of the dead are swirling around the trees. Shivers curl up my spine as a hundred people board the decorated bus as we are about to embark and stop at key locations in the struggle for healthcare for all. Underneath the props to animate each different queer venue, the conversations on the bus energised the deeper transformations. The small conversations between people from different generations and different cultures on the bus created a wider tapestry of meaning for everyone on board to truly acknowledge and recognise their worth in the ongoing journey of queer humankind.

Ahead of the day, Hope Winter Hall from the Sisters of Perpetual Indulgence – a brilliant movement that utilises drag, particularly wearing nun habits, to call out religious and sexual intolerance – shared her plans to take the ashes of her late husband, Rev. Virgil Hall on board. Now aged 65, remembering the peak of the crisis they told us, 'In 1981 I was in New York and I remember the rumours and conspiracy theories starting about what was called "GRID" or 'Gay-related immune deficiency'. In spring I came home to London where people began to get sick and die. Then I got sick. I know HIV is no longer a death sentence now but as we approach the 40th anniversary of the first diagnosed cases, I dream of AIDS being over before I die – that dream can only come true if we never give up the fight.'

We travelled from Middlesex Hospital in Fitzrovia, where some of the first cases were diagnosed, heading to Trafalgar Square, where huge protests for medication were held in the 1980s. Slowly weaving through the traffic to our last stop we finally got to the Dean Street clinic.[1] The finale here was to highlight where, after such an epic battle since HIV began, the fight is now and to host a party to celebrate the staff and their massive contribution to the 90 per cent reduction in HIV diagnosis.

Standing on top of the bus in the cold air and under the Christmas lights, at moments like this my heart swells for my city.

David Stuart works at Dean Street clinic as the Wellbeing Support Services Manager. A fearless lioness he practices and consoles hundreds of people caught in the toxic spider web of chemsex, internalised stigma and HIV+ each week. The love he has for his queer family practically glows off him.

David took the mic:

We've had some exciting reductions in HIV diagnoses recently in London. But we remain aware of the challenges ahead and queerstory of HIV and AIDS in London. The legacy and collective trauma of all the AIDS deaths, or all the injustices afforded homosexuals, still rattles in our souls; it's too recent a trauma for us to be able to fathom this new epidemic of deaths and traumas that accompany chemsex. The deaths. Deaths, amongst brilliant brilliant gay people, simply pursuing the joy and intimacy of sex and love, and finding it complex; needing drugs [chems] to find the pleasure in it where it can be complicated. And dying, or suffering in the pursuit.

Approximately two gay men die in this pursuit in London each month.

Varying similarities in other cities around the world.

I can't stand it.

So I am an activist, and I don't stop.

Join me. I insist.

While both dressed in some kind of busman's holiday meets 'Hi-de-Hi' drag, Nell and Dan then hyped the crowd with a final rendition of 'The Queers on the Bus Say Save Our Spaces!' while I sat with Stuart for a moment to gather my thoughts.

Stuart looked at me and said 'In the good old times of Gay Lib we talked a lot about having a retirement home for old acid queens, one with wide corridors we could whizz around on our electric wheelchairs hidden beneath our crinolines. But never in the plague years that followed did I ever imagine boarding a "Queer Tours of London mince through time – AIDS BANG BUS" to visit those places where we said goodbye to so many of our nearest and dearest. A bus with Fabulous Hostesses to entertain us, play quiz games and encourage us to share our memories. A mystery tour that three hours earlier picked up a bunch of strangers, set down a group of friends, the BANG BUS was one of the most anarchic events I've ever experienced. It had all the elements of a trip on LSD. I thought at one point I was in a modern version of Fellini's *Satyricon*', as he left the bus smiling.

Beyond the striking message this was an opportunity to remember. A refusal to be defined by the pain of what happened, which is exactly the point.

How to Organise a BANG BUS

1 Light the 'soul-fire'! Collaborate with the organising crew by asking, what is meaningful? What brings love and power to you and your community?

2 Build a crew of 'glamorous assistants' for the BANG BUS to enchant the crowds and support the protagonists, speakers and story-tellers. Glamorous assistants make every show or project a million times more pleasurable.

3 Attention to detail. Use space on the bus and in the bus stops for art, creativity and power.

4 Catalyse fun and interactiveness amongst the chaos through quizzes, songs, games; 'eye spy with my little eye' on top of the BANG BUS provides hours of fun.

5 Instead of a reductive loophole feedback, organise a 'feed forward' discussion in a debrief by asking 'what worked? What could be better next time?'

Stigma-induced pain is particularly acute when it comes to love, sex and dating. For people living with stigmatised conditions, fear of rejection is huge and going on a date can be terrifying. Feeling like damaged goods, unlovable and unattractive as a result of an HIV diagnosis is commonplace for so many across the world.

After the BANG BUS adventures, ACT UP had a plan to bring back our show 'HIV Blind Date' for the next World AIDS Day. It is a cabaret that platforms the powers of love in stigma-heavy communities. The idea was hatched after the passing of Cilla Black, famous for hosting *Blind Date*, with sparkling charisma and her 'what's your name and where dya come from' introductions from the contestants.

Built around dating questions to incorporate the realities of both HIV+ and inter-related Hepatitis conditions, the show is interspersed with performances. It is an appreciation of how living and loving with stigmatised conditions is totally interdependent on our systems of support. Fundamentally the show is a celebration of how we navigate sexual freedom, owning our differences and of life itself. It is a celebration of where we've got to because of people fighting till the bitter end, patting ourselves on the back and then saying 'Right, we still have more to do'.

The venue was booked and contestants recruited so off I went to meet Silvia to write the script.

Artist, feminist, yoga instructor, fashion icon, revolutionary activist and living openly with HIV since 2005, Silvia is now the CEO of Positively UK, the only UK HIV charity led and run by people living with HIV in the UK, whilst also spearheading ACT UP Women, working together with women with HIV to empower themselves and own their space in the healthcare struggle. She is a tour de force to say the least.

Her yoga classes for people with HIV are such a healthy tonic for me and I am so grateful for people like Silvia who ground me. In her office training room grounds she looked at me while I held the blank script-writing sheets and explained, 'Living with HIV today is still fraught with incredible stigma and difficulties. Women living with HIV continue to be diagnosed later and are more likely to experience violence, as well as living in poverty and having poor mental and emotional wellbeing. The cuts on support services has had an incredible negative impact on our lives. To address the structural power imbalances women with HIV face we need sustained programmes that put us at the centre, and provide opportunities to amplify our voices and develop leadership skills so that we can live our lives with dignity.'

We then started to thrash out the questions for Cilla to ask contestants to bring to life issues of diagnosis, disclosing, health, intimacy, sexual relationships and sexuality.

1   What are the positives of being HIV positive?
2   We are on a date and I've just forgotten to take my anti-psychotic medication (because mental health affects us much harder in the HIV/HEP community). What do you do to calm me down?
3   You are stuck in a lift with Richard Branson – knowing that he successfully sued the NHS after losing out on a £82m contract, pocketing £2m of public money in the process – you look in your handbag and you find handcuffs, a pie and a pig. What do you do?

4 I'm feeling really lonely because isolation and depression hit our community harder. What would you do to cheer me up and what song would you sing to me?

The questions refer to the understanding that in the face of the condition the participants and audience gain a deeper perspective on love, life and death. Importantly, once you are marginalised in society, you are able to gain a more critical understanding of the system of power. As Penny Arcade, legendary queer performance artist and international icon of creative resistance, teaches us, 'I prefer to be in the margins and lead a libidinal life that's rooted in culture, and sex. Pleasure is a radical action.'[2]

One month later and a day before the 'HIV Blind Date' World AIDS Day Special show I was staring out my window dazed at the amount of work to do. It was a slow Sunday morning in November 2018 and the leaves shedding off the trees outside my window were golden and beautiful.

I knew what I needed to do – to dance without any responsibility. I could spare two hours before the mayhem began, and it helps that I've always been a daytime-shift raver. It's 7am and Dan has just minced home honking of a sordid night thrashing about in a raucous filthy Hackney squat party. So off I trot to the base bins. I don't want to hear a word about HIV, campaigns, a new project to protect queer space or a new action coming up. Leave me alone to get lost in the vibrations.

Dancing with my friend Lee, kindred spirit of parties and defiance since we were teenagers, together we balanced on upside-down beer crates to a brave new world of hopeful blissful dimensions.

We spend our lives fighting to reclaim spaces, for ourselves and for other marginalised people to express their souls, love, loss and dreams in a city that increasingly seems to prioritise space for the moneyed and elite, but deep down I know that London is a beast that can never be tamed – of many layers of a cake that refuses to be squashed. A city of 10 million stories of communities who live on top, beside, against and for each other. It's a web that is ever growing and will not be untangled – no matter how hard either the establishment or our own often-segregated campaign demands try to pincer apart and compartmentalise.

After getting home, a long shower and a little disco nap I jump into a taxi with the props to the dress rehearsal, staring at my phone picture of Dan, missing him. After all the incessant actions, 'empowerment' workshops and campaigns he is always there to calm my nerves. Chatting with the driver about how he is looking forward to getting home to his wife and kids, he turns to me and asks 'Do you have children?' Looking around at my bags of feather boas, sequined pants, HIV/HEP anti-stigma leaflets and cabaret 'applause signs' he looks up at me and smiles,

'Oh I see, you are a lovely boy . . . so who is that on your phone?'

'It's my brother', I mumble.

Fuck the journey is long.

Five minutes later we arrived at the venue. The first person I see is ACT UP activist Jarek, but this time with a difference, a bulging black eye. A pioneer of the London Polish LGBTQIA+ Network, he was beaten up on the street for being foreign and gay. Holding a sheet of paper and standing next to one of London's most legendary drag queens, 'Charity Kase', they are definitely pushing through the pain and preparing their opening 'HIV Blind Date' speech, but still nervous, because tonight's show is in tribute to Jacob Alexander, a trailblazing HIV artist and respected anti-stigma advocate.

I first met Jacob dancing in a leather jacket as one of the glamorous assistants at the first 'HIV Blind Date' back in 2015. Often big-hearted people who spend so much time advocating for others don't leave time for themselves. Last month he killed himself and we for sure weren't going to let Jacob's legacy be just another statistic in the rising LGBTQIA+ or the HIV+ communities' suicide list.

It's 7pm and it is time for the show. The crowd is getting bigger and the lights come on, and out steps Jarek and Charity Kase looking fabulous with the glamorous assistants by their side, to read Jacob's Mum's speech. I'd spoken for hours with her throughout the week and the grief was too heavy for her to come in person. The crowd went silent as they started. 'Welcome to "HIV Blind Date" everyone! Before we begin the show we want to pay tribute to Jacob who we lost a couple of months ago. Please take a moment as we read a statement from his mother.'

Hi Everyone, Good evening my name is Jacqueline, The message I'd like you all to keep in your mind and heart going forward is that change really can start with just one person.

That is how we can all help to stop the stigma for those living with HIV. Talk about your story. Don't be concerned about the ignorance of others. You never know, if just one person is listening then you have the possibility to change their thought process and that's where change begins with education. When Jacob was diagnosed on the morning of his 22nd birthday, he found the usual information, but there was nothing to connect him to other newly diagnosed young people or people with HIV. So Jacob created his app 'The Positive Project'. We could stop the stigma before it has a chance to grow and that really could make a difference. Thank you for listening, I hope you all have a fabulous evening, love from Jacqueline, Jacob's Mum.

Silence. People hug each other in the crowd and as the emotionally charged atmosphere intensifies amongst new friends, the music slowly gets louder, blasting out Aretha Franklin's heart-wrenching classic 'Say a Little Prayer (for You)'.

It's five minutes to go until drumroll for the contestants and LeaSuwanna is busy doing the last of her make-up behind stage. One of the contestants, she is bringing to life her slinky character archetype, the 'secretary by day, dominatrix by night' personality. LeaSuwanna is part of ACT UP Women and Positively UK with Silvia and they recently won 'event of the year' for 'The Catwalk Power, Resistance and Hope' at the Sexual Freedom Awards 2018. The Catwalk Power project is a community-building initiative focusing on how HIV/AIDS impacts on women's lives. The activism generated by this community group raises public awareness about HIV stigma, inequality, and power. The framework of fashion carries a strong political message while recognising the resilience and strength with which women living with HIV can be empowered.

Looking absolutely incredible and full of life I had to inquire more.

'LeaSuwanna what made you want to be part of tonight's show?'

'For too long, HIV+ has been dominated by white men's stories . . . only thing missing was the voices and faces of the people they were discussing. For me it acknowledged a massive black hole in Women's culture, background and knowledge on sex. Dating is scary because of so many reasons, but my main one is women not having the confidence to ask for what they need sexually. We don't often have the knowledge that we are also sexual beings and deserve good sex and are not just there for someone else's pleasure. Side note its #MasturbationMonth for me that's a daily thing, helps with stress!' she giggles and applies striking lilac lipstick.

'Let's welcome our three fabulous contestants to the stage!' we hear Silvia bellowing from the front. 'Oh shit that's me, better go!' and LeaSuwanna legs it through the door chanting 'The Power's Ours! Amandla Awethu!'

'Hello beautiful audience, remember we have power in community so let me ask you a question first', Cilla radiates.

'If you are an HIV-positive woman and you want to give birth to an HIV-negative baby, how many months during pregnancy do you have to be on the drugs?'

Cilla pauses and waits for any answers, 'Well the answer is three months during pregnancy'.

'Now question number one for our lovely panel. If you could go back in time, what would you tell your younger self when you first got your diagnosis?'

LeaSuwanna takes the mic, 'Self-love is everything to me. I have a family, friends, activism, studying 'Knowledge Is Power' and many more things I take responsibility for. However, if I have no time for myself, no time to appreciate my accomplishments and especially no time for pleasure then I will also have nothing to give to the long list that needs my full attention.'

The rest of the night the contestants laugh, giggle and sweat responding to the other questions. As the show climaxes the glamour girls storm the stage with a choreographed dance, and need to be shooed off. Cilla triumphantly kisses the contestants, releases them from the stage and says, 'Well sadly that's all we have time for but hopefully we'll see you soon. Tara!' LeaSuwanna then hits the decks playing a sizzling set starting with Miguel's 'Sure Thing', a triumphant ode to pristine love.

Everyone is on the dancefloor going wild. Searching for my sequinned jacket backstage in the dressing room I find ACT UP activist Andria taking off her glamorous assistant outfit.

'Why did you come backstage Andria, are you ok my dear?' I ask.

'Jacob's story really moved me tonight, Dan. The idea that people who are unwell should be discriminated against is unconscionable. It's completely crass and disgusting. You wouldn't see an old person who needs help walking down the street and cross the road. You don't start giving them hell . . . you don't start telling them off. Or a child whose acting out because they're just doing what we all do sometimes. If you see vulnerability, regardless of whether they are called alternative communities or marginalised communities or whatever they are, the response should be to want to care and to help. Next year is the 50th anniversary of Stonewall, a time for celebration but also reflection . . .', Andria trails off.

She then looks up at me, straight in the eye, and continues, 'I do think we should be prepared to die for the struggle, like Marsha and Sylvia did because in the end it seems to me . . . it seems like there's been very little major change without thousands of deaths . . . you know sometimes it's hard not to cry.'

As the great Australian indigenous activist Lilla Watson says, 'If you have come here to help me, you are wasting your time. But if you have come because your liberation is bound up with mine, then let us work together.'[3]

How to Organise an 'HIV Blind Date' Show

1 Meet people and connect directly 'where they are at', emotionally, practically and spiritually, rather than where you want them to be.
2 Create each character to be unique and archetypes of the key themes.
3 Weave in community games such as 'Love Is Power', speed dating or a raffle.
4 There are no limits. If Cilla wants a gaggle of gimps to support her on stage them make it happen – unleash it all!
5 Combine theatre and activism by incorporating an 'action element' in the show and by investigating sites of social injustice in the

---

local neighbourhood. When the show is done take the audience out to a nearby target such as a pharmaceutical company with giant confetti cannons and flares. Always flares.

When you are 21 and you're diagnosed HIV+ it can be the most lonely thing ever. Fast forward ten years and when you've clocked on that HIV+ is not just your issue to deal with but society's – you can't get a moment's peace.

The journey to owning your body, identity and voice is precious. It wasn't so long ago that I couldn't even say the words 'gay' or 'HIV'. Every day you know that life's not promised. This then helps make you walk down the street and fall in love. Not just with people but with situations that fuel you to take the necessary steps to look after yourself and join movements to take collective action. Jacob's spirit will always be with me and I have the words of Doctor Seaton, my first HIV doctor, to push me on too 'Dan, I don't know what it is you're doing [after my health rapidly improved] but whatever it is you're doing – keep at it.'

Always, and especially in these bleak times of austerity and looming ecological collapse, draw strength from painful places. We need to find the celebratory, life-affirming and raucous ways of wrestling those demons inside us because at the end of the day, when you feel that sense of loss, it enhances your sense of love.

Pharmaceutical greed and the global export of homophobia have left people looking at the compass for a new direction, a new hope and a harbour on this Earth, to berth and call home. Turbo-capitalism that prioritises profit over human life is a historical development that has outlived its social usefulness and the marginalised and disenfranchised will seek to overthrow it even if things get worse before they get better.

It often seems like the world is spinning out of control. The space for genuine civil disobedience is atrophying, so for all of us at the margins, when hoisting the flag and seeking change, we must refrain from naivety. In the era of corporate globalisation and gross inequality, those living within cycles of poverty and spiralling debt are treated as criminals, and protesting against further impoverishment is terrorism. The only way to make democracy real is to begin a process of constant questioning, permanent provocation and continuous public conversation between citizens and the state. When the establishment's grip at the centres of power becomes too tight, all of us left out at sea are connecting to challenge power, shouting, 'Ahoy!' as flares for alternative development blaze across the sky.

We know deep down that a community's well-being simply has to do with the quality of the relationships and the cohesion that exists among its citizens rather than what lines a few people's wallets, what we can call real social capita. Incredible examples of creative community resistance can inspire us to attain this. At the turn of the nineteenth century Harriet Tubman utilised networks of antislavery activists to free countless slaves, contributing to the dissolution of slavery.[4] In 1967, countercultural anti-war and revolutionary 'Yippie' protesters dropped bags of money into squabbling bankers at the New York Stock Exchange to denounce the Vietnam War, expose the greed of capitalism and call for the 'death of money'.[5] In 1999 French farmer José Bové's 'dismantling' of a McDonald's restaurant generated movements across the world against genetically modified food and large-scale destructive agri-business.[6] That same year, Bolivian Oscar Olivera, successfully mobilised factory workers against water theft by the Bechtel Corporation that threatened access to water for their cities' poorest citizens.[7] All these examples are just a sprinkling of movements across the world fighting for the poor and oppressed. These are our planet's beacons of hope in the night storms.

There is an alternative. A world where we re-ignite our indicators of development and live within the limits of the natural world and more fairly with each other, locally, nationally and globally. A world where we focus on the things that really matter and apply our core human values to what is really valuable. Britain's value system must have a total decolonial overhaul where social and environmental justice should be the central goal of policy-making. Today the marginalised are demanding change. From the 'Save the NHS' campaigns to community projects for queer freedom and all movements for social justice across the world we dream that queers, all people oppressed by sexual bigotry and all marginalised communities intentionally trapped under the late stages of capitalism's trapdoor, for the last time, are put first. Community empowerment programmes, strategised effectively in key stages, can enable this.

Firstly, localising resistance and re-skilling ourselves from agriculture to manufacturing to the provision of local finance means returning our economy to an appropriate scale. This means equipping ourselves with the means to do so through restructuring an 'ecology of finance' of private, public and mutually owned institutions designed to meet local needs. Importantly, this shift in local economic choice must be situated firmly in an international context. Reframing concepts of 'development' must incorporate colonialism and its consequences, regulate inheritance, prosecute companies built off the violence of imperialism and unpack development 'aid' in relation to the continuation of empire through the back door, or 'neo-colonialism'. Last but not least, reparations must be made that include explicit acknowledgements, apologies and compensation packages and a returning of all assets of all queers punished through global colonialism, neo-colonialism and domestic imprisonment because of homophobic legislation such as the Buggery Act and Section 28, with all such punishments being immediately investigated and assets accounted for.

Ultimately, all of these alternative economic choices need to be delicately structured and critically analysed so as not to perpetuate the problem. But they must start now before it is too late, before the doors of cultural amnesia close around us and the status quo is entrenched for good.

Humans are beings of praxis. Praxis involves strengthening a culture of dialogue where those at the peripheries can search for and find sooner the lighthouse that will guide them to safety ahead. The point is to start the change that stops manufacturing inequality. This will change these cycles of violence from repeating themselves in the form of co-option of Pride, and throughout austerity Britain today.

14

Spirit of the Camp Road

I want say that Pride should be a platform to raise our voices for LGBTQIA+ rights. People who live in London may have some of their rights but it doesn't mean the entire world has been changed. There are millions of people suffering and being tortured every day in different parts of the world. (Mazharul Islam, LGBTQIA+ freedom fighter and Patron of ReportOUT)

It's torturous to be thinking about both oppression and homosexual liberation all the time but Maz, Nettie, Ted, Andrew, Stuart and the others I've met in queer justice movements on this bumpy ride know that there is an end in sight. Connecting local and global struggles are the key to achieving LGBTQI+ liberation, and absolute freedom for all, across the world. Generating hope is part of our essential human story and, I now see, our treasure. The words of a favourite writer resonate here. Dutch mystic and liberation thinker Etty Hillesum teaches us from her diaries before she was killed in Auschwitz.

> They can harass us, they can rob us of our material goods, our freedom of movement, but we ourselves forfeit our greatest assets by our misguided compliance. By our feelings of being persecuted, humiliated, and oppressed. By our own hatred. By our swagger, which hides our fear. We may of course be sad and depressed by what has been done to us; that is only human and understandable. However: our greatest injury is one we inflict upon ourselves. I find life beautiful, and I feel free. The sky within me is as wide as the one stretching above my head. (Etty Hillesum, Westerbork Transit Camp, 1942)[1]

One thing I will always remember about my Nan, Michalina, is her unbelievable optimism. As a child I was so confused when she used to have fits of hysterical laughter after sharing the saddest gut-wrenching stories. Humour and self-deprecation, I have now grown to deeply appreciate, are life-savers as they help alleviate the pain we carry to face life in all its glory.

Recently I started a new job taking groups of young people on anti-war education tours across Europe tracing the footsteps of my grandparents' experience, underground resistance movements and legendary queer anti-fascist fighters. We travel through the battlefields of Normandy, the cabaret hotspots of the Weimar era where Hitler unleashed his first attack against the queer community and onto the present-day migrant camps where the inhabitants live in fear of Neo-Nazi attacks. We visit migrant communities, activist movements that support them and finally end up at Dachau Concentration Camp, the first regular Nazi-established concentration camp, as a final hard-hitting learning curve.

One hundred thousand lesbians and homosexual men were arrested during the Second World War, many perished in the concentration camps and many fought back as part of the underground resistance too. The current political climate demands that we go beyond sombre memorialisation and scrutinise the conditions that permitted the Nazi holocaust that still exist in the world today. Right-wing extremism still poses a threat legally, publicly and politically as society witnesses an upsurge in European fascist movements. Far-right populist upsurges in British politics and the European Parliament lead to rising hate crime, mass armament, corporate dominance, austerity induced 'welfare reforms', violations of international law and immigration policies – all of which endanger the integrity of the 1950 European Convention on Human Rights, which was born out of the 'end' of the war. If we are ever to truly see the Nazi Holocaust as the past we must continue to say

'NO PASARAN' (they shall not pass), take to the streets and stop fascism everywhere we find it.

Every time I visit Dachau I learn more than I could ever imagine. Lessons of hope, courage and conviction that persecution will end. I think the most gut-wrenching situation I have ever learnt was from the remaining stories of homosexuals who survived the camps. When the camps were liberated and all the inmates could begin to smell freedom, homosexuals were incarcerated because it was still illegal to be gay in Germany. If I was alive then that would have been me. It's no wonder my soul is filled with queer rage.

Last time, upon leaving the barracks a sign caught my eye in the centre of the barracks under a tree. Small and rectangular, in classic Nazi font, it stood lonely between two giant pine trees. Here is where the inmates met, looked after each other, shared stories, loved and planned their freedom, it was known as 'the spirit of the camp road'.

The word 'camp' has for centuries been regarded as the stereotypical behaviour homosexuals theatrically inhabit. At moments like this it is a reminder that our identity, and our reclamation of it, is nothing less than life and death. It is priceless.

Finding beauty, meaning and optimism in the ongoing struggle for LGBTQIA+ freedom and justice at large we need this 'Spirit of the Camp Road' today, in all its meanings. Deportations and death camps have always been a key mechanism at the heart of homophobic cultural apparatus. The rise in illegal detainment for migrants and their children, the daily torture and lack of healthcare for people fleeing war and conflict that the UK started and the forced removal of a generation of migrants with legal status 'back to where they are from' all spell danger.

News headlines have just revealed that far-right Britain First activists have been joining the Conservative Party in numbers,[2] emboldened by the Conservative landslide in December 2012, so I'm having dinner with Saph in Brick Lane wondering what to do.

'There is so much pain that you have to go through in order to fight oppression. I think this is evident throughout life. How nothing really is won by being silent or just by writing poems. Justice is won by fighting back and yeah, sometimes violence. The brutality of the state is the worst. They have more gadgets, more guns and more prisons. We need more revolutions like Stonewall, especially now.'

'And who needs confronting today?'

'Margaret Thatcher, who else? All the well-known bigots – Nigel Farage, Tommy Robinson, Steve Bannon, Donald Trump, Katie Hopkins, Piers Morgan – we need to defy them all!' Saph responded, leaving my heart swelling with hope that the situation can change.

From the time of the exportation of the 1533 Buggery Act through the British Empire, World Wars and to the current web of power and powerlessness we are in, the oppressed will always resist. Learning what has gone before and taking action in the present, that knowledge will guide us. Only through having a very wide conception about what's gone on in the world can we fully comprehend the dangers of exceptionalism.

It's 6.30am and the next morning I am sitting with Andrew, other GLF activists and about a hundred other people on a bus singing the song 'Solidarity Forever' treasured in the film *Pride* about Lesbians and Gays Support the Miners (LGSM). The solidarity bus is heading to Chelmsford Crown Court to support 15 activists convicted of a terrorism-related offence for chaining themselves around an immigration removal flight at Stansted airport.[3] Many of the defendants are part of LGSM who recently helped launch the first ever Peckham Community Pride – a strongly political event, firmly rooted in social engagement to explore the intersecting issues for migrants, people threatened by deportation. On a freezing morning in March 2017 they occupied Stansted Airport runway to stop 60 vulnerable migrants being sent back to Nigeria and Ghana, former British colonies where the anti-sodomy laws are entrenched because of the British Buggery Act of 1533.

Public outcry erupted over what human rights defenders branded a heavy-handed prosecution and the group became known as the 'Stansted 15'. Lyndsay was one of them. In between leading 'Queer Tours' Lyndsay has been juggling the constraints of the trial. I wave to her from the public gallery, and clutching her necklace, our matching 'Sonder' chains, she smiles.

The oldest, and most fabulous people there are of course the GLFers. Speaking at the front of the demo outside court, Andrew steps up to the mic.

I cannot call myself a very significant activist today. What inspires me is the younger people. I'm deeply inspired by the Stanstead 15 who are on trial in Chelmsford, on charges of terrorism for stopping a Nigerian lesbian being forced onto an aircraft and sent to a husband who had threatened to murder her. That's what I admire the most now, activism around deportation.

Later Lyndsay came to share with us in the court waiting room.

'It all started when we were chatting to someone who was part of the Bristol Bisons gay rugby club in Bristol. He was incredibly involved in loads of community events, such a lovely guy, and then the Home Office threatened to deport him. He's built his life here and they just want to send him to Nigeria, a place where he could get gang raped, gang murdered for being gay. In Britain we are not reminded often enough that this country deports our queer family who live besides us to countries where they will get homophobically attacked. Homophobically attacked because there are still colonial anti-sodomy laws in place. That's a British colonial legacy. It's there now. It's just the truth and it's fucking horrible.'

'How are you coping Lyndsay?' I ask, completely in awe of her resilience sitting in court day in and day out, her profound spirit of deep love and justice being demonised by the prosecution.

'When I was speaking on trial in my justification defence, the pain ran deep. It's been so stressful but it's also been the purest way I could express love. Because rage is love, and is something that needs a voice. Rage is just love that's seeking a different expression. It needs to be heard as that. The dark part of that light is really very, very dark, so I'm trying to find a way to look after that so it doesn't fuck me up. I ain't no strip light', she said.

'I ain't no strip light.' Iconic. I am sure Marsha P. Johnson and Sylvia Rivera would be proud of Lyndsay and the 'Stansted 15'.

Outside in the solidarity demonstration crowd stood Sinthia with bulging bright tearful eyes and a story to tell. Along with Maz they knew this reality all too well. They had both fled to the UK from Bangladesh. On 25 April 2016, Xulhaz Mannan, the publisher and co-founder of *Roopban*, the first ever LGBTQIA+ magazine in Bangladesh, and another LGBTQIA+ activist were brutally murdered by religious activists.[4] Maz got word that he would be the next target so he swiftly made his moves. They are now campaigning for justice for Xulhaz Mannan and Mahbub Rabbi

Tonoy and also want the Commonwealth leaders to take necessary steps to abolish the '377 Penal Code' law against homosexuality, that yet again, the British Empire started.

The next week, along with 40 other Bangladeshi queers, we took to the steps of the Bangladesh High Commission demanding justice for Xulhaz and Mahbub Rabbi Tonoy.

On the tube to the Bangladesh High Commission I stick on one of my favourite tunes by Miriam Makeba, popularly known as 'Mother Africa'. Singing from the South African townships she sings the blues for those living the brutal nightmare of Apartheid, where one type of human is considered superior to the other.[5]

'They say "Khawuleza Mama", which simply means "Hurry Mama, please don't let them catch you"', she sings.

How true these words rang today.

Everyone present at the demonstration faces daily fears that they could be exposed in pictures or the media, endangering their lives in London and their families back in Bangladesh. This is on top of the daily brutality of living in London's poorest boroughs with no financial support and in fear of the hostile environment. The levels of danger could be felt in the air. Their courage is outstanding.

Standing in a sharp suit on the steps of the High Commission in well-to-do Kensington, Maz raised his hand to knock on the front door, turned around and addressed the crowd.

This is something no one has done before. I am the first queer person with a Bangladeshi passport to make this protest before the Bangladesh High Commission. I have to think a lot about my security and especially my family security back in Bangladesh. If the government wants then they can find out my parents any time and harass them.

Commitment in his eyes and shakes in his hands, Maz continued,

My friends were brutally murdered. Bangladesh is one of the commonwealth countries and Bangladesh still follows the British colonial laws. The Penal Code 377 states 'Unnatural offenses'. Whoever voluntarily has carnal intercourse against the order of nature with any man, woman or animal shall be punished with imprisonment and liable to a fine. LGBTQIA+ activists around the world should come forward to work together and make a strategic plan to abolish the laws against homosexuality. We should change the world before we die so that future generations can live in a world where homophobia doesn't exist so that we don't need to leave our own country, family friends and live in another country with refugee status.

Maz then turned around and handed the petition to the staff. He made them promise to respond, before they claim ignorance or stuff the petition in a drawer. The sun was fading and it was time to leave. Crammed in, on the tube back home together to East London, we were standing next to a few South Asians, maybe Bangladeshi. They saw the 'LGBTQIA+ World' placard in Maz's hand, looked at each other and immediately moved away. As the doors opened at his tube stop, Maz looked at me defiantly and said 'this reminds us that we have a long way to go'.

Meanwhile that evening, news reports had broken that hundreds of people were being rounded up because of their sexuality or perceived sexuality by authorities in Chechnya.[6] They were subjected to beatings and electric shocks in secret prisons, provoking international condemnation and sanctions. Hoping to put my feet up after this emotionally exhausting day, the phone was going wild. Reports from the Russian LGBT Network described a new terrifying wave of kidnappings where innocent LGBTQIA+ people were being removed to illegal detention centres.[7] Ramzan Kadyrov, the Chechen leader, denies the existence of LGBT people in his country. At the same time the growing news stories of homosexuals spending 12 days in a blood-soaked cell, starved, humiliated, beaten and subjected to extreme torture, 'honour killing' incitements encouraging families to denounce their queer relatives and never-again-heard-of voices, like famous pop singer Zelim Bakaev, would not be out of place in Nazi Germany.

Learning about the LGBT+ internment camps in Chechnya, I shiver that night wondering what to do. It was January 2019 – a few weeks before Holocaust Memorial Day when for many descendants of survivors the world becomes clearer. I spoke to my Nan in my dreams and her words 'Never Again Ever' leaped from my mind into the next day. Surviving the war by living undercover in the Warsaw Ghetto she was a pro at 'hiding in plain site'. A lesson so true in Russia today.

Action stations, and a 'QUEER POWER' demo was organised over the coming weeks for Holocaust Memorial Day on 27 January 2019 outside the Russian Embassy to demand the government and United Nations take action, and that we open up our borders to support those fleeing. Far-right LGBTQIA+ groups like 'LGBTQIA+ Trump' were making the issue even more apparent by rejecting calls for solidarity – the silence was deafening. It planted a seed; fast-forward ten months and I found myself standing in the cold streets of Moscow. I was invited by the Russian LGBT+ Network to address their annual conference on 'international solidarity for global LGBTQIA+ freedom' along with a delegation of LGBT+ and HIV+ activists. The event's aim was to mark the 16th anniversary of the repeal of Section 28, and build international understanding and solidarity for those across the world affected by its legacy. Ten years after Section 28 was repealed, Putin took up the model and created the 'Gay Propaganda Law', a similar model but much more deadly.[8]

After two weeks on the delegation I found myself getting really emotional. Maybe it's because I was knackered or maybe it's because after you've been talking about the same issues in meeting after meeting, taking photos of your new connections, you become numb. Only when you get back to your bed do the cracks begin to appear and the gravity of it all becomes too real.

I met many courageous people through Arina, a young razor-sharp queer woman hungry for community. I first met Igor Iasine, who not only has been part of creating LGBT+ freedom parades and interventions in Russia – a country that bans Pride marches and any form of sexual education outside of the nuclear family – but trail-blazed a movement when the news of the LGBT+ murders in Chechnya began. At the beginning of the uprisings, in a country where most protest is illegal, Igor and the other activists were wondering what to do, so they held 'teach ins' and *Pride* film screenings to inform and equip them with a toolkit to challenge this.

However, I am learning that the crisis is deepening. The sexual repression and tyrannical homophobia have led to approximately one in ten gay men and 1 per cent of Russia in general are living, loving and dying with HIV+. According to the UN, Russia has one of the fastest growing HIV/AIDS epidemics in the world.[9] But campaigns to create sex education, stop the extrajudicial violence and hold those responsible to account are simultaneously growing.

'A few years ago a homophobic campaign began, and the state openly involved itself in the oppression of LGBT people. It has complicated the lives of LGBT people on the one hand, but on the other, it has allowed us to undertake discussion of the problems and rights of LGBT people on an unprecedented level', Igor fervidly told me.

Later in the delegation, I met Valentina who works night and day in Moscow's underground and over-filled LGBT+ Centre where people flee homophobia in the family, workplace and the streets from all over Russia to come and seek respite in the hope of human connection that this world denies them. 'You know that scene in the film *The Pianist* when they [the Jews] were realising what was happening [Nazi invasion] but didn't want to quite believe it was going to be that bad ... well that's what's going on here', she said.

Aware that reacting to a tyrannical system is never enough Valentina knew it was time to fight back. So four years ago she helped found 'Barents Pride' alongside FRI, the Norwegian-Helsinki Committee, Amnesty International Norway, Queer World and Russia team, on the Norwegian side of the Norway and Russia border because the 'Gay Propaganda Law' bans the promotion of homosexuality in Russia. From the border sidelines they watch the police stand in defence and they dream of a Pride in Russia. Valentina and the Barents Pride team are going to make this happen. Today they need musicians and artists from all over the world to join them.

Another long-time activist is Yury, who in all his spare time helps coordinate Russia's HIV+ Network. Because of the 'Gay Propaganda Law' that compounds the nuclear family as the only way to exist, any other form of sex education is banned. LGBT+ and HIV+ people, if they can, flee. Many to places like Uzbekistan where, as being LGBTQI+ is a criminal offence, they are immediately imprisoned and die without healthcare.

How dare anyone call this 'propaganda'.

Chelyabinsk is in Central Russia by the mountains. In 2015 this is where the famous meteorite fell from the skies. Today Yury is busy launching a life-changing moment of his own, Russia's first PrEP trial. In a country where not only is being 'gay' shameful but being 'ill' also brings shame, he is defiantly creating a system where having sex is not a crime and asking for healthcare is supported. If PrEP trial statistics are anything to go by, the introduction of PrEP could stem the tide of the HIV+ epidemic here where over 1 million people currently live with it and people still regularly die of AIDS.[10]

'You must meet "Action"', the residents at Moscow's LGBT+ Centre told me. Eve, Viola and Nastya are part of the new movement 'Action' – young, smart lightning-rods of creative resistance for a tired, traumatised, older LGBT+ movement. Since the 'Gay Propaganda Law' was introduced, street interventions and political protests have died out. Kicked out of their family homes, and bullied in school (Nastya's classmates stole her Pride flag and burned it in a ceremony in the playground and the video went viral) – they have nothing to lose and everything to gain. On 11 October this year – international 'Coming Out' day – they protested the gay concentration camps in front of the Chechen government office to bring to life their vision of a Russia free from legislated homophobia and the creation of an LGBT+ protection law.

They have huge, growing arrest fines and court fees to pay. Some of them are 18 years old.

When I come back to the UK I will have to try to find a neat, simple campaign message to verbalise, knowing people will ask 'what was it like and what can we do?'

But the reality is it's far messier and socially complex but through people and actions like these much more emotionally beautiful than I could have ever imagined.

That night, at goodbye drinks, while Eve painted eyeliner wet through wine from her glass (impressive) on her best mate whilst wearing a badge which said 'HELL – Admit One', Viola turned to me with a fierce look in her eyes. A progressive queer Jew in an Orthodox conservative country she is active in the new socialist lesbian movement. She hugged me and quietly said into my ear, 'It is all about hope. We love our family and friends here in Russia. We don't want to go abroad. We have to show that we have the power inside, not just the power but brought to life through smart actions. There are some parts of the world where you can't be yourself – you have to fight. Together we must build this roadmap.'

Wondering if and how I could let off some steam in an LGBT+ club after so many intense conversations I keep asking around where I should go. 'Popoff Kitchen',

I was told on repeat, and this is where I found Nikita Egorov-Kirillov.

When the 'Gay Propaganda Law' was introduced Nikita had his face smashed in and his arm broken by homophobes; he could have fled. He soon found himself on the 'LGBT+ Blacklist', a fascists' bucket-list of those they intend to attack; again Nikita could have fled.

Instead Nikita drew a line in the sand and decided to navigate the system and build a queer revolution inside. When safe spaces for queers to congregate were abandoned he knew what he had to do. He started a party and a handful of friends came along. The next party there were more and the next even more. The media found out but he said nothing, aware that this space was sacred. Through compassion and strategy he let eros weave through the parties. HIV+ testing, posters on sex+positivity and self-care, play rooms, nudity, performance, laughter and queer love – it wasn't long before a couple (consensually) made love on the dance-floor. He knew that things were changing. Now Popoff Kitchen has thousands of people attending each month, queer parties, raves and sexual awakening is multiplying across Russia, and Nikita is in demand around the world.[11]

'But what about the propaganda I hear about at home?' I asked.

'Don't leave us isolated. We need you to see what's really going on here and us queers across the world must stick together.'

'And what can we do in solidarity?' I ask.

'The key strategy on the road to freedom then is "MASS VISIBILITY" to push the issues up the political agenda and provide a true assessment of the criminal damage at hand in order to counter government "statistics" that are constantly lowering the numbers of people with HIV+ and affected by hate-crime and domestic violence. The government wants us to believe that we are "invisible", that no one will touch us, but actually the opposite is true. The destruction not only happens in attacks in alleyways and people being left to die without medication in villages across Russia but we turn inside and kill ourselves.

'There are no laws about violence against LGBT+, no laws protecting HIV+ people or any marginalised group so they can live without fear of violent attacks. People then become their own worst propaganda and censor themselves when actually we must unite to abolish the "Gay Propaganda Law" and, even deeper, confront the government's wholesale legislative control of the right to protest and freedom of expression. Civil action overturned Section 28 and it can happen here too. It must.'

The last person to meet on the delegation was Boris, the first publicly out LGBT+ HIV+ artist in Russia. One of the many amazing actions of which he was part seized press attention and captured the public imagination. In the St Petersburg main square, in response to the government's AIDSphobic rhetoric, along with his friend who is HIV negative they drank each other's blood, mixed with vodka, to show that we are all human and sex is a fact of life – to remember the dead. Very Russian. Gives a totally new meaning to 'Bloody Mary'.

He shared that whilst he is known for his actions there is also the work he does on the ground. Boris works everyday in anti-domestic violence shelters and AIDS support centres to connect different marginalised groups to actively destroy the patriarchal foundations that oppress everyone. I knew we would be friends. Then, when he started talking about 'ACT UP', our awe for each other was cemented. The words 'ACT UP', whether whispered in heavily repressed environments or bellowed on a megaphone, are always a code to transformative Narnia.

'LGBTQIA+, Black, Women's and HIV groups are always treated as lesser; all of us across the world have to stop being submissive', said Boris.

Before we left he looked at us with a twinkle in his eye and said, 'People need carnivals, such as Pride which is currently banned, to cope with the fact of death. Only through holiday can we celebrate life before coping with the fact of death. Carnivals reconcile people with death through celebrating life.'

With people like Boris I'm sure it won't be long before Pride becomes a reality in Russia – just like how the GLF established it in the UK 50 years ago – a protest, an alchemical display of grief and a carnival of hope.

And off he minces and my heart swells so much I can feel it pounding.

Reaching home and seeing Dan's face I couldn't say a word. The joy of just being in his arms and being able to show affection in public was enough. It was time to rest before the final queer tours and GLF 'Think Ins' of the following year kicked off. To escape from this escalating action, my early New Year's resolution was to do more weird and wonderful things, partly for fun and partly for self-care.

So that Sunday evening I'm sitting with my best friend Duncan in Canning Town, East London, letting off steam in the backyard of Docklands Spa, an iconic Russian schmeissing centre. 'Schmeiss' is a Yiddish word meaning 'whip', and the practice of schmeissing was introduced to the East End by Jewish immigrants in the early twentieth century. It was recommended by my Grandad and is frequented these days by Russians, Jewish taxi drivers and curious folk like Duncan and me.

Just below us we see goats gnawing on their ropes whilst we have a ciggie and coffee underneath the morning's grey clouds.

'See there's a goat in the backyard, oh wait, there's two!'

The sauna is heaving with 30 manly Russian men, some naked and some in wet towels, smashing or rather schmeissing each other, wearing braces and tiny little upside-down-flower-pot style hats. This is the best place to unwind after the intensity of my time out in Russia, but my mind still wanders. I know the Russian government is complicit in homophobic genocidal crimes by setting up the gay concentration camps in Chechnya – but what's that got to do with a goat in the back of a spa in Canning Town?

Everyone needs community, love and affection. In this part of the world these Russian men continue their age-old custom of schmeissing, which has for many years kept their souls clean and their skin crisp in saunas in freezing cold Siberia. I'm grateful that they've brought it to us here in East London, but whilst I'm enjoying the show my mind wanders to those Russian men currently in another cramped place, in detention centres, with other men. How can these men not see – either on the surface of their minds or in the subconscious of their souls, or even feel it in the swirl of their groins – the homoerotic contradictions in this bizarre scenario?

After a long deep sauna-induced sleep it was back to pounding the streets in support of the Russian LGBT Network.

Welcome everyone to 'Queer Tours of London – Queer Freedom Everywhere Special' with your fabulous tour guide Kat. I would like to start with my interpretation of the poem 'Caged Bird' by poet Maya Angelou:[12]
The caged bird sings
with a fearful trill
of things unknown
but longed for still
and his tune is heard

on the distant hill
for the caged bird
sings of freedom.
So thank you for coming out on this cold, rainy afternoon when we could easily have hidden under the
covers. But maybe you're as sick of hiding depressed
under the covers as I am, as I am sure many of us
are.

Today I am so chuffed to be standing next to Kat. Members
of the LGBTQIA+ community and supporters from various
Commonwealth nation diasporas are standing outside the
Ugandan Embassy on a blowy and bright winters morning
to pay tribute to the ground-breaking work of Ugandan
LGBTQIA+ and HIV/AIDS activist David Kato. It is
the eighth year since he was bludgeoned to death in his
home in 2011. He was murdered just weeks after assisting
in securing a high court injunction against a local tabloid
that printed the names, photographs and addresses of gay
people that explicitly called for their execution.

The huge crowd is from Uganda, Bangladesh, Nigeria,
Russia, Trinidad and Tobago and the UK. People have come
with sponges to 'wash the homophobia' off the embassies
we will visit. The atmosphere is electric. Unpeeling multiple layers of structural injustice and the innate truth that
queerstory is told by those who write it, means that there
are always people and communities whose story is traditionally left out of the picture, like the Trans community,

people with HIV+, queer migrants or David Kato – until someone kicks off.

The crowd surrounds Kat and first to pay tribute to David Kato is Edwin Sesange of African Equality Foundation:[13]

The fight claimed his life. This is why we launched, a movement driven by refugees and asylum seekers, adamant at speaking out for themselves, instead of being spoken to or about as vulnerable people – a strength perpetuated by Kato's example. Kato's activist legacy and the reality of his absence wrought measurable impact. The loss of David is a tragedy for the activism he would surely have instigated, as well as being a point of uprising amongst freedom fighters who challenge injustice in his name. He was murdered for being queer; his surviving family, endangered.

The target of the tour is a conference taking place that week, 'The Commonwealth Heads of Government Meeting, or CHOGM Conference is here and we are on the streets of London to agitate for a global movement of creative activism to decriminalise homosexuality everywhere!' Kat shouted across the crowd and then read a message from GLF activist and renowned campaigner Peter Tatchell that was sent for the occasion.

The Commonwealth is a bastion of homophobia. In defiance of the human rights principles of the Commonwealth Charter, 37 out of the 53 Commonwealth countries criminalise LGBTQIA+ people. Nine use life imprisonment. In parts of two countries, Pakistan and Nigeria, the death penalty can be used. Even more Commonwealth countries fail to protect LGBTQIA+ people against discrimination and hate crime and reject dialogue with their local LGBTQIA+ organisations. For six decades, the leaders at Commonwealth summits have refused to discuss, let alone support, equality for the estimated more than 100 million LGBTQIA+ citizens living in the member states.

Fresh after a night out at her favourite karaoke bar and covered in a bundle of balloons, Kat radiates good energy. 'Love' in many different ways has been tattooed on her body as it is her compass. After so many devastating sharings of homophobia from around the world, her outfit is exactly what the crowd needs to lift their spirits. So many great revolutionary movements to overturn injustice look fabulous. We can look to the hot-pink sari-wearing Gulabi Gang in India defending against rapists, to the traditional African cloth that the Black Panthers wore to promote racial pride or to the ACT UP activists with their tight graffiti-art T-shirts.

Today the hostile environment strategy is provoking the far-right, Neo-Nazis and homophobic street-bashers to step up their game. Emboldened by politicians' and right-wing media's xenophobic statements like 'plagued by swarms of migrants and asylum seekers, shelling out benefits like Monopoly money' or a 'bunch of migrants' or 'processing migrants',[14] fascists are getting organised in the streets, but not in the dressing rooms. Kat beats them to it and shows just how fabulous and fierce the resistance are. Next tour I'm wearing my sequinned bomber jacket as my contribution to dazzle them back to where they came from.

Kat came to London from Botswana as a Master's candidate and left as a knowledgeable, part-time queer historian. Guided by a principle in Setswana called *botho*, which loosely translates to compassion and humanity, Kat feels that no situation is too big if you view it from a place where you are led by '*botho*', or without bias. Kat is also the first openly trans-identifying public figure from Botswana. As a Motswana who is trans-identifying, Kat sees herself and others like her as trapped within legal systems with misinformed societal impressions influenced by vague interpretations of these laws by the key-holders. Her mission is to 'redress the scar tissues of our oppressions' and to 'develop the nerve to possess yourself' as she shares with and empowers the group that day.

Kat faces the crowd:

> Everyone, the fact that we, as queer people, embody our courage to go out into the streets and say to everyone, 'We have a queerstory, We are not new!' and have it backed by well-informed research is essentially what makes today, and all the queerstory tours and events we do, so important. By claiming our queerstory, we are able to mitigate regressions in the present and plot for stronger futures.

A five minute mince from Trafalgar Square, our next stop is the Nigerian Embassy. Aderonke Apata stood in front of the building and explained why they had set up the 'African Rainbow Family'.[15] The network connects and builds strength for the queer African diaspora in the UK and also currently campaigns to repeal Nigeria's anti-gay law.

> We know not how many people are infected or dying of HIV/AIDS, and from prejudice-incited murder and oppression. It is pertinent that someone stands up to oppose the ignorance of Nigerian leaders that fuels homophobia and persecution of LGBTQIA+ Nigerians. This homophobia in turn causes Nigeria to lose some of her brightest people and consequently leads to a backward economy.

A formidable force to be reckoned with, Aderonke is now training to be a human rights barrister.

Our last stop is the Royal Courts of Justice in the
Strand. We stomp there together in the rain. Standing outside the High Court Aderonke bellowed to the crowd:

> This is where a judge refused to believe that I was
> fleeing persecution and deserved asylum status sim-
> ply because I have a child! It is inconceivable that in
> the UK, in this age, a top government lawyer can
> express such a vile opinion in a court as if being a
> lesbian means being sterile or infertile! This kind of
> statement only goes to show that underbelly institu-
> tional homophobia is endemic in some parts of the
> establishment!

As the crowd hugged and cheered, the energy dissipated.
Kat, in her knowing way, sensed my need for a hug and we
cocooned each other holding onto the High Court gates
and I spotted a tattoo on the side of her neck I had not
noticed before.

'Is that a new tattoo?' I ask.

'I've had this "Live Love Learn Laugh" one for a
while', Kat replied.

'Tell me more my love', I respond.

'It reminds me everyday that when I wake up, I affirm
that I will Live. As I live, I will make time, always, to
Love. Through love, I hope to Learn. While I learn, no
matter what, I will remember to Laugh. This is why I
don't advocate for the "underdog" or "finding the light"

narratives because they sometimes convince you that you must suffer a certain length of time before you can graduate to your higher consciousness. It's about rejuvenating, emboldening, being absolutely fabulous, recognising love of self, of things, and of others and being kind enough to help untangle it from whatever's binding it however much you can.' With words like this and spellbinding visions like those shared by Kat and Aderonke, a new dawn opens.

That was the soul ammunition I needed to generate energy for the final tour of 2019, and before the 50th birthday celebrations of the GLF in 2020 begins. Racing over to Soho I check my bag.

Trusty pink clipboard – tick.

Large plastic bag to stand in the 'notorious urinal' – tick.

Cottaging vs. Cruising Quiz signs (a picture of a pot of cottage cheese and one of Tom Cruise's face) – tick.

Queer Crime Quiz – tick.

Outsavvy (LGBTQIA+ ticketing company) sign-up sheet of punters – tick.

Hanky code guide – tick.

GLF demands – tick.

List of countries where it is still illegal to be LGBTQIA+ – tick.

The British Home Office guide to migration – tick.

Stack of iconic London LGBTQIA+ queerstory postcards – tick.

That's all I need and I'm ready to go! One day soon I promise our guides will have their own sparkly jazzy diamante bomber jackets and multicoloured umbrellas, and I have had many a dream of a bike sound system – fuck it we deserve a rainbow chariot of fire. But deep beneath the surface of our pink clipboards and well-versed and rehearsed Polari exercises, backward-glance mincing theatrics and retelling of homoerotic stories of love and loss, we all carry our real life stories of queer grief. I know I do. I'm mincing not just for the tour punters or for the love of retelling queerstory, or to make enough cash for a night out through building our queer economy – where our sexual wellbeing is liberated within and not exploited by the economic system. I'm not mincing even for the love of changing the world for the better. I'm mincing these streets for the well of rage that boils inside us. I do this because I want revenge. As I mince past Old Compton Street to meet the tour group the war stories of my Nan, of the queers who perished in Dachau, the queer migrant voices from this morning's tour, the struggle for justice in Bangladesh and recent news from Chechnya were reverberating around my mind and it was all getting a bit much.

I want revenge for my London queer family who are two delicate steps from falling through the social welfare net. For everyone who has been turned away from landlords for being queer, refused a department store job because they don't fit the bill of what 'sales people should look like' and who have ever had their identity, relationships, desires and dreams – affirmed at best – invisibilised at worst.

I want revenge for every gaping hole in our understanding of the world and the meaning of life that should have a shining glorious queer role model and icon in it.

I want revenge for every Marsha P. Johnson or Willem Arondeus that isn't taught in schools, for vapid celebrity culture, TV soaps or brochures selling us fucking perfumes.

I want revenge for every single fucking queer that threw themselves in the Thames or hung themselves in a threadbare Soho attic because they couldn't see another way.

I want revenge for everyone who has disregarded their beautiful, weird and queer bodies as nothing but phenomenal works of art.

I want revenge for everyone who contracted HIV+ or all manner of other STDs because not only were we refused any sex-education that actually means anything because of Section 28, but because we were too busy running, running, running up that hill to get fucked by the first person who would recognise our existence as real humans.

Getting fucked, not making love. All I wanted to do as a teenager was to get fucked. Psychologically, emotionally, spiritually, practically – so that no pore of my body, mind or soul would have to make sense of the prison I was locked in.

I want revenge for me and my playground of inner children who've been left to fend for themselves. Children. These children who had more stories of self-hatred by the age of ten that no amount of My Little Pony queer magic could make up for.

Today, thankfully, that rage is no longer targeted at myself. I'm still here simply because my sight isn't solely targeted at the giant red self-destruct button that as a child took the place of my heart. I'm here because of my queer family – my school friend Jess or my college mate Kathy who could see that beneath the bravado was an aching queer child yelping for help and everyone in the sexual freedom movement fighting back.

Anyway let's not let emotions get in the way of tour-guiding eh?

Yeah. Right.

The reason that exploring queer liberation on the streets has struck a chord with the public is exactly because they strike a match within our hearts. Audre Lorde, Etty Hillesum, George Michael, Paulo Freire, Steve Biko, Amy Winehouse, Nina Simone, Freddie Mercury and every other icon of harnessing wholehearted grief as a flame for unravelling our soul powers that teach that emotions are everything and love is at its root. We take to the streets with the triple powers of the head, the heart and the hand. The intellectual understanding of the systems of power that dominate us and how we break free, the practical campaign skills that our community have employed and I have been lucky to learn about. From abseiling into the House of Lords against Section 28, to 'die-ins' in Trafalgar Square protesting against government inaction at the height of the AIDS epidemic, to mass public 'kiss-ins' in response to homophobic street attacks, or further afield to using our very own beloved's AIDS ashes as tools of protest, but most importantly our emotions. For every layer of emotions that has been trapped like a vice in our insides for fear of upsetting the status quo, there is a melancholic tidal wave in all of us.

I dream of taking the government to court for the harm done because of Section 28 for every queer in Britain. It may not be successful but it's damn well worth a try.

Denied the right to be human.
Denied the right to exist.
Denied the right to express our core.
Denied the right to live, love, learn, laugh.
Denied the right to communicate, validate or share our pain and to learn not to inflict that on others.
Denied the right to be happy, smile and to hold our heads up high.
Denied! Denied! Denied!

Just because a government or establishment says a law has been overturned doesn't mean the damage is over, that the sun suddenly shines through the fog and we all skip like

Bambi away from the fire and over the waterfall into the sparkling rainbow.

What would justice look like? What would the sweet revenge of Section 28 taste like?

One of the bravest things you can do is to heal from your own trauma, because it allows you to hold your feelings and connect with others. To utilise our cultural inheritance, not to dwell on our sorrows but to fight injustice around us to enhance people's possibility of revival, collective joy and sheer ecstasy at being alive.

And now release.

Hello everyone! Welcome to the tour. Now before we begin can we all speak to someone new and share for five minutes 'what makes you proud to be queer' or 'what in your community makes you proud for its contribution to queer freedom?' There's no right or wrong answer and there's no time to waste – there's power in our community and no-one's gonna spark it apart from us! Now go! Five minutes and counting.

After the tour was over and the moon was rising in the sky, around the corner, back in the basement of the London School of Economics, the GLF were hunched around a table to hear the response from Pride in London to their new demands sent those few weeks ago.

'This was the Pride Community Advisory Board (CAB) Chair's response to our letter on the issue, I can't believe it!' Nettie screamed and everyone craned their necks to read it.

I'm sure our views are similar with regards to concern around war and arms but as we try to be the most inclusive Pride, every organisation is reviewed for entry to the parade by CAB and just because the company may have a policy that we find difficult to agree with, that's no reason for its LGBTQIA+ employees not to be part of the Parade. That is the CAB view as a whole but that doesn't mean to say we can't find other ways to highlight some very serious issues which you rightly raise.

'Their response is pathetic! I can't imagine that I'm the only LGBTQIA+ person in London with enough experience of violence, war, xenophobia and conflict that seeing the police and military, doesn't make me feel able to express my sexuality', Nettie cried out.

The news had recently revealed that BAE Systems would be the primary sponsor of Surrey Pride 2019. In a particularly vacuous toxic display of weapons over people, Theresa Palmer of BAE Systems Applied Intelligence had announced:

BAE Systems is extremely proud to be headline sponsor for the first ever Pride in Surrey. We feel strongly that visible support of such openly inclusive events is key to driving the type of diverse workplace we are striving for. That makes this particular event even more personal for us as it represents our neighbours and as a local employer, we want to make clear to our community that they have a welcoming, supportive business on their doorstep.[16]

Nettie stood up and continued, 'I'm really angry about BAE Systems sponsoring Surrey Pride this year. We need to demand the unreserved withdrawal of the invitation of BAE Systems to march on this year's parade. Enough is enough of BAE using what we began as a branding exercise to divert attention away from how they are complicit in war crimes and needless human suffering.'

Nettie wasn't going to settle for Pride in London's response. She wasn't going to let what her and her fellow GLFers created be stolen so easily. Later in the week she had snuck herself a place at BAE Systems Annual General Meeting amongst 150 shareholders. Under a giant picture of a warship, she took her seat and waited to be called to the stand and when it was time, took the microphone and cleared her throat.

We have been learning from the media that BAE now has a policy of welcoming lesbian, gay, bisexual and transgendered + employees to its workforce. BAE is clearly proud of its policy of non-discrimination, diversity and inclusion. We note that this year you are even sponsoring Surrey Pride, Blackpool Pride and have involvement in London Pride. I am here representing the Gay Liberation Front and we wonder how BAE Systems reconcile the export of arms to regions with poor human rights records who torture, execute and imprison this same group of people – that is LGBTQIA+ people. The weapons you sell are also used to kill LGBTQIA+ people in conflicts. I can't see how these actions can be reconciled. Your thoughts on this issue would be valued.

BAE Systems chairman Sir Roger Carr waffled on about how wonderful diversity was and how what happened in other countries was quite separate.

Nettie stood up again, ruffled her pink hair and said firmly, 'Thank you for sharing your thoughts but I think you are part of the problem not part of the solution'. She continued, 'Because we take Pride in radically challenging gendered and sexual oppression, not in assimilation to the status quo. Because an injustice to one is an injustice to all. Because there is No Pride in War.'

And she left the building, head held high, pink hair shining in the sunshine.

How to Organise an International Campaign

1 Acknowledge where you are in the global web of power, your privileges and your freedoms.

2 Dig deeper and get to the root of where the issue began, like the 1533 Buggery Act that instigated the criminalisation of homosexuality.

3 Build what playwright Carla Harryman calls 'comprehensive knowledge', the weaving of multiple dimensions, double entendres, maybe even triple entendres, that are still clear and empowering for the public to digest.[17]

4 Explore the points of intervention as the phenomenal art-activist toolkit 'Beautiful Trouble' explains: 'A point of intervention is a physical or conceptual place within a system where pressure can be put to disrupt its smooth functioning and push for change.'[18]

5 Join the dots that connect the web of multiple oppressions such as how Pride's military support maintains the military-industrial complex which directly kills LGBTQIA+, and so many other communities, around the world.

15

Liberation or Slavery

Power without love is reckless and abusive, and love without power is sentimental and anemic. Power at its best is love implementing the demands of justice, and justice at its best is power correcting everything that stands against love. (Martin Luther King Jr)[1]

I needed to get away to be able to think clearly, as this poignant quote reminds us, about the best ways forward to build love in our community and obtain the justice we deserve. The situation in Chechnya was too close to the bone. I know I am not getting the balance right between action and reflection, between the struggle and self-care, as the infrastructure of our growing global queer family becomes more connected and more people become more empowered to take the necessary action, because phew! It is a lot of work.

At the end of the year's final 'Think In', I sat with Ashley, now a celebrated film director for his striking celebration of LGBT+ movements *Are You Proud?*, reading the paper with excitement that justice in an oppressive framework, rather than merely rights that should be a basic standard, can be fought for, and won.[2] The news that day announced that 'Pride in London could ban LGBT+ employees of arms manufacturers and fossil fuel companies'.[3] Ashley looked over, held my arm and said to me 'Dan, remember self care is key. Allowing yourself to disconnect from the struggles and enjoy human connections in their fullest is an important part too. And it's often in these moments that the best ideas blossom.'

Exhaustion, or 'burn out', in struggles for justice is so commonplace that it emphasises the importance of a liberation psychology that transforms our relationship with ourselves as well as practically addressing the socio-political impoverishment within which marginalised people exist. The silver lining of living with HIV, a stress-related condition, is that it makes me sensitive to the fact that if I get stressed I get sick, so I'm constantly trying to balance the wisdom of two of my revolutionary icons. These are Paulo Freire who reminds us to practice 'humanisation, healthy dialogue and understanding the oppressor consciousness'[4] and the iconic mantra of American feminist and civil rights activist Audre Lorde who said 'Caring for myself is not self-indulgence, it is self-preservation, and that is an act of political warfare'.[5] But that evening after the 'Think In' Audre won and I finally freed myself to take a break.

It's snowing outside. Beautiful and chilly. It's so cold now my hands are learning how to write again. I'm writing this on a train back from Edinburgh after spending time with my best friend, Baba. What a wee joy. It's so good being in Scotland. Space. Space. Space. It opens up the mind and the heart to be kind, think of others and BE ROWDY! In London, it's easy to constrict, however great many characteristics there are.

Space. Unravel. Unfurl and harness the spirit of the eagle

Eagles fly alone at high altitude. The eagle tests before it trusts. Eagles invest in training others. Eagles rejuvenate. Eagles do not eat dead things. Eagles love the storm.[6]

Hold your chin up and belly laugh.

You can't predetermine the outcomes of healing but you can commit to acting on love as a verb. You can't predict what will happen when people reclaim their identity and begin to inhabit their true selves. However, we can get an idea of what happens when divided communities come together and join the dots. Strong, connected communities that intervene in the status quo and celebrate our 'beautiful mistakes' in the process, flex our heart muscles and reach our utmost humanity to provide meaning, becoming whole again.

Queers are seekers with a lot of stolen time to make up for. Who are we really behind the versions of ourselves we inhabit in order to survive? Can we tell a different story than the ones that imprison us? Can we ask questions that are often uncomfortable in the search to find a home?

To answer any of these, firstly you have to choose to acknowledge the search.

When we are faced with understanding our human purpose, not just of what to eat for lunch, or which word to use instead, it is a choice. A choice involving branches with roots in your heart, where there are so many blossoming fruits to consider and where you might find a patch of disease that needs culling. How does a person decide which is best when the roots go further than just one heart, one tree, one Earth? On my own I can't untangle the shimmering threads or retrace the invigorating roots as the fruits are connected to more than I can conceive. Yet my heart stays grounded and everything still remains, close. I think it's because I trust the people that teach our queer spirit of Gay Liberation – that together we all make up one collective spirit. What I've had to come to terms with, however, in this quest for purpose is pace – pace and practice – for it is in the inner world of self-love and the outer world of community and respect that we fully flourish.

Stepping back, refreshed, onto the London pavements I love so much, it's time to mince off to the rehearsal of the recreation of the first Pride in London for the 50th anniversary next year. On the way into the building I catch Ted with a tear in his eye. Clutched in his hands, a gorgeous picture of a young beaming Ted wearing blue jeans and tight T-shirt smiling out of the world jumps out at me.

'What are they Ted?' I ask.

'I've actually brought 36 pictures to share with everyone. These are pictures of the first GLF march against the Age of Consent restriction laws, which went from Hyde Park, along Oxford and Regent Streets, down Haymarket to its rally in Trafalgar Square. The first public gay and lesbian march through the centre of London, presaging even the Gay Pride Marches, pictures which have never been published anywhere. I've also got videos, photos, brochures, newspaper clippings, correspondence covering a range of campaigns and issues in my archive at home, starting in 1971. There's also video and press material on our work that helped produce "Why Civil Liberties?", the campaign against Buju Banton's murderously homophobic dance-hall record "Boom Bye Bye",[7] against virulent homophobia in the media such as *The Voice* newspaper, our support for out gay black football hero Justin Fashanu[8] and so much more, you should come and have a look.'

If there were 100 hours in a day Ted would devour them all. He has a mission to complete.

Time ticks by, queerstory is over and the present moment is here. It is five minutes to 6pm and the meeting is about to start.

'Ted, are you ok?' I ask noticing his hands shaking as he puts his photos down.

'No, not really. Actually, I am really stressed. Earlier this week, my partner was attacked in his elderly home. He's living with dementia and can't grasp what's going on but I know it is homophobic. I've been around the block', he answered quietly, clenching his jaw tightly. We had a long hug and the tension released.

There isn't one LGBTQIA+ elderly home in the whole of London. Regularly queers face attacks at the hands of homophobes in their elderly homes and often having to go back in the closet. The cruel irony of legends from the GLF like this suffering homophobia at the end of their lives is enough to make a skull smile.

As we entered the room Ted looked at me without saying any more words and his warmth cracked something deep inside. He unlocked a vice I didn't know I had. A fear that sticks inside me, that however many people you search for in this struggle for queer meaning, you are always alone.

Grief can be powerful. We chuckled. A friendship was born.

Behind every expressionless tense face there is a person. Behind every person there is a story. Behind every story there is tragedy, behind tragedy there are emotions and behind emotions there is love. That's the web Ted weaves and the light the founders of Pride legacy leaves us all.

We join the group and everyone's excitedly sharing their favourite GLF stories to put into the 50th anniversary press release.

In a tight cream shirt with a ravishing smile and a relentless spirit of mischief I am sure that Andrew had fun in the communes he has told me about. With a glint in his eye he scans the room and says, 'I think for my part, I'd say what we can see looking back is that this was a revolution. It's a revolution in the same sense there was a French Revolution, an American Revolution, you name them. The name GLF probably comes originally from the Vietnamese Liberation Front because of the impact of that during the Vietnam War. So, this meets the problem of education. In schools and colleges, it should be taught that there was a gay revolution – you can call it the Stonewall Revolution. And that is a world event.'

Stuart was next to take the baton, 'I think one of the things I'm most proud of is the GLF street theatre group. We dressed up as nuns and stormed the Methodist Central Hall stage doing the can-can and releasing mice amongst the crowds of the religious homophobic "Festival of Light" in 1971. People were utterly staggered. They couldn't believe their eyes, nuns exhibiting themselves in public. We at the GLF had campaigned to equalise the age of consent for all sexualities and had joined protests in support of abortion rights and full sexual freedom for all. Three years later the festival organisers were trying to recriminalise abortion and homosexuality so we infiltrated, wreaked havoc and defeated their inaugural rally in Westminster Methodist Central Hall, their rally in Trafalgar Square, and the major rally in Hyde Park afterwards was also disrupted.

'The whole movement collapsed.'

Nettie followed, 'I think what GLF means to all of us is absolutely life-changing. It changed us and it changed us forever. Still today the bond we feel between each other is extraordinary. The people in this room that I've known for nearly 50 years, we're really really close now. I mean, how many people can say that? It's not just the people in this room, it's the other people in GLF and the younger activists as well. There's a real bond between us all. It's a pretty good time.'

As the clock on the wall tick tocks the 'Think In' is coming to a close. Everyone's excited. The speech has been drafted for the 50th anniversary celebration. Stuart stands tall.

'We are a few remaining activists from the original GLF, who started Pride. In our culture we invert the pink triangle to honour the memory of all those who died in the gas chambers of the Nazis and the Stalinists.'[9]

'And gay women wore, of course, the black triangle!' Nettie yelled.

Stuart smiled and continued 'Of course. We were all part of the first openly public demonstration by homosexuals in this country and present on the first Gay Pride March. Others are millennials, activists from ACT UP who celebrated the achievements of GLF in 2015 and we all came together in 2016 to prepare and celebrate the 50th anniversary of the partial decriminalisation of homosexuality in 2017. Did Pride in London Corporation honour the activists of the 1950s and 1960s who fought the government and won the Sexual Offences Act repeal? No, it refused to.'

'GLF stands for liberation: the choice is always there – liberation or slavery.'

'Join us to recreate the spirit of the GLF 1970 and Pride March of 1972. Feel the zeitgeist of the years that changed the world for LGBT people ... and for everyone else!'

The younger activists in the room were captivated and the energy was so palpable no more words could do justice.

One month later, in the spring sunshine, one hundred of us released banners across the centre of Trafalgar Square. We stood by the lions under banners stating 'We are the radical roots of Pride', 'GLF – 50 years out' and 'We are STILL the people your parents warned you about.'

Ted stepped up to the mic, paused and then opened up his lungs,

We are taking to Trafalgar Square to remember and reinvigorate the fires that fought back against centuries of oppression and the seemingly overwhelming odds. I'm proud and inspired by the Stonewall uprising's 50th, GLF's 50th and Pride's 50th anniversaries. I want all these celebrations to be joyous yet maintain a core of radicalism. This is necessary as a tribute to the queers who suffered victimisation in the past or who fought for our freedoms, and that around the world many queer people are still victims of archaic sexism and homophobia. Life for LGBTQIA+ activists means combining domestic life with maintaining contact with other activists plus preparing for the next event, publication, demonstration. Very few such activists ever stop their campaigning completely. We must always keep awareness that there are powerful forces who will want to take all our rights away. We must be ready to defend ourselves.

The demonstration was focused, lively, radical and productive. All the best action ingredients. Hyped on my way home I decided to actually live a sexually charged queer life rather than always talking and writing about it and so off I minced to Liverpool Street Station toilets – a notorious cruising spot. It was wild, I felt like I was in a Joe Orton novel. I sucked off a guy with a cherry tattoo on his hip. Now I knew where I wanted to put my tribute to Willem Arondeus, who for so long I have admired for saving thousands of people in Nazi Germany from being found and murdered, and possibly many of my own family too.

So I had a pin-up of Arondeus emblazoned on my hip lying on the beach. For all he did, he deserves to relax in the sunshine. The heat reminds us all how injustice ignites a flame in all of us and to carry the torch without getting burnt out.

'It's over, THE END!' waved a tall, smiling, middle-aged man as the toilet staff came in and we all giggled and fled.

But there was one more mission I felt called to do before Pride season truly began. It's not often you get the opportunity to go back to your roots for where your 'coming into' queerstory began. There was something big I had to do.

I had been invited to Warsaw to connect with activists currently threatened by the rising prejudice from the 'Law and Justice' party and their 'LGBTQIA+ free zones'.[10] These are municipalities across Poland that proclaim themselves to be free from LGBTQIA+ ideology and actively refrain from promoting equal rights as part of a broader attack on the queer community. It also happened to be the 76th anniversary of the Warsaw Ghetto uprising, where resistance began by Polish Jews under Nazi occupation on 16 May 1943 to the forced deportations from Warsaw to the Treblinka extermination camp. The revolt was crushed four weeks later.

On the trip I brought with me my Nan's survival story because her last words jumped out at me.

In Poland, there was generally no sympathy for the Jews. We, who had false papers, were more afraid of being recognised by the Poles than to be discovered by Germans. Poles who lived so long with the Jews, knew all the minutiae of the Jewish soul, and sometimes a sad frightened facial expression was enough to give us away. But there were some noble and righteous Christians who helped Jews by hiding them at a great risk to themselves. Some did it for money, some out of a deep humanity. And thus, these Poles exonerated the nation. In my small way I pay tribute to them.

Now it was my turn to pay tribute to her.

The next day I went to the Jewish Archive in Warsaw in search of details of her life and where she lived. I found the house from where she saw the sky ablaze as the ghetto burned down.

On the final day, in my own small way I paid tribute to Michalina and everyone everywhere resisting bigotry. I went to the building and found the abandoned flat and kicked the wall in for that schmuck who messed with my Nan and read this:

We are all in the gutter, but some of us are looking at the stars. (Oscar Wilde)[11]

Fitting that I'd just found out that her birth surname was Sternlicht or Starlight.

Building Loving Community

1 Cultivate joy and hope.
2 Remember that life is short.
3 Live in awe and wonder.
4 Cherish each human's unique revolutionary potential.
5 Defy the stereotypes by refusing to be pigeon-holed.

And one more for luck – get a revolutionary homo-erotic hip tattoo.

Let it be known that homosexuals are not cowards. (Willem Arondeus, 22 August 1894 – 1 July 1943)[12]

Notes

Foreword

1   Gerada, L. and D. Laverick (2015). *Another Pride Is Possible.* Novara Media.

2   Freire, P. (1996). *Pedagogy of the Oppressed.* Penguin Books.

Chicken Soup

1   Quoted in Calkhoven, L. (2008). *Harriet Tubman: Leading the Way to Freedom.* Sterling.

2   Arendt, H. (1998). *The Human Condition.* University of Chicago Press. Quoted in Newman, J. (2014). Hannah Arendt: radical evil, radical hope. *European Judaism: A Journal for the New Europe* 47(1): 60–71.

An Inalienable Right

1   From the poem 'Two Loves' (1892), published in *The Chamelon* in December 1894.

2   Dolye, J. (2014). Willem Arondeus: the openly gay, anti-fascist resistance fighter. Ozy.com. www.ozy.com/ flashback/willem-arondeus-the-openly-gay-anti-

fascist-resistance-fighter/32825/ (accessed 15 January 2020).

3   Jacobs, J. (2019). Two transgender activists are getting a monument in New York. *The New York Times*.

4   Iqbal, N. (2017). Munroe Bergdorf on the L'Oréal racism row: 'It puzzles me that my views are considered extreme'. *The Guardian*.

5   Friedkin, W. (dir.) (1973). *The Exorcist*.

6   Davis, C. (2005). Hauntology, spectres and phantoms. *French Studies* 59(3): 373–379.

7   Nodin, Nuno, Elizabeth Peel, Allan Tyler and Ian Rivers (2015). *The RaRE Research Report. LGB&T Mental Health: Risk and Resilience Explored*. Queer Futures.

8   Freire, P. (1996). *Pedagogy of the Oppressed*. Penguin Books, p. 14.

9   *Pink News* (2018). What was Section 28? The history of the homophobic legislation 30 years on.

10   Todd, M. (2013). Margaret Thatcher was no poster girl for gay rights. *The Guardian*.

11   *The Telegraph* (2012). Margaret Thatcher saved career of police chief who made Aids remarks.

12   British Universities Film and Video Council (1986, 18 December). Bill Brownhill on gay people with AIDS.

13   Todd, M. (2013). Margaret Thatcher was no poster girl for gay rights. *The Guardian*.

Shafted?

1   www.rebeldykes1980s.com; *Time Out* (2017). Meet the lesbian punks who've been written out of London's history.

2   *The London Economic* (2019). Atos, the firm at the centre of disability assessment appeals, awarded new £25m government contract.

3 Einstein, A. (2014). *The World as I See It*. CreateSpace.

4 Landon, A. (2019). The famed london bookshop at the heart of the LGBT+ rights movement: Gay's The Word. *Secret London*. secretldn.com; wwwgaystheword.tumblr.com.

5 Bartal, Y. (2019). The true story of 'Pride': Lesbians and Gays Support the Miners were communists. *Left Voice*. leftvoice.org.

6 Winterson, J. (2012). *Why Be Happy When You Can Be Normal?* Vintage, p. 33.

7 Feather, S. (2016). *Blowing the Lid: Gay Liberation, Sexual Revolution and Radical Queens*. Zero Books.

8 Gay Liberation Front (1971, rev. 1978). *Manifesto*. London.

9 Friends of the The Joiners Arms. www.thejoinersliveson. wordpress.com.

10 University College London (UCL) Urban Lab. 'Queer Spaces' report.

11 Schulman, S. (2013). *The Gentrification of the Mind: Witness to a Lost Imagination*. University of California Press, p. 14.

12 Kat Kai Kol-Kes (TED Fellow). www.kkolkes.wixsite.com/ kkolkes.

13 Sheerin, J. (2018). Matthew Shepard: the murder that changed America. *BBC*.

Sprawling Anthills Deep Underground

1 *The Dictionary of Obscure Sorrows*. www. dictionaryofobscuresorrows.com.

2 hooks, b. (1996). *Reel to Real: Race, Sex and Class at the Movies*. Routledge, p. 149.

3 hooks, b. (2016). *All about Love: New Visions*. HarperPerennial, p. 4.

4 Huxley, A. (2005). *Island*. Vintage Classics, p. 253.

Leave the Gay Donkeys Alone

1 Fisher, M. (2014). Is it still possible to forget? *Spike*. www.spikeartmagazine.com/articles/qa-mark-fisher. Mark Fisher is a cultural theorist, music critic and blogger who lives in London. His collection of essays *Ghosts of My Life: Writings on Depression, Hauntology and Lost Futures* was published in 2014 by Zero Books, and his much-discussed book *Capitalist Realism: Is There No Alternative?* appeared (also from Zero Books) in 2009, in the wake of the financial crisis.

2 Marx, K. (1844). *On the Jewish Question*. www.marxists.org/archive/marx/works/1844/jewish-question/.

3 Hope, A. and S. Timmel (1984). *Training for Transformation I: A Handbook for Community Workers*. Training for Transformation Institute, p. 86.

4 Biko, S. (1978). *I Write What I Like*. University of Chicago Press, p. 68.

5 Watt, N. (2014). Keep HIV-positive migrants out of Britain, says UKIP's Nigel Farage. *The Guardian*.

6 Rasmussen, T. (2015). Fighting the silence that still surrounds HIV/AIDS. *I.D. Magazine*.

7 Duffy, N. (2014). UKIP kicked out of London offices after HIV activists dump horse s**t outside. *Pink News*.

8 Stevenson, A. (2014). Russell Brand ripped Nigel Farage to shreds on Question Time last night. *Metro UK*.

9 *Political Scrapbook* (2014). UKIP: Disability benefit claimants are 'parasitic underclass of scroungers'.

10 *Evening Standard* (2014). Farage 'felt awkward' on train.

11 Nianias, H. (2015). UKIP candidate Donald Grewar investigated after gay people labeled 'paedophiles' and 'fascist perverts'. *The Independent*.

12   Dearden, L. (2014). UKIP candidate: 'Gay donkey tried to rape my horse'. *The Independent.*

13   Bienkov, A. (2017). Here are all the times UKIP has called for NHS privatisation. *Business Insider.*

14   Wintour, P. (2014). UKIP wants a five-year ban on new migrants, says Nigel Farage. *The Guardian.*

15   Ward, B. (2013). UKIP's energy and climate policies under the spotlight. *The Guardian.*

16   Aldersley, M. (2019). Arron Banks 'spent £450,000 on Nigel Farage in year after Brexit vote – providing him with £4.4m Chelsea home, £32,000 Land Rover Discovery, close protection driver, furniture and even utility bills'. *Mail Online.*

17   Niven, J. (2019). If you think Nigel Farage is a 'man of the people' here's one word of warning for you – Trump. *Daily Record.*

18   Barnett, R. (2013). *Jews and Gypsies: Myths and Reality.* CreateSpace.

19   Holbourne, Zita. (2017). *Striving for Equality, Freedom and Justice: Embracing Roots, Culture and Identity.* Hansib Publications.

The Golden Egg

1   Allen, K. (2019). Around 5 million people attended WorldPride in New York City over the weekend. *ABC News.*

2   *Hackney Gazette* (2018). Lavinia Co-op on how the Bloolips brought radical drag to the mainstream – and the Hackney Empire.

3   *The New European* (2018). The rise and fall of Milo, the alt-right poster boy.

4   Chesterman, J. (1971). The Gay Liberation Front (GLF) Demands. https://gayliberationfrontuk.home.blog/demands/ (accessed 15 January 2020).

5   Debord, G. (1994). *Society of the Spectacle*. Rebel Press.

6   Frith, M. (2012). Mayor's £650,000 offer to keep gay pride in the pink. *Evening Standard*.

7   Gerada, L. and D. Laverick (2015). *Another Pride Is Possible*. Novara Media; House of Commons Committee of Public Accounts Tax Avoidance (2013–14). Ninth Report of Session 2013–14.

8   Chakelian, A. (2014). Meet Ukip's seal-hating, gay-baiting, victim-blaming Newark candidate, Roger Helmer. *New Statesman*.

9   *Attitude Magazine* (2015). Ukip candidate: 'being an arse bandit is nothing to be proud of'.

10 James Wentzy with Jerry Lakatos at DIVA TV. The Ashes Action (1992). AIDS Community Television weekly series. https://actupny.org/diva/synAshes.html (accessed 15 January 2020).

11 Schulman, S. (2013). *The Gentrification of the Mind: Witness to a Lost Imagination*. University of California Press, p. 14.

12 *Al Jazeera* (2018). Yemen: 85,000 children may have died from starvation. www.aljazeera.com/news/2018/11/yemen-85000-children-died-starvation-181121041742347.html (accessed 15 January 20).

13 Rodney, W. (2018). *How Europe Underdeveloped Africa*. Verso, p. 10.

14 Sleigh, S. (2019). Kensington and Chelsea 'richest' area in UK with residents earning three times the national average. *Evening Standard*.

15 McCormack, C. (2013). The price of economic barbarism: an uncomfortable truth. *The Australian Community Psychologist* 25(1) (June). www.psychology.org.au/APS/media/ACP/ACP-25(1)-McCormack.pdf (accessed 15 January 2020).

16 Fanon, F. (1963). *Wretched of the Earth*. Grove Weidenfeld. http://abahlali.org/wp-content/uploads/2011/04/Frantz-Fanon-The-Wretched-of-the-Earth-1965.pdf (accessed 15 January 2020).

17 'The Outside Project'. The UK's first LGBTIQ+ Crisis/Homeless Shelter and Community Centre. www.lgbtiqoutside.org/.

18 Harvey, D. (2004). The 'new' imperialism: accumulation by dispossession. *Socialist Register* 40: 63–87.

19 Federici, S. (2017). *Caliban and the Witch: Women, the Body and Primitive*. Autonomedia.

20 Sears, A. (2005). Queer anti-capitalism: what's left of lesbian and gay liberation? *Marxist-Feminist Thought Today* 69(1): 92–112.

21 Wilson, L. (2012). *Steve Biko*. Reprint edition. Ohio University Press, p. 145.

22 Gurney, J. (2012). *1649 Gerrard Winstanley: The Digger's Life and Legacy*. Pluto Press, p. 162.

Coming Into

1 Robinson, T. (1978). Sing if you're glad to be gay! https://gladtobegay.net/versions/glad-to-be-gay-87/. Tom Robinson was the first gay rock star to be out-and-proud from the off.

2 Newton, H. (1970). A letter to the Revolutionary Brothers and Sisters about Women's Liberation and Gay Liberation. www.historyisaweapon.com/defcon1/newtonq.html.

3   LSE (2017). Sociology and the Gay Liberation Front – Bob Mellors at LSE. https://blogs.lse.ac.uk/ lsehistory/2017/02/06/ gay-liberation-front-bob-mellors/.

4   Dass, R. and M. Bush (2018). *Walking Each Other Home: Conversations on Love and Dying.* www.ramdass.org/ wp-content/uploads/dlm_uploads/2018/08/MKT1988-Walking-Each-Other-Home-Excerpt.pdf (accessed 15 January 2020).

5   Zapata, E. www.no-gods-no-masters.com/ (accessed 15 January 2020).

6   X, Malcolm (2007). *Autobiography of Malcolm X.* Penguin; Suleiman, O. (2020). Malcolm X is still misunderstood – and misused. *Aljazeera.* www.aljazeera.com/indepth/ opinion/malcolm-misunderstood-misused-200221054407806.html (accessed 15 January 2020).

7   Osborne, S. (2019). Uganda announces 'Kill the Gays' law imposing death penalty on homosexuals. *The Independent.*

Janine

1   Counter Terrorism Intelligence Unit (CTU). www.npcc. police.uk.

2   Clews, C. (2012). 1982. Gay London Police Monitoring Group (GALOP). *Gay in the 80s: From Fighting for Our Rights to Fighting for Our Lives.* www.gayinthe80s. com/2012/12/1982-gay-london-police-monitoring-group-galop/.

3   OutRage! is a broad-based group of queers committed to radical, non-violent direct action and civil disobedience to (1) ASSERT the dignity and human rights of queers (2)

FIGHT homophobia, discrimination and violence directed against us and (3) AFFIRM our right to sexual freedom, choice and self-determination. www.outrage.org.uk.

4   Ogbar, J. (2017). The FBI's war on civil rights leaders. *The Daily Beast*.

5   Police Spies Out of Our Lives. www.policespiesoutoflives. org.uk.

6   *Tech Register* (2019). The Home Office is facing public pressure to release a report called 'Left Wing Activism and Extremism in the UK'.

7   Cavendish Knights. www.cavendishknights.com.

8   Shaxson, N. (2011). The tax haven in the heart of Britain. *New Statesman*.

As Soon as this Pub Closes

1   *Urban Pamphleteer #7. LGBTQ+ Night-time Spaces: Past, Present + Future* (2018). www.ucl.ac.uk/urban-lab.

2   Focus E15 Campaign – Social Housing not Social Cleansing! www.focuse15.org.

3   Angelou, M. (1978). Still I Rise. In *And Still I Rise: A Book of Poems*. Random House.

4   Rosenberg, D. (2019). *Rebel Footprints*. Pluto Press.

5   Property Awards. The UK's leading and most prestigious annual awards dedicated to the full spectrum of the commercial property industry. www.awards.propertyweek. com.

6   Musby, M. (2019). Homeless households in England rise by 23% in a year. *The Guardian*.

7   Streets Kitchen. A UK and Ireland grassroots group working to help the homeless community, providing daily outreaches with food, clothing and information that benefits

our streets. We work in partnership with others across the UK and beyond. www.streetskitchen.org.

8 FRONTLINERS. www.tht.org.uk/our-work/about-our-charity/our-history/1980s/.

9 The John Mordaunt Trust. The Trust regularly publishes the User's Voice blog and newsletter. www.usersvoice.org/.

Here We Dare to Dream

1 Spiegelhalter, D. (2015). Is 10% of the population really gay? *The Guardian*.

2 British Library Collection. The Criminal Law Amendment Act, 1885. www.bl.uk.

3 Houlbrook, M. (2006). *Queer London: Perils and Pleasures in the Sexual Metropolis, 1918–1957*. New edition. University of Chicago Press.

4 mudlark121 (2018). Today in queer history: acid-drag queen commune Bethnal Rouge opens, Bethnal Green, 1973. Rebel History Calendar. www.pasttenseblog.wordpress.com.

5 Waters, S. (2003). *Fingersmith*. Virago.

6 Clews, C. (1986). 1986. Lesbians and Gays Support the Printworkers. *Gay in the 80s*.

7 Holland, B. (2019). How the Mob helped establish NYC's gay bar scene. www.history.com.

8 Boal, A. (2008). *Theatre of the Oppressed (Get Political)*. 3rd edition. Pluto Press. https://warwick.ac.uk/fac/arts/english/currentstudents/undergraduate/modules/fulllist/first/en122/lecturelist2019-20/theatre_of_the_oppressed.pdf (accessed 15 January 2020).

9 McLaughlin, R. (2017). Ed Webb-Ingall: 'I am a product of lesbian history and a child of Section 28'. www.studiointernational.com.

10   Disability Discrimination Act. www.legislation.gov.uk/
     ukpga/1995/50/contents.
11   May, A. (2013). The tao of Kate Moss: never complain,
     never explain. www.purplerevolver.com.
12   Hepple, J. (2016). If you're a disabled, gay
     twentysomething, Grindr is a godsend. *The Guardian*.
13   Lampert, N. (2007). Erratic George Michael's new shame.
     The Daily Mail. www.dailymail.co.uk/tvshowbiz/article-
     397227/Erratic-George-Michaels-new-shame.html
     (accessed 15 January 2020); Hind, K. (2006). George: 'No
     shame in cruising'. *The Daily Mail*.
14   Barton, L. (2016). George Michael's songs were more than
     simple tales of lust and longing. *The Guardian*.

Sex Litter

1   Green and Black Cross. wwwgreenandblackcross.org.
2   Brown, Adrienne Maree (2019). *Pleasure Activism: The
     Politics of Feeling Good*. AK Press.

Over Our Dead Bodies

1   Salk, Jonas (1992). Are we being good ancestors? *World
     Affairs: The Journal of International Issues* 1(2): 16–18. www.
     jstor.org/stable/45064193 (accessed 20 December 2019).
2   Campbell, D. (2018). Sexual health service cuts will increase
     spread of STIs. *The Guardian*.
3   World Health Organization. Global Health Observatory
     (GHO) data. www.who.int/gho/hiv/en/.
4   Travis, A. (2013). Immigration bill: Theresa May defends
     plans to create 'hostile environment'. *The Guardian*.

5   Terrence Higgins Trust. HIV statistics. www.tht.org.uk/
    hiv-and-sexual-health/about-hiv/hiv-statistics.

6   Randhawa, K. (2018). There's an HIV drug with 99%
    success rate ... now let's make it available to all. *Evening
    Standard* (AIDSfree appeal).

7   Cooper, C. (2018). Government under pressure to overturn
    NHS's 'truly shocking' decision not to fund revolutionary
    HIV drug PrEP. *The Independent.*

8   Lessons from the AIDS movement: Peter Staley interview
    transcripts. www.meaction.net/tools/case-studies/how-to-
    survive-a-plague/peter-staley-transcript/ (accessed 20
    December 2019).

9   Staley, P. (2008). On September 5th, 1991, I put a giant
    condom over Jesse Helms' house. www.poz.com/blog/
    in-memory-of-je.

10 *Gay Star News* (2015). Larry Kramer gives blistering speech
    on AIDS: 'I believe genocide is being inflicted upon gay
    people'. www.gaystarnews.com/article/larry-kramer-gives-
    blistering-speech-aids-i-believe-genocide-being-inflicted-
    upon-gay-people/ (accessed 20 December 2019).

11 Pharma Greed Kills (2016). On 1st April 2016, activists
    across the world are protesting against the greed that blocks
    access to essential medicines. www.pharmagreedkills.com.

12 I Want PREP Now was created to raise awareness and access
    to PrEP, with all the information in one place so that you
    can access PrEP now. www.iwantPrEPnow.co.uk.

13 Ipsos-Mori (2012). Britons are more proud of their history,
    NHS and army than the Royal Family.

14 Campbell, D. (2019). Private firms given £9.2bn of NHS
    budget despite Hancock promise. *The Guardian.*

15 Gallagher, P. (2013). Is Simon Stevens really the right
    person to run the NHS? *The Independent.*

16 Gallagher, P. (2018). Virgin Care Services: no corporation tax paid as profits from NHS contracts rise to £8m on £200m turnover. *Inews.*

17 Forster, K. (2017). NHS cuts blamed for 30,000 deaths in new study. *The Independent.* www.independent.co.uk/news/ world/americas/us-politics/nhs-cuts-excess-deaths-30000- study-research-royal-society-medicine-london-school-hygiene- martin-a7585001.html (accessed 20 December 2019).

18 Campbell, D. (2017). Richard Branson's Virgin healthcare firm scoops £1bn of NHS contracts. *The Guardian.* www. theguardian.com/society/2017/dec/29/richard-branson- virgin-scoops-1bn-pounds-of-nhs-contracts (accessed 20 December 2019).

19 Berry, C. (2019). Thatcher had a battle plan for her economic revolution – now the left needs one too. *Open Democracy.* www.opendemocracy.net/en/oureconomy/ thatcher-had-a-battle-plan-for-her-economic-revolution- now-the-left-needs-one-too/ (accessed 20 December 2019).

20 Thatcher, M. (1988). 1988 May 21. Margaret Thatcher – Speech to General Assembly of the Church of Scotland. www.margaretthatcher.org/document/107246.

21 Boffey, D. (2012). Jeremy Hunt is criticised for his role in £650m Virgin hospital deal. *The Guardian.*

22 House of Commons Hansard – UK Parliament – NHS Outsourcing and Privatisation, Volume 641 (2018). www. hansard.parliament.uk.

23 Lowe, J. (2016). Jeremy hunt is one of the UK's least popular politicians, says poll. *Newsweek.*

24 Gregory, A. (2018). Jeremy Hunt avoids £100,000 stamp duty by exploiting Tory tax loophole and buying flats in bulk. *The Mirror.*

Homo Hope

1   Dean Street is a friendly, convenient and free NHS sexual health clinic in the heart of London. The service – based in Soho – also offers full outpatient HIV clinic services. www. dean.st/56deanstreet/.

2   *Attitude Magazine* (2015). Queer performance artist Penny Arcade: 'Pleasure is a radical action'. https://attitude.co. uk/article/queer-performance-artist-penny-arcade-pleasure-is-a-radical-action/8285/ (accessed 15 November 2019).

3   'Sister', a film by Brenda Davis – an intimate portrait of a global crisis. www.sisterdocumentary.com/action.html (accessed 15 November 2019).

4   National Women's History Museum. Harriet Tubman ca. 1820–1913. www.womenshistory.org.

5   Boissoneault, L. (2017). How the New York Stock Exchange gave Abbie Hoffman his start in guerrilla theater. *Smithsonian Magazine*.

6   Northcutt, W. (2003). José Bové vs. McDonald's: the making of a national hero in the French anti-globalization movement. *Journal of the Western Society for French History* 31: 326–345.

7   Olivera, O. (2006). The voice of the people can dilute corporate power. *The Guardian*. www.theguardian.com/ society/2006/jul/19/comment.guardiansocietysupplement (accessed 15 November 2019).

Spirit of the Camp Road

1   From Etty Hillesum's *An Interrupted Life*, quoted in Coetsie, Meins G.S. (2014). *The Existential Philosophy of Etty Hillesum: An Analysis of Her Diaries and Letters*. Brill, p. 525.

2   Townsend, M. (2019). Britain First says 5,000 of its members have joined Tories. *The Guardian*.

3   Britton, B. (2019). They saved migrants from deportation: then they faced terror-related charges. *CNN*.

4   Hammadi, S. and A. Gani (2016). Founder of Bangladesh's first and only LGBT magazine killed. *The Guardian*.

5   Onyebadi, U. and L. Mbunyuza-Memani (2017). Women and South Africa's anti-Apartheid struggle: evaluating the political messages in the music of Miriam Makeba. www.igi-global.com/chapter/women-and-south-africas-anti-apartheid-struggle/178005.

6   *BBC* (2019). Chechnya LGBT: dozens 'detained in new gay purge'.

7   Gilbert, D. (2019). Chechnya's new LGBT purge has already claimed two lives, activists say. *Vice*.

8   Belyakov, D. (2018). Russia's 'Gay Propaganda' law iperils LGBT youth. *Human Rights Watch*.

9   Cain, M. (2017). How homophobia feeds Russia's HIV epidemic. *The Guardian*.

10 Roth, A. (2019). Russia wants to make HIV/Aids denialism illegal to halt epidemic. *The Guardian*.

11 Fedorova, A. (2018). These people are leading Russia's blossoming queer clubbing scene forward. *Dazed Digital*.

12 Angelou, M. (1983). Caged Bird. www.poetryfoundation.org/poems/48989/caged-bird (accessed 15 January 2020).

13 African Equality Foundation is a Non Profit and Non Governmental Organisation inaugurated with the purpose of promoting Inclusion And Empowerment.

14 Usborne, S. (2015). Katie Hopkins has just written a piece so hateful that it might give Hitler pause – why was it published? *The Independent*.

15 African Rainbow Family. Support for Lesbian, Gay, Bisexual, Transgender and Queer (LGBTIQ) people of African heritage including refugees and wider Black and Asian minority ethnic groups. https://africanrainbowfamily. org/.

16 Houston, R. (2019). Pride in Surrey name lead sponsor BAE Systems. *Queer News. The Home of Worldwide LGBTQ News.* www.queer-news.co.uk/?p=238 (accessed 20 December 2019).

17 Schulman, S. (2013). *The Gentrification of the Mind: Witness to a Lost Imagination.* University of California Press, p. 75.

18 Beautiful Trouble is a book, web toolbox and international network of artist-activist trainers whose mission is to make grassroots movements more creative and more effective. www.beautifultrouble.org.

Liberation or Slavery

1 *Beacon Broadside* (2017). Martin Luther King, Jr.'s 'Where Do We Go from Here' turns 50. www. beaconbroadside.com/broadside/2017/06/martin-luther-king-jrs-where-do-we-go-from-here-turns-50.html (accessed 15 January 2020).

2 Bradshaw, P. (2019). *Are You Proud?* Review – bold, vivid celebration of LGBT rights movement. *The Guardian.*

3 Duffy, N. (2019). Pride in London looking into major shake-ups, such as banning fossil fuel companies and moving the parade. *Pink News.*

4 Freire, P. (1996). *Pedagogy of the Oppressed.* Penguin Books, chapter 2. www.historyisaweapon.com/defcon2/pedagogy/pedagogychapter2.html (accessed 15 January 2020).

5   Spicer, André (2019). 'Self-care': how a radical feminist idea was stripped of politics for the mass market. *The Guardian*. www.theguardian.com/commentisfree/2019/aug/21/self-care-radical-feminist-idea-mass-market (accessed 15 January 2020).

6   7 powerful life lessons from the eagle. *Medium*. https://medium.com/@carla.ibanzo/7-powerful-life-lessons-from-the-eagle-ed1a318c1305 (accessed 15 January 2020).

7   Murder inna dancehall – nuff with the chi-chi man songs. www.soulrebels.org/dancehall/d_history_1976.htm.

8   Harris, D. (2017). John Fashanu on brother Justin: 'He was my shining light. He became my arch enemy'. *The Guardian*.

9   Mullen, M. (2019). The pink triangle: from Nazi label to symbol of gay pride. www.history.com.

10 Noack, R. (2019). Polish cities and provinces declare 'LGBT-free zones' as government ramps up 'hate speech'. *The Independent*.

11 Wilde, O. (2016). *Lady Windermere's Fan*. CreateSpace; Statue: Oscar Wilde reclining. Erection date: 30/11/1998. *London Remembers*. www.londonremembers.com/memorials/oscar-wilde-reclining (accessed 15 January 2020).

12 Dolye, J. (2014). Willem Arondeus: the openly gay, anti-fascist resistance fighter. Ozy.com. www.ozy.com/flashback/willem-arondeus-the-openly-gay-anti-fascist-resistance-fighter/32825/ (accessed 15 January 2020).

Bibliography

Angelou, M. (1978). *And Still I Rise: A Book of Poems*. Random House.

Angelou, M. (1984). *I Know Why the Caged Bird Sings*. Virago.

Arendt, H. (1998). *The Human Condition*. University of Chicago Press.

Baim, T. (2015). *Barbara Gittings: Gay Pioneer*. CreateSpace.

Baldwin, J. (2001). *Go Tell It on the Mountain*. Penguin Classics.

Barnett, R. (2013). *Jews and Gypsies: Myths and Reality*. CreateSpace.

Biko, S. (1978). *I Write What I Like*. University of Chicago Press.

Boal, A. (2008). *Theatre of the Oppressed (Get Political)*. Pluto Press.

Brown, A.M. (2019). *Pleasure Activism: The Politics of Feeling Good*. AK Press.

Calkhoven, L. (2008). *Harriet Tubman: Leading the Way to Freedom*. Sterling.

Carbado, D. (2015). *Time on Two Crosses: The Collected Writings of Bayard Rustin*. Cleis Press.

Carrico, A. (2010). Elevated suicide rate among HIV-positive persons despite benefits of antiretroviral therapy: implications for a stress and coping model of suicide. *Amercian Journal of Psychiatry* 167: 117–119.

Clinton, C. (2005). *Harriet Tubman: The Road to Freedom*. Little, Brown and Company.

Coetsie, Meins G.S. (2014). *The Existential Philosophy of Etty Hillesum: An Analysis of Her Diaries and Letters*. Brill.

Dass, R. (2018). *Walking Each Other Home: Conversations on Love and Dying*. Sounds True.

Davis, C. (2005). Hauntology, spectres and phantoms. *French Studies* 59(3): 373–379.

Debord, G. (1994). *Society of the Spectacle*. Rebel Press.

Dercon, A. (2009). The political economy of development: an assessment. *Oxford Review of Economic Policy* 23: 173–189.

Egremont, M. (2014). *Some Desperate Glory: The First World War the Poets Knew*. Picador.

Einstein, A. (2014). *The World as I See It*. CreateSpace.

Fanon, F. (1963). *Wretched of the Earth*. Grove Weidenfeld.

Feather, S. (2016). *Blowing the Lid: Gay Liberation, Sexual Revolution and Radical Queens*. Zero Books.

Federici, S. (2017). *Caliban and the Witch: Women, the Body and Primitive*. Autonomedia.

Fisher, M. (2014). *Ghosts of My Life: Writings on Depression, Hauntology and Lost Futures*. Zero Books.

France, D. (2012). *How to Survive a Plague*. (www.surviveaplague.com).

Freire, P. (1996). *Pedagogy of the Oppressed*. Penguin.

Freire, P. (1997). *Learning to Question: A Pedagogy of Liberation*. Continuum.

Fromm, E. (1995). *The Art of Loving*. Thorsons.

Gerada, L. and Laverick, D. (2015). *Another Pride Is Possible*. Novara Media.

Gurney, J. (2012). *Gerrard Winstanley: The Digger's Life and Legacy*. Pluto Press.

Gyatso, Tenzin, His Holiness the Dalai Lama (1999). *Ancient Wisdom, Modern World: Ethics of the New Millennium*. The Berkley Publishing Group.

Harvey, D. (2004). The 'new' imperialism: accumulation by dispossession. *Socialist Register* 40: 63–87.

Helminski, C. and Helminski, K. (1996). *Rumi – Jewels of Remembrance*. Threshold Books.

Hillesum, E. (1996). *An Interrupted Life: The Diaries, 1941–1943 and Letters from Westerbork*. Picador.

Holbourne, Zita. (2017). *Striving for Equality, Freedom and Justice: Embracing Roots, Culture and Identity*. Hansib Publications.

Hone, M. (2015). *Homosexual Warriors*. CreateSpace.

Hone, M. (2020). *Mattachine Society: The Trojan Horse That Introduced Homosexuality into America Paperback*. Independently published.

hooks, b. (2016). *All about Love: New Visions*. HarperPerennial.

Hope, A. (2007). Building a convivial society: insights from Nyerere and Friere: Julius Nyerere. Annual Lecture on LifeLong Learning, UWC.

Hope, A. and Timmel, S. (1984). *Training for Transformation I: A Handbook for Community Workers*. Training for Transformation Institute.

Houlbrook, M. (2006). *Queer London: Perils and Pleasures in the Sexual Metropolis, 1918–1957*. New edition. University of Chicago Press.

Hubbard, J. (2012). *United in Anger: A History of ACT UP*. (www.unitedinanger.com).

Huxley, A. (2005). *Island*. Vintage Classics.

Jarman, D. (2018). *Modern Nature: Journals, 1989–1990*. Vintage Classics.

Kahane, A. (2010). *Power and Love: A Theory and Practice of Social Change*. Berrett-Koehler Publishers.

Bibliography

Kramer, L. (2015). *American People: Volume I, The Hardcover.* Farrar, Straus and Giroux.

Martin-Baro, I. (1994). *Writings for a Liberation Psychology.* Edited by A. Aron and S. Corne. Harvard University Press.

Marx, K. (1844). *On the Jewish Question.* www.marxists.org/ archive/marx/works/1844/jewish-question/.

Marx, K. (2013). *Capital: Volumes One and Two.* Wordsworth Editions.

Max-Neef, M. (1991). *Human Scale Development, Conception, Application and Further Reflections.* Zed Books.

McCormack, C. (2009). *The Wee Yellow Butterfly.* Argyll Publishing.

McCormack, C. (2013). The price of economic barbarism: an uncomfortable truth. *The Australian Community Psychologist* 25(1) (June).

McIntosh, A. (2004). *Soil and Soul: People versus Corporate Power.* Aurum Press.

Milligan, D. (2019). *Gay Liberation: A Brief Moment in Turbulent Times.* (www.studiesinanti-capitalism.net).

Mold, A. (2015). *Placing the Public in Public Health: Public Health in Britain, 1948–2010.* London School of Tropical Medicine and Hygiene.

Newman, J. (2014). Hannah Arendt: radical evil, radical hope. *European Judaism: A Journal for the New Europe* 47(1): 60–71.

Nodin, Nuno, Elizabeth Peel, Allan Tyler and Ian Rivers (2015). *The RaRE Research Report. LGB&T Mental Health: Risk and Resilience Explored.* Queer Futures.

Northcutt, W. (2003). José Bové vs. McDonald's: the making of a national hero in the French anti-globalization movement. *Journal of the Western Society for French History* 31: 326–345.

Pierson, P. (1995). *Dismantling the Welfare State? Reagan, Thatcher, and the Politics of Retrenchment.* Cambridge University Press.

Puar, J. (2017). *Terrorist Assemblages.* Duke University Press.

Rodney, W. (2018). *How Europe Underdeveloped Africa.* Verso.

Rosenberg, D. (2019). *Rebel Footprints.* Pluto Press.

Salk, Jonas (1985). *Anatomy of Reality: Merging of Intuition and Reality.* Praeger.

Salk, Jonas (1992). Are we being good ancestors? *World Affairs: The Journal of International Issues* 1(2): 16–18.

Schulman, S. (2013). *The Gentrification of the Mind: Witness to a Lost Imagination.* University of California Press.

Seale, B. (1991). *Seize the Time: Story of the Black Panther Party and Huey P. Newton.* Black Classic Press.

Sears, A. (2005). Queer anti-capitalism: what's left of lesbian and gay liberation? *Marxist-Feminist Thought Today* 69(1): 92–112.

Sennett, R. (2003). *Respect: The Formation of Character in an Age of Inequality.* Penguin Books.

Smith, L.T. (1999). *Decolonizing Methodologies: Research and Indigenous Peoples.* University of Otago Press.

Thatcher, M. (1988). Speech to the General Assembly of the Church of Scotland (www.margaretthatcher.org/document/107246).

Thayer, T. (2012). A colony for HIV patients. (www.aidsresponseeffort.org/2012/03/21/a-colony-for-hiv-patients/).

Thomas, K. (2011). *Human Life Matters: The Ecology of Sustainable Human Living vs the Rule of the Barbarians.* CreateSpace.

UNAIDS (2012). Stars and activists turn out to 'Unite for an AIDS-Free Generation'. (www.unaids.org/en/resources/

presscentre/pressreleaseandstatementarchive/2012/
july/20120721prkennedycenter/).

Waters, S. (2003). *Fingersmith*. Virago.

Weller, F. (2011). *Entering the Healing Ground: Grief, Ritual and the Soul of the World*. Wisdom Bridge Press.

Wheen, F. (2001). *Karl Marx: A Life*. Norton.

Wilde, O. (2016). *Lady Windermere's Fan*. CreateSpace.

Wilkinson, R. and Pickett, K. (2009). *The Spirit Level*. Bloomsbury Press.

Wilson, L. (2012). *Steve Biko*. Reprint edition. Ohio University Press.

Winterson, J. (2012). *Why Be Happy When You Can Be Normal?* Vintage.

Wojnarowicz, D. (2017). *Close to the Knives: A Memoir of Disintegration*. Canongate Books.

X, Malcolm (2007). *Autobiography of Malcolm X*. Penguin.

Young, I.M. (1988). Five faces of oppression. *The Philosophical Forum* 19(4): 270–290.

Index

Index

Index

Index